The Road to Exile

Didier Nebot

Translated by Henri-Michel Moyal

Alef Design Group

ISBN# 1-881283-16-X

Copyright © 1998 Didier Nebot

Translation Copyright © 1998 Henri-Michel Moyal

Published by Alef Design Group

All rights reserved. No part of this publication may be reproduced or transmitted in any form or by any means graphic, electronic or mechanical, including photocopying, recording or by any information storage and retrieval system, without permission in writing from the publisher.

Alef Design Group • 4423 Fruitland Avenue, Los Angeles, CA 90058
(800) 845–0662 • (213) 582-1200 • (213) 585–0327 fax

MANUFACTURED IN THE UNITED STATES OF AMERICA

The Road to Exile

TEMPLE EMANU-EL
HaSifriyah
Haverhill, MA 01830

Chapter 1

MAY 1493

Never lose sight of the coast. Navigate by guesswork, as close to the wind as possible. Make the best of the current's fits. At night, rely on the stars. Most important, never let up your vigil. Not even for an instant.

Simon Benavista-Zarka had not slept in two days, perhaps three. He was not at all sure anymore. Fatigue made him sluggish, but he still held on to the helm with all the unwavering strength of his determination. And the boat sailed on, obstinately, toward the East, following a most improbable course: far, always farther away from that accursed Spain with, at the end, a near impossible and fantastic aim—Italy.

The stifling heat of that month of May was weighing him down. He let go of the helm for just a moment in order to freshen his face. He felt better. David was asleep at his feet, curled up on the bottom of the small boat, his head resting on the carefully wrapped Book. Simon cast a tender gaze upon him, and Spain came rushing back into his mind. He thought of its hatred-ravaged people and of their deceptive argumentation and shrill justifications. He thought of his own helpless people who had to escape, dragging along the burden of their ancestral fate.

He had had to run about and make deals and beg to get that wretched boat. Then, land faded in the distance. That land now abhorred for the suffering that sprung up among its olive groves, land now mourned, now shunned, and now just a thin diminishing line. Soon it disappeared completely and the horizon became one with the universe.

"Eastward, eastward," Simon recited to spur himself on. "It is in the East where the sun will shine." Simon banished Spain from his thoughts to concentrate on the task at hand. Relax one muscle at a time and breathe easy. And understand? No, little David, it is too late for that. We will later, much later. Right now, we must stay strong and survive and land over there, in Italy.

A bad cough had settled in his chest and an obstinate and throbbing fatigue was gripping him. Simon now knew that he would never set eyes on his promised land. That boat would be his last homestead, but without informers for neighbors, without burning homes, without gangs of looters, rapists and murderers. Hope was mingling with sadness and he wanted to cry. He would not see his own son grow up. Yet, he was at peace.

David had now relieved him at the helm. He was careful to hug the coast as long as it remained visible, his eyes fixed on the East where the sun, at times friendly, at times unbearable, appeared with each new dawn. Although the boat was bobbing upon the waves, they were making progress.

David was fifteen. What could he remember from that year's events? Did he understand why his mother and sister were not there? Would never be there? Why his father, his aunt Myriam, the cousins with whom he so much enjoyed playing, why these peaceful families had to abandon Spain in haste?

"Because we are Jews."

He might have been able to come to terms with that answer gleaned precipitously amid sobbing and fright but time was of the essence. He had to run, and walk, and run. And David had run, and walked, and run to join Simon and had not asked any questions. All the way to the harbor, to that pathetic boat lost on the Mediterranean Sea.

Simon was no longer scared. His suffering was more intense. A piercing pain was boring his back. He had overestimated his own strength when he thought he could lift the small boat unaided: he had cracked a rib. Usually not a fatal accident but Simon was gasping for air: he knew he was going to die. But why now? After having been through hell? Now that they had hope again? He made enormous efforts to move as little as he could to forget the pain and, with it, the "before." As the hours wore on, the "before" faded in his hazy memory.

They had been at sea for five days. Simon was dying little by little. "David, dear little David, I am going to die." That was the thought that welled within him when he caught the young man's trusting gaze. "When you reach a safe harbor, and if you do not lose your faith, you will live as a free man, free to worship God and to practice proudly our ancestral rites. You are strong, my son, keep our spirit alive and think of me when I am gone, when I have joined Rachel, your dear mother, and our beloved Judith. At night, in your thoughts, tell me of Italy where they say nature is beautiful. Share with me your grief, your doubts, your affections...." And David, diligently practicing the lesson he had been taught, was staring to the East. He understood, without the need for any words, that he was becoming the sturdy sapling whose turn it now was to sustain the sick old tree. He could not conceive that his father could die. To him, his father was eternal. Simon, troubled by such faith, could not muster the courage to prepare his son for what was to come.

As days followed, there came an afternoon when Simon no longer coughed, no longer moved. He could not open his eyes and David understood that this day would be unlike any other. He rushed to his fading father, begging him to hold on.

Simon died peacefully at last transcending his suffering. His soul so longed to meet his Creator that he hardly felt himself slipping out of this world. His lifeless body remained warm in David's motionless embrace. And David never could decide if the faint song he then heard came from his father or from above in the sky. In its symphonic dirge, the sea rushed everything in a tumultuous chant.

Melancholy replaced fear. He was gripped by sadness and boundless fear. David held his father in his arms: they would never again share reassuring glances and conspiratorial smiles. The relentless sea blew its deafening requiem and the wind began a long wail. Simon was smiling in death; David was sobbing.

Much later, David reluctantly turned the body over to the waters. The sea swallowed him unto its dark depths. Indifferent, it returned to its lethargic self. Standing in the boat, David looked at the diminishing point where he had taken eternal leave of his father. He began to cry. He was alone, somewhere on the Mediterranean Sea.

Then came hunger. With time it overwhelmed sorrow. Tenacious hunger. David had fasted before but he never faced thousands of miles with only a few dry crackers. There would be no feast to break the fast, no lavish confections spread on a table to mollify the shooting, gut-crushing hunger that raged in his head. "Help me!" he would shout to the sky, "help me, I am afraid." Panicked, he drank all his remaining water. Maddened, he let go of the helm.

The sun scorched his eyelids. At night he shivered. The sea came back at him each morning urging him to give up. He let the boat be taken by the fits of the current and spent long delirious hours. The small boat sailed on, an insignificant speck upon the sea's immensity. David was shriveled and exhausted. Nothing but the vast engulfing mire mattered anymore in his raving mind. Death awaited at the end of the sojourn, entrancing, like a horrid nightmare.

He opened his eyes. A ghostly boat, huge in the sun, was straying toward him on the calm sea. He stood up and waited.

As in a dream, the silent sun-baked hull drifted nearer. The sea was blinding with sun-lit sparkles. The ship was but a few strokes away. The stillness of the air was such that he could hear the grating of the keel. He called out but received no answer: the craft was empty. When the hulls collided nonchalantly, David tied a rope round his waist and hoisted himself aboard the ship. Then he fastened his small boat. With utmost caution, he explored the deserted ship. It was a merchant vessel: this part of the Mediterranean was much traveled. David could find no one. In the hold, he came upon barrels of water and provisions. He screamed when he found them. All this seemed so unreal and his amazement was such that he received this divine gift without surprise. He quickly returned to retrieve the Book, his father's ark of the covenant. Then he settled on board, captain of his ship after God.

He ate dried fish and nibbled on some dried fruit. His strength was returning slowly. He felt his blood pulsing in his temples. He was alive! Then the haze in his mind lifted and memories rushed in: his sheltered childhood, Spain, the screams, the deaths of his father, mother and sister, all mingled in a din. The future took on the face of little Lea, his cousin, and he could still see the sign she made when she fared her adieu: " Good-bye," she was saying. "Soon we'll be adults and we'll be happy." She was waving her small hand; she was smiling.

David gazed at the vast sea and for the first time thought that there were lands beyond the horizon. The world was big; bigger than the

Mediterranean sea and, moreover, to the East, Italy was awaiting. He straightened up and drew in deep breaths. It made him dizzy. All at once, life was racing through his veins. He decided to fight and stay alive for many more years. He did not want his parents' sacrifice to have been for naught. He balled his fists, then poured cool water over himself. Although he was lost it would have been sheer folly to pilot the ship without knowledge of the sea, but it did not matter. An unshakable determination was giving him new life.

A sudden downpour brought him a temporary but tepid gift. He took it as a token from the Heavens. It was telling him that God had not abandoned him. The young man busied himself with making his living quarters more comfortable. Then, his belly full, his spirit calm, he settled himself under the clear sky with the Book in his hands.

Simon had been careful to wrap the Book and to protect it during the voyage. At sea, he carefully wrapped it in a blanket. "This is the Book." A mythical phrase. Overwhelmed with emotion, David had agreed. "The Book," enigmatic, loaded with resonances. Up to now, the child had not been able to bring himself to open it, expecting, it seemed, to receive a sign. That day, he did not hesitate.

He unwrapped the blanket and sat down next to the helm, enjoying the afternoon sun. Then he undid the strings, parted the patches of material and inhaled the salty air with full force.

He opened the Book.

Chapter 2

SUMMER OF 1391, TOLEDO REGION

Of all the despots who had fought over this land, the sun had always emerged the victor. It permeated every stone, every young tree, every speck of dust. Pity whoever challenged it when it had reached its zenith, as the afternoon Eli was returning home, exhausted.

He had left at dawn. The road was long—his mule slow. The mule was willing but slow like the vine that requires so much care so that one day wine will flow like dark blood. Eli could behold his vineyard as he came up the hill: it was a lot of work but he was proud of it. The soil, baked by too much sun, had been stingy. Eli, like his father before him, struggled to produce grapes and to tend them to be full and ripe enough to give up their dark ooze. On that particular day, he had traveled to the village of Aro, a good 40 miles away, to take delivery of three delicately curved hoes that he had ordered a month earlier from the village blacksmith. He had groomed the mule, patted its neck and they had left for the village. The blacksmith's reputation had spread throughout the entire region. He had decided to deliver the hoes the day after Saint Anna's day. Eli had flinched when he realized that it corresponded to the 17th of Tamouz in the Jewish calendar, a day of prayer and fasting. But what did the blacksmith care about the celebration of Nebuchadnezzar's capture of Jerusalem. Secure in his talent, he felt entitled to princely whims and did not take kindly to being questioned. Eli, thus, had agreed, not daring to ask that the date be moved up a day. On the way home, while his mule plodded under the unyielding sun, he admonished himself for having been so coy.

Nevertheless, he had observed the fast. He had not eaten a thing. He only gulped some water while muttering a lame pardon between his cracked lips. But God would not have wanted him to die of thirst, alone on that long deserted road. Rocked by the hobble of the exhausted mule, he felt happy to go back home to his wife.

Esther! For two years now, nothing had eroded their passion. Every day began a new exploration of their love. Though not much of an artist, Eli had carved the dark-wood cradle that was to receive the first fruit of their wondrous union. Lazarus, now ten months old, kept them busy with his happy babble and voracious appetite. Eli never tired of telling Esther how beautiful she was. Esther always blushed and stammered: "No, I am not, look at the Benayoun girl, she is so much prettier, I'm just …" Eli would laugh: "Our son too, is the handsomest."

Eli was nearing the Santa Luisa's farm. He gently patted the mule's neck and said: "You're the most beautiful mule in all the world and soon you'll drink till your gut busts." He thought of the coming Fall and of the vines rid of pesky insects thanks to the tools gleaming in his pouch. What a harvest to come! What a full and happy existence!

Santa Luisa's farm came into sight, simple and white in the blinding sun. Absorbed in his thoughts, Eli had forgotten about the heat battering his temples. He drew in a deep breath. He was almost home but decided to pay his neighbors a quick visit, partly for the poor animal that was panting heavily but also because he wanted to greet the Santa Luisas, whose hospitality and cheer he enjoyed. After dismounting, the mule rushed headlong toward the pond. Tired, he paced the ground.

He did not become aware of the silence immediately. He didn't hear old Santa Luisa's booming voice inside the cool walls of the farm house, nor his sons noisy bickering and chasing after each other from building to building. Eli smiled. What miracle had taken place? In all the years he had visited his Christian neighbor, the two boys had always been squabbling noisily. Strangely, today there was silence.

He called out. Maria did not yell back her customary "Yeah, yeah, yeah!" She didn't come out of the kitchen wiping her hands. She was responsible for all selling and bartering of cheese for wine, and she did it all with a handshake. Then, she would holler to her husband that there was wine for the men. Eli would never overstay his welcome because he felt ill at ease in that commotion.

No one was around that evening. Eli called again. His call was answered by the feeble minded farmhand, his hair ruffled and his mouth agape: "Nobody's home. Went to town. They were all screaming. They said to guard the house." He pointed to the pitchfork he was dragging behind, a pitiful weapon to ward off thieves.

Eli's belly rumbled, hunger was stirring within him. "To town? All of them?" The lad nodded: "Yeah, all of them." Eli, showing disbelief, shrugged his shoulders. "Well, I'll be back another day. Take good care of the farm." Baffled, he climbed on his mule and resumed his journey.

His winery. It was famous throughout the entire region. This year its production would be another success. Even noblemen loved the pungent-sweet nectar. Legend had it that in 1085 King Alfonso VI, having benefited from Mathias Benavista's timely and critical help, rewarded Eli's ancestor with a few acres of fertile land right outside the Castillian capital. Since then, the Benavistas had been renowned wine-makers.

But Eli was troubled by other thoughts at the end of his sojourn, now that the sun was setting majestically on the other side of the hills. The silence at the Santa Luisa's farm worried him. Why did they have to leave their home in the care of that cretinous farmhand? What had happened? Everything, however, looked normal on the farm.

Soon, he would drop off his new tools in the small house at the foot of the vineyard where Samir and Ahmed, his trusted employees, lived. Then he would ride the other mule home. The fast was to end at sundown: he would eat well. Later, he would fall asleep in his wife's arms, while Lazarus, wrapped in the warmth of his cradle, would dream peacefully, fast asleep, clenching his little muscular fists.

Samir and Ahmed were not there. Eli frowned. It was not like them to have left the vineyard at the same time: one of them always kept an eye on it. Their absence did not bode well. But he was hungry and tired and his mind refused to make sense of it all.

On the road, he pondered the recent events in Sevilla, being careful, however, not to give them too much importance. Rumor had it that two months before the Jewish quarters had been attacked by Christians, whipped into a frenzy by archdeacon don Hernando Martinez. The Jewish community of Toledo was only prepared to see in it an isolated, though horrible, incident. Only God knew what unneighborly jealousies had prompted the Christians and don Hernando Martinez with his virulent speeches to commit the horrible massacre. None of this would ever happen in Toledo. "Would it, father? Will it ever? mother." These were the questions the anguished Jews of Toledo would fearfully whispered, at night, to each other. "We are not hurting anyone, are we? It only happens to others, right?" Then, fears would ease and, once the candle was snuffed , people slept peacefully.

Eli, riding his mule home, wanted to hurry to make sure that Esther was fine, as well as Lazarus and all the residents of the Jewish Quarters.

Go across Toledo. How long a ride it still was. A whole day of travel under a torrid sun, without anything to eat while all the Jews of the world were at prayers. Why didn't he speak up when the blacksmith set the day! He was still debating vexingly with himself, searching for something or someone to blame for terrible things he was imagining, when his mule reached the outskirts of Toledo, a fortress perched high on a mountain like an eagle nest against the flaming sky. He had it: why did he not ask his cousin Raphael, also a blacksmith, instead of that sneering Christian? Forty miles, forty long miles to satisfy a whim. Eli urged his mule on. But it had not been a whim, for his cousin was so unskillful that he would have understood little of the specifications required. "That's why, inept cousin of mine!"

Eli was becoming angry. In his mind, images flashed in rapid succession. Anxiously, he tried to brush them aside.

Run little mule, run for I am afraid. What if something happened to my dear Esther, my Lazarus? It will be my fault and that of that worthless cousin, and of the nasty blacksmith, and of that mule too, that rode so laboriously the entire day, and of the August sun and of the Christians! Why did they become so crazed, like in Sevilla? Why did they attack the peaceful Jews who wanted nothing more than to live according to their own customs? Why, when they lacked a pretext, would they invoke that eternal crime against the Christ? What did the Jews have to do with it? What did Eli Benavista, his wife and son have to do with Christ who died fourteen centuries ago?

The mule stepped on the Alcantara bridge. This was the same bridge where, during other troubled times, Moors and Christians had fought many times. Eli was shaking his head, hardly noticing that the royal guards, whose duty it was to watch the entrance to the bridge day and night, were not at their sentry-posts. His entire world was turning upside down and the silence in Toledo was rending his racing heart. He was now conversing with Esther, a hurried speech, to somehow keep her alive and well: "I'm coming, Esther, wait for me, wait for me." He got off on the tired, slow moving mule and hurried on foot in the streets now eerily empty.

He ran along the city's walls, unconcerned with the animal toddling along behind him. He ran toward the Jewish neighborhood of Montichel located clear across the city. He ran toward Esther's smile whille begging her to be well. Stumbling his way through the foul smelling streets, he finally caught sight of people's shapes. His fogged vision only retained frozen postures, petrified gestures. There was no time to stop. He hardly recognized Maria Santa Luisa among the multitude of shadows coming toward him. He barely made out the comforting words she was shouting at him: "We tried to tell them." Old Santa Luisa was right behind her nodding his head: "Eli, they did not want to listen to us." But Eli was already gone.

The Jewish neighborhood began there and so did the nightmare. Women cried, men prayed, others were helpless. Eli rushed toward his house. Amoyal, a wan look on his face, tried to stop him: "Don't go in, don't." Letting out a grunt, Eli broke away. He pushed open the front door half way unhinged, stepped inside his home and collapsed, breathing haltingly. His friends filed in silently. Myriam Amoyal was carrying a screaming baby in her arms. Esther was lying on the floor as if asleep. Her belly had been ripped open.

Eli stared at his wife, haggard, unable to move. Neighbors held him up gently telling him words he did not understand. He let them, unaware of his surrounding. A few sobbing women were at the entrance of the house; they too had lost a child or a husband and their suffering merged with Eli's despair. Finally Myriam came forward and placed the baby in his arms. Eli looked at it an instant not understanding. Then, little by little he began to recover from his numbness and smiled to the child. It is then that he began to cry.

One by one, his neighbors returned to their homes. Myriam and her husband stayed with Eli. Christians had swooped down on the Jewish area. Who was responsible for this murderous onslaught? No one knew though all of Christian Toledo had risen against the nameless enemy. From house to house news of the great gathering spread like quick fire. The Santa Luisas had misunderstood what holiday it was and found themselves amid the euphoric crowd of Toledians. They, like a few others, understood too late that a massacre was about to unleash and their attempts to stop it were in vain. They heard the cheers when the first skull was cracked open against a wall and they saw the hacking of the two Benoiel boys at the hands of the hooligan-leaders.

The blood-thirsty mob had knocked in the doors of the synagogues. They set upon the congregants mercilessly and then cast their victims' still warm corpses to the bonfires. The jews had barricaded themselves in their houses quickly but devastation struck those whose doors gave in. Others were spared thanks to the sturdiness of a piece of timber. In her panic, Esther hid her sleepy child in the back of the house. When she rushed to the front to secure the door, Christians were already tearing it down. Five, maybe six men, saw the beautiful jewess and threw themselves on her. They raped her, then stabbed herin the belly. She died uttering Eli's name. The murderers were already going away to extend their frenzied visit to other houses. When the sun disappeared behind the hills, they went home, their consciences clear.

Wrapped in his blanket, little Lazarus had just been fed. He began to cry when he did not hear his mother's voice. Myriam and Moshe and all the other survivors slowlycame out of their houses, trembling. Their dazed-looks crossing. The survivors fell in a parent or a friend's arms. They had entered homes with smashed doors and had wailed in horror when they discovered the victims.

Myriam let out a piercing scream when she saw Esther dead, her belly open. She had looked for Lazarus, expecting the worst. She heard his crying and rushed to him. She took him in her arms, sobbing. She had a fleeting thought for Eli who, perhaps, would find a reason to go on because of his son.

It took Eli a long time to accept the impossible. He could not come to terms with Esther's death. It would have been so easy to retreat from reality, so simple to take refuge in madness. But Eli could not because the son he held asleep in his arms needed him. He had his mother's large eyes; and if they stayed blue they would bear forever sweet Esther's bright look.

That day, Eli had aged fifteen years.

Myriam asked a young mother to come to the house and serve as wet-nurse for Lazarus. Her name was Rachel and her eyes still held the horror of the carnage. She fed the child as the same time as her little Deborah.

Your ancestor, dear little David, lost in the middle of the Mediterranean sea, that insatiable baby who will grow up never knowing his mother, was ten months old when the murderous folly went on a rampage and killed thousands of Jews in all four corners of Spain.

Chapter 3

Hundreds had died in Toledo. Satisfied, the Christians relented. Life gradually returned to normal. For the Jews, however, life had been irrevocably changed.

But that restlessness did not stop in Sevilla or Toledo. A rumbling antisemitism lived deep in the heart of all Christians. It came to life with the news of the merry massacres in both cities. Pitchforks were raised, swords were honed and when archdeacon Martinez came to town with his entourage and his message of death, shrieking war- and hate cries thundered everywhere.

With the news of four thousands dead in Sevilla, a religious frenzy took all of Spain in a vise. Evangelization, they intoned, from Burgos to Valencia, from Majorca to Cordu. Let us avenge Christ and let us spread our precepts of love and peace. It had been so long since these honest peasants, those well-thinking townsfolks had been able to hate so gleefully. Of course, there had been the usual sporadic canings. But they were isolated incidents, nothing more. This time, however, from Pamplona to Cortes, from Montoro to Andujar, the love of Christ pulsed at the end of their sticks and torches. From Jeen to Ubeda and from Bunel to Ablitas, one cry: let us love one another and let us kill those who resist us: let us do them violence, let us burn them alive and God will then measure how eager we are to please Him.

The Jewish quarters were not at all prepared to offer any type of resistance. No one wanted to believe that disaster would strike—not on the street over here, nor in that particular house over there. It was only when the cries of death could be heard close to their quarters that some ran away to take refuge in the environs of their cities or in neighboring villages. Others, unwilling to abandon their homes, tried to barricade themselves in. But some were made to convert at the hands of zealous priests all too happy to use a weighty argument: "They, after all, were not murderers!" As for the others, most were burnt alive.

In Barcelona, the mayhem was total. For three days and nights, the mob slipped furtively in all the nooks and corners of the Jewish quarters, killing, burning, plundering. Then came the throngs of thieves attracted by the prodigious flames that bloodied the night: they fell upon the city that the Barcelonians, exhausted, had left for scraps. The terror-stricken survivors took quick cover behind the tall walls of the Castillo Nuevo. But the fortress fell to the attackers who butchered men, women and children. On Saturday, August 5, 1391, the children of Israel had been entirely decimated in Barcelona the Proud. Realizing the extend of the devastation, the gaon of Castilla, spiritual leader of the Israelites/Hebrews, asked for queen Leonora's protection.

He offered her a considerable amount of money which the queen refused declaring that "never would she ask any favor of this people, so that they, in turn, could never curse her silently."

In all of Spain the will to survive took on a name: conversion. Surely, an atavistic hatred was to blame for these killings but, above the populace, the powerful catholic establishment pulled all the strings of that strangely organized destruction. Here was its opportunity to impose once and for all its control on the country. Life was of no value and given the sword or the cross, Jews did not hesitate. But what new Christians did the Church tally? Bewildered prisoners who, pushed and clubbed on their way to baptismal fonts, repeated three words in Latin before turning back, branded catholics, to the ruined homes where beyond generations everything pulsated with the Hebrews' ancestral faith. Did they really think that they would let go of twenty centuries of customs with a shaking yes, granted to a enemy priest, in order to sport the clothes of the believers? Between the cross and death, they did not hesitate.

The Christians sniggered: those wretched creatures would never possess the unequalled bearing of the princes of Holy Castilla. Aware of the humiliation they were subjecting these pariahs, they would clap with each aspersion of holy water, like children playing near a fountain. A horrible game it was, but survival was at stake and some even ended up believing that, however cruel, the unique God of the Christians seemed more powerful and better organized than the same unique God of the

Jews. And wasn't the new Bishop of Burgos, the great Santa Maria, ex-rabbi Halevy!?

They traded their names, took up residence away from the neighborhoods where they had grown up and life resumed its course. Others, however, did not understand the significance of the drops of holy water. They assumed that they had to eradicate the memory of their origins, that the cross was more than just the material prize of a hastened conversion. Lost between their ways and their new allegiance, they were harassed by Christians communities, happy to indulge in a new society game and they also met the scornful gaze of their old coreligionists. They never knew peace. Neither did, for that matter, those who, fanatical in their beliefs, refused to cede. Those kept a serene soul, but at what price? They slept with great difficulties and that for the many years during which fear cropped up from behind every shadow.

Tempers quieted only with the coming of Fall. The vineyards and the orchards, full of fruit, were ready, and it was not as hot and, also, there were better things to do than to waste time in futile demonstrations: soon harvests would fill up people's lofts and hearts. The country let itself lull into the calmness of the new situation, however confused it still was. The important Jewish areas, once peaceful surburbs existed no more. On the other hand, many a small village saw its Jewish population increase with the arrival of converted or non-converted families, who hoped to find in the remoteness of the village an oasis of tranquility for their children. Life returned to normal.

How does one forget? The great rabbi of Castilla, after his unsuccessful attempt with the queen, turned to the Council of Regents, made up of noblemen and high church dignitaries. These Lords had been little affected by that summer's fever: they allowed the populace to find a diversion in those tasks. The representative of the Hebrews spoke to them in a dull voice about what had been inevitable. Perhaps to get rid of the old man and in order to alleviate the weight on their conscience, the members of the Council promised him that the killers would be sought and punished. Each nodded convincingly. They talked about it in the halls of power, and they forgot about it very quickly. How do you punish several thousands criminals? Why render justice, anyhow? So that but a thousand inhabitants people the holy soil of Spain! For everyone or just about everyone had been a participant and if it would have been easy to point to archdeacon don Hernando Martinez as the instigator of the merciless slaughter, he was not even bothered. The harm was done, and the Spanish dignitaries had other businesses to attend, perhaps more mundane ones but very time-consuming nonetheless. So, what's done is done! Let's return to business as usual!

A new attempt was made. The new converts found themselves quite often at a loss never knowing what was expected of them, exiled in a faith they knew nothing about. Rabbis beseeched the proper authorities to void the forced conversions. But what a splendid job had been done! What other salvation did the Jewish pagans think of now, now that they were reborn in the love of Jesus Christ! The church, never doubting its mission, expressed its satisfaction with the work done with the lost souls. It would have been impossible to translate the fervent Catholic discourse into jewish anguish. What about our traditions, our history, our language and our lithurgy! Glory be to God to have saved those souls, the high church officials incanted. Jewish pleas fell into deaf ears, as if Spain had lived in error for centuries only to see the light in the summer of 1391. The Catholics, with their well-heeded arrogance and radiant taste for self-punishing, had asserted their authority over Spain and allowed generous room for those who did not adopt their spirituality. This would be no more. The history of Holy Spain was yet to be mapped out. Let the would-be spoilers beware.

So be it. Amen.

Chapter 4

Eli feared what awaited him: to live among the deafening echo of the dead. Esther's absence permeated the walls, spread out between them as surely as the emptiness of the rooms. It wormed its way into Eli who felt forlorn. Why fight when Esther was no longer alive?

Lazarus was the answer. In the midst of his mental confusion, Eli thanked God for having spared his son. He remembered the gurgles and the coos he made as a baby, and his blue eyes, and the answer was clear even though he sometimes refuted the obvious. Lazarus was the living portrait of Esther. That memory, however, produced in him as much hope as sadness. Finally, he decided to resume work for Lazarus: he would repair his fire-ravaged house. Raise the walls, strengthen the posts, give a coat of whitewash to the blackened walls.

He spent most of his time inside his house, giving little thought to his vineyard. Sometimes, Moshe would help him while Myriam and young Rachel cared for the baby. Once in a while, Eli would freeze for just a second, a stone in his hand. He would hold that posture, dazed, then he would awaken and slowly complete his task. He was fighting depression but the smallest piece of wood he fitted in the wall reminded him of the old happy house and of Esther… His friends did not know what else to do; they were hoping that time would heal his wounds.

Then the damages were repaired. Eli entrusted Lazarus to the Amoyals and locked himself in. He closed the shutters, shut the door, and lay in his bed.

What was to become of him? He did not want to think, he only wanted to close his eyes and awaken from that terrible dream. She is dead, dead. Night passed. He was not able to sleep. He heard the early morning blackbirds, the village waking up, the bells of the citadel. He remained motionless, neglecting his personal hygiene and his prayers because he was resolved to let himself die. His neighbors grew concerned and went to Ezra.

Ezra-the-Patriarch had miraculously survived the massacre. When the murderous gang burst into the synagogue, he was there with a few others. All had died but him, who had fallen to the ground curled-up. Strangely, the assaillants who brushed past him many a time spared him as if, in answer to his prayer, God had made him invisible. He was the memory of the Jewish quarter, he had seen all the children being born. He himself did not know how old he was, but his wisdom was great. He listened attentively to Moshe. True, Eli was suffering, but no less than so many others in their destroyed neighborhood. But Ezra remembered the intensity of the love between the newly-wed Benavistas and he recalled the emotion he had felt when he witnessed their perfect happiness. He thanked the Amoyals and slowly walked toward Eli's house.

He knocked a long time. Then, he called out lamely. A tired Eli got up and, staggering, came to open the door. In the darkened room, the two men spoke a long time, then they went to the synagogue to pray. After the service they took leave of each other and, holding Eli's hands in his, Ezra said: "God will help you." Eli thanked him warmly. His heart was now at peace.

He straightaway went to visit his worried neighbors. When they saw him, they knew that the patriarch had been successful in calming him. They smiled, and Myriam prepared a nice meal, and Moshe made him sit down. Eli seemed as if he was rediscovering the world. He asked for news of all those who, in the haze of his mind, had disappeared.

He had almost forgotten his vineyard in all that commotion. Thank God, his loyal Samir and Ahmed had not waited for any instructions to take good care of it. They did not belong in this violence-ridden century. A long time ago, their ancestors had chosen to remain in Toledo when the Arab communities had moved south. Both men loved Eli, with whom they had grown up. They loved their painstaking work and never even entertained the thought of leaving the Benavistas in their difficult time.

Moshe reassured Eli: "Samir and Ahmed took good care of the vineyard, Eli, don't you worry. Rachel cares for Lazarus more and more and her husband is getting jealous! The Bibasses left a week ago to visit their cousins on the coast; the Perezes converted, and many others…

"Converted?"

"Yes, they became Christians because they were afraid for their children."

"Christians?"

"Yes, Eli, and the lost mule found its way back to the vineyard. Samir saw it coming back, famished. And Myriam is pregnant. Life is starting anew. And Lazarus, oh Lazarus! he is always smiling."

The memory of Esther was always present. He knew she was watching over them from above. He taught Lazarus how to say "mother." He would point to the clouds: "Mother is up there," and the child, not fully comprehending his father's words, would repeat "mama", a finger pointing toward the sky.

At harvest time, he had little time to spend on the house. He came back at night, exhausted, only to leave at the crack of dawn. He was relieved to have so much to do, to have to spend all of his energy under the unending heat of that later part of September. His two helpers were pleased to see him tend to his vineyard again; they put their hearts into the harvest, in the hope that with the black wine streaming abundantly, their master would regain a sense of purpose. "Boss, you're gonna be happy, your grapes are fat and the whole region will be drunk with your wine, the princes and the paupers. For once they taste it they won't be able to quit it." Eli smiled, wiped his forehead and poured another basket into the wine press.

He wouldn't have minded continuing this solitary widower's existence, dividing his time between nostalgia and hard work. But his neighbors confused him: "Eli, a feminine presence would be good for Lazarus and a man is not meant to remain by himself, it's the law of nature according to God." He shook his head incredulously. A woman! They could understand his refusal: Esther would never be replaced in his heart. "Eli! Myriam is pregnant; she won't be able to take care of two households. Rachel has never complained but she has so much work to do and her in-laws came to live with her. Eli! Lazarus goes from one home to another; how is he going to grow up, eh?" Eli stammered: "Isn't he happy? He's always laughing! I'll take better care of the house. Sorry,

Myriam, to have let you do it all by yourself, but don't worry, from now on I'll take care of everything!" They preferred not to insist.

Once more, he was all alone, Despair crept back, insidious. Again, he couldn't find sleep, crushed as he was by the task that awaited him. He would take Lazarus's hand while pointing to the clouds: "We're gonna be happy, you and me," he whispered, "your mother in the heavens above will protect us. We don't need anyone." But at Lazarus's slightest sobbing, he felt helpless.

Go along with their suggestion to remarry? That would reopen his wounds. I will always see that woman as an intruder, I will betray Esther. No, he heard himself answer, maybe you will find someone who's understanding, who will love Lazarus, who will bring you tenderness—not love, no—but an adequate measure of comfort, and you will age peacefully. He sighed, not believing it.

But life afforded him little respite. In tranquil Toledo, the future had to be built upon the ruins of a bloody past. The irrepressible institution of the matchmakers sent spies in every delegation, snooping in every street, in every family, on the lookout for single women ready to be remarried. Eli smiled when he saw them: if he had wanted to remain a widower he would have had to move to the desert to escape them. They described him in their register as an energetic, hard-working man, with a good physique and with a litte boy. Of course, a match was found: Sarah Monsonego, also a widow but childless, the daughter of the powerful Isaac Monsonego, a very wealthy merchant. The matchmakers waited for the end of the mourning period with baited breath… Ah! What a beautiful marriage this will be! They were made for each other… at least, it will be a beautiful wedding. Eli got wind of their plans and sighed once more. Sarah…

Their grandmothers were cousins. The Benavistas and the Monsonegos had lived side by side for many years. Sarah and Avi Monsonego had grown up on the same street, had attended the same synagogue until Isaac Monsonego's fantastic rise separated them.

Isaac Monsonego had a passion for travel. He had defied the seas, traveled over entire continents, cementing along the way solid friendships in the far away countries of the east. His energy, his spirit and his prodigious business acumen had made him one of the richest men of Castilla. This rotund giant spoke six languages and had his entrees with high dignitaries of Italy as well as Turkey and Greece, all of whom he had charmed with his explosive laugh. He feared no one except, perhaps, his wife. He had established many outlets for his businesses and hired his representatives from among the local Jewish communities, paying them generously, —one of his secrets. Everyone in Castilla knew the mythical Isaac and his fantastic commerce of the rarest products. His ships were ploughing the seas, loaded with the finest materials, strange spices, oils and aromatics that incensed the senses. Isaac Monsonego incarnated the mysteries of the orient.

His story took on the airs of a fairytale when he focused his ambition toward Africa and its marvelous natural wealth: gold. The grandees of Spain would have sold their souls for the metal with the destructive sparkle: Isaac went to fetch it and, to their amazament, brought it back. He was the Court's magician; noblemen entertained him, eager to possess the magical powder; ladies swooned when mention was made of perfumes that drove men mad and of fabrics so fine that they felt like a light wind blowing. Isaac Monsonego became don Monsonego and, because it served their interests, noblemen forgot that the man they were now celebrating belonged to that same strange religion of the killers of the messiah and even went so far as to greet him from the tip of their feathered hats.

After having traveled the world, Isaac came back to settle in Spain. He lived many years in Barcelona and Sevilla. He took charge of the education of Avi, his son. Then, when his hair had turned white and his back had grown weary, he returned to Toledo. The home he had built on the shores of the Tagus, in an area reserved for affluent Spaniards, delighted the passers-by's gaze with its thickets of colorful flowers, its tall lime-trees giving a generous amount of shade and its white marble fountains. The house itself was made of stone, its fish-scale roof robbed the sun of its brilliance. He resolved to retire to it without any second thoughts. He would reflect long periods of time while watching the Tagus change with the seasons and only expressed anger when he heard his wife's piercing voice coming out of the main building. He couldn't stand that voice but he never dared tell her so. Senora Monsonego did not know that her shrill screams were partly responsible for the many travels her husband had undertaken which, in turn, became the source of his immense wealth!

He entrusted the business to his son Avi. Don Monsonego II had inherited from his father, if not his adventurous spirit, at least his practical sense. On his balcony, his father was reflecting on the twists and turns of his life. No one knew how little he cared about his money or that he had no interest in court's festivities. His real wealth was the changing landscapes of the deserts he had crossed; it was the friendship he had forged with the prince of a nomadic tribe or the storm he had weathered on the African coast. But he had lived a full life and now had began to study the Talmud to transform the adventurer into a wise man while secretly awaiting the arrival of grandchildren to whom he would recount his extraordinary adventures.

In the summer of 1391, when troubles erupted, Isaac's heart was touched. His daily reading of the Bible brought him closer to the people from whom, because of his eventful existence, he had distanced himself. When, from the window of his mansion, he saw the fires run through the Jewish quarter, he felt his throat tightening. Later, he paid the devastated neighborhoods a visit, dressed simply. He secretly paid masons to help in the reconstruction of houses and synagogues, then resumed his meditation, his eyes fixed on the huge sun that was now sinking into the river.

The summer the massacres took place, his daughter Sarah had only been married one year to Youda Bitton, his representative in Barcelona. They were still childless. Sarah, miraculously, escaped the carnage.

Youda Bitton worked at the harbor. Sarah tended to her domestic chores and was alone in her garden, folding the beautiful seawind-dried sheets she did not tire of touching while singing in a soft voice. She couldn't stand being idle and was impatiently waiting for God to allow her to bear children. She heard a faraway rumble but, absorbed as she was in her task, gave it little attention.

The uncontrolled mob fell upon the city like a cloud of grasshoppers. All of a sudden, howlings could be heard all around Sarah, followed by unbearable screams. Humans forms were running about before collapsing to the ground; farther down, a bloody head hung on a tree limb. Within ten seconds, Sarah Bitton's tranquil life turned into a nightmare, and she lost consciousness, falling all of one piece over the sheets.

The young Christian maid they had hired two months earlier was mistaken for the mistress of the house. She died after a cruel beating.

Youda had rushed home at the height of the massacre. He had barely enough time to catch a glimpse of a burnt body when a pitchfork pierced his belly. He fell to the ground, groaning.

His screams caused his wife to regain consciousness. Sarah opened her eyes only to witness her husband fall to his knees, pierced through and through by the pitchfork's tines. Then, closing her eyes before the unbearable, she lost consciousness again. That's how she was spared, in the dark abyss of the unconscious, while the massacre that would forever haunt her and of which she'd preserve but a few confused images, went on. The Christians, buoyed by their crazed frenzy, went to extend the massacre farther down in the Jewish quarter. Sarah came to only at dawn. She got up, frozen, surrounded by an apocalyptic silence. The entire quarter had been razed. She was but one of the few survivors.

As she recovered, mad horror went through her. Recognizing nothing and no one, she stumbled forward, dazed, stepping over dead bodies, parts of destroyed walls, streams of blood. She walked like an apparition, her stomach turning with each step. She screamed with fright at the slightest noise; columns crumbled; farther down, rats crept amond the ruins. She bit her nails, dug them into her skin, and ran to hide inside a house that was still standing. She found some food. She ate and drank furtively like a wild animal.

Lost and not knowing what to do, she went home. Digging through the piles of debris of what had been her home, her eyes brimming with tears, she found a small box with some gold which her mother had given her. She screamed, perhaps to convince herself that she wasn't dead too, or so that another living soul might hear her, be it friend of foe, it mattered little, in order not to remain alone in that huge mass grave.

Her soul and mind wearied, she got up and began to walk toward the countryside. People were going to kill her but she didn't care, she almost wanted it. She went on. Night fell.

Three peasant couples were going toward Madrid in horse-drawn carts. The Jewess rushed toward them, her eyes marked with dark circles, their color washed out from so much crying. They lifted her up on the hay where she collapsed. They let her sleep. When she awoke, she felt better and, to thank them, she tendered a gold coin. This could have proved a fatal mistake, but Sarah was too dazed nor did she have her father's cautious nature either. The peasants, however, took the gold coin with their eyes opening wide. A gold coin! If they had sold the entire contents of their cart, they wouldn't even have gotten half as much!

She told them about her father, the great Isaac, the adventurous seafarer. She couldn't stop recounting his exploits as if to exorcise the very thought of the carnage that came knocking on the window of her consciousness. She told them about delicate materials, unknown perfumes, and the fantastic adventures she'd heard during her childhood.

The trip lasted four days and went on without a hitch. When she saw the front gate of her parents' home, she jumped out of the cart and rushed through the gardens while calling her mother. Her mother came running out, crying and screaming all at once in her shrill voice. The two women fell in each other's arms. Then, Sarah introduced the six peasants who will long remember the incredible meal they were treated to and how they became intoxicated by inhaling rare perfumes and stroking their cheekswith the silky materials senora Monsonego gave them. Sarah's nightmare was over.

Within her family, Sarah found a comforting sense of security. With time, the events in Barcelona lost some of their concreteness and became but a bad dream. She wanted to erase the last image she had of her husband run through by a pitchfork; then, it was the entire year spent with him she rejected. That union, anyhow, had been arranged to serve her father's interests, not love. She began to feel like a maiden awaiting a husband to come along. She'd listen to her mother talk to the matchmakers. When senora Monsonego told her about Eli, Sarah smiled submissively.

Her mother sighed: "True, he doesn't have a real good profession but you don't have much of a choice yourself." Sarah didn't understand and awaited a decision.

After many hesitations, Eli accepted. Sarah had a bland personality, she was meek and obedient. Unlike her mother, however, she wasn't always screaming; she knew how to manage a household and, more importantly, she was Isaac Monsonego's daughter. If Eli wasn't up to looking after his own interests, his friends were. "Sarah is a good match, Eli. She has suffered a lot, like you. She'll take care of Lazarus and you'll have children together. And her father is so wealthy..." No one would have understood if he had passed such an opportunity. So be it, then. But there was always that small pang deep in his heart of hearts to remind him that he would love Esther forever. The wedding day was set.

Avi, Sarah's brother, invited Eli to his wonderful property. By taking over his father's business ventures, he had assured for himself a power that could not easily be contested. Eli was surprised to hear that his small house in the Jewish quarter could not suit Sarah. He hardly reacted; for him, that place had held so much happiness. But the Monsonego family held other values. "When I got married, I was able to give my wife a comfortable lifestyle. Think about it! You see, Eli, Sarah has always lived in luxurious homes. After all she's gone through you wouldn't want her to have to get accustomed to a different lifestyle!" Eli didn't care. At any rate, Sarah's living where Esther had lived would have been too much. "There's no need to wait. Join me on the balcony." Both men went out. "Look."

The window overlooked the surrounding countryside; the river rolled its murky waters between the vales scorched by the winter. The view was fantastic. "Everything you see is ours! We'll build you a house. Over there, perhaps. You and Sarah will be safer here than in Toledo. Here, there are only Christians. And us! Don't frown like that, Eli. There will be gardens, a real paradise! Go then and get ready for the move, you can also bring the furniture you're attached to."

Eli went home slowly and greeted his home as he would have a friend. Leave everything. He well realized that since Esther's passing he had not been consulted about anything. His friends and his neighbors, the matchmakers and the Monsonegos, all had imposed their view regardless of what he might feel. Lazarus wouldn't be seeing his godmothers anymore, nor would he see the other children with whom he played... Did he have to get married, give up his habits, betray his memories? He lowered his head. How much had he needed the tools he had gone so far away to fetch the day of the massacre? If he had stayed, he would have saved Esther. Destiny was cruel. He was going to be married to Sarah Monsonego, change homes and be under Avi's control. His life had become meaningless. He shrugged.

Tradition required that the mourning period last a full year. However, in cases of extreme necessity, that period could be reduced to a few months, but no less than three, in order to ascertain that the widow didn't carry the man's child. Once that was established and five months after that bloody summer, Eli and Sarah were married, neither for the better nor for the worse. He was melancholy; she, somewhat disinterested. They never were in a festive mood. The wedding ceremony was simple. Isaac was rid of a worrisome problem, his wife was reassured of her daughter's reputation and future, and Avi, proud to have arranged everything, only invited the persons closest to his family. Everything returned to normal.

After the ceremony, when Eli led Sarah toward their newly built home, he felt the wound in his heart reopen. He didn't want to touch that woman. Sarah was smiling, happy to have wed the handsome Eli, and was waiting for a gentle command to obey. She was met with indifference. She wasn't much pained by it at first but once she realized she had married a man who, for the rest of her life, would never even look at her, her heart filled with sadness. It was as if she didn't exist. She had to beg him to fulfill his husband's duty in the hope that one day she might have a child that would smile to her, would speak to her, would need her. Eli forced himself and implored Esther in the heavens above, to forgive him this betrayal. He closed his eyes perhaps in order not to cry. The house was beautiful, the view magnificent and the Tagus flowed gently through a pacified Spain.

Lazarus was one year old when he came to live in that pretty house: he felt lost. The sad lady who lived with his father lacked the cheer of his Toledan "mothers". She didn't sing, didn't take him in her arms to cover him with kisses like Rachel, she didn't indulge in baby-talk, like Myriam. He didn't feel any animosity but, rather, a lack of warmth. He couldn't understand that every time he pointed to the clouds while happily shouting "Mommy!" he was hurting Sarah, who languished in her uselessness.

She held for him the same reserve she held for his father, the smiling baby impressed as much as Eli and she grew afraid that a show of affection on her part might be met with indifference by the little boy. Thus, they studied each other; Lazarus with his large blue eyes and Sarah with her sad gaze. She prayed for a child. Lazarus, wouldn't you like me a little if I gave you a little brother? And your father, wouldn't he be more interested in me if I gave him another child? And days passed spent in that painful thought.

Sarah's dowry enabled them to acquire several properties in the area. They planted vineyards because the soil was fertile and the river close by. Eli plunged headlong in the cultivation of his lands. He spent days in the fields, escaping the large house as soon he could, only going back there to kiss Lazarus. He hoped that with time his home would be more tolerable and he also wished he could grow closer to his new spouse, shed the cold indifference he had for her; that poor girl had suffered so much already... Eli chided himself, but the temptation the vine held for him and the perspective of mindless labor were stronger. With time, perhaps...

For now, he worked very hard. He had just hired many peasants and delegated greater responsibilities to Samir and Ahmed. If Christians always considered Jews with suspicion, the two Arab men harbored no such prejudice. They couldn't care less about Isaac and Avi's wealth, about material considerations or the gossips that feed tensions between families. They lived in a small house near the vineyard, the one they had refused to abandon. They had agreed once to some minor improvements but insisted that not too many were made. Eli liked their company and thought of them as oriental wisemen. He often stayed with them in the small house awaiting nightfall before heading back home. When Lazarus began to walk, Eli often took him along—to his friends' delight.

As for Sarah, she sought her mother and Avi's wife more and more often to bathe in the warmth she had known in her youth. The family atmosphere helped her bear her husband's indifference. She was so depressed that her mother could often be heard asking Sarah in her shrill voice: "Tell me, my daughter, what's wrong?"

"Everything's fine," Sarah would answer in a subdued voice. "I'd like to be with a child, that's all."

And then her belly grew round. One morning, she knew that the child she had so much expected was on the way and she rushed to announce the good news to her family. Orpha, Avi's wife, bit her lip and pleaded with God that such a happy event soon be also hers. Her mother was screaming at the top of her lungs and, for once, Isaac, in the left wing of the house where he had retreated, paid attention to his wife's ear-splitting screams. A son! Sarah is expecting a son! He shrugged. What a fool! It will probably be a girl! He decided against going downstairs to congratulate Sarah. But Sarah was used to her father's absence and didn't think anything of it. She waited for nightfall to tell Eli. She was brimming with hope, convinced that now he would look at her differently. Thanks to her talkative mother, the entire country now knew about her pregnancy.

When Sarah finally told her husband, he glanced at her, seemed confused and then he lowered his head and frowned. Her disappointment was too great. She turned away to hide her tears and fell, prostrate, on the ground. In spite of his powerlessness to act, Eli was moved. He came closer to Sarah and ran his hand in her hair. Between sobs, she told him about her dull life, yelled that she should have died in Barcelona with all the others and pointed to Lazarus who frightened her.

Unable to comfort her and feeling guilty for having driven her to such unhappiness, Eli was torn. He tried to clear his head. While Sarah wept, ridding herself of much bitterness, he told her how his own life had been shattered by Esther's death. She didn't quite understand Eli's flow of words; he was telling her about another woman, about a past life in which she had no part. He said nothing about her or about their future together. It was only much later that, exhausted, she calmed down but also after Eli had confessed how ill-at-ease he had been in his new life and had implored her to try to understand him and had promised that he would try to be more considerate in the future.

And a new child would be so nice! Even a girl! A little sister for Lazarus! Everything will turn out fine, "Trust me, Sarah." Deep in his heart, he knew he didn't mean what he had said but he couldn't find the words to soothe her unhappiness; he kept his head down and didn't take her in his arms. At least, she had spoken her mind and had asserted that she mattered. Soon, too, a child would be there to receive all of his mother's love and unfulfilled longings.

Eli looked at Lazarus and began a dialogue with him in his own mind: You're a little man now and a new child is on the way, about to be born in empty comfort. You were born amid love and violence but you're a sturdy plant, nothing will ever abate your appetite for life. Lazarus, my son, when I was about to give up on life I realized I had to go on for your sake because you are the living memory of Esther; you must preserve her memory for a long, long time…

The news of the impending birth had an impact on Eli's state of mind: though he wasn't fully aware of all it meant, he was no longer turned to the past. He began to think about the future. Slowly, Esther's image faded. The labor of the vineyard no longer served as an outlet to his malaise; he found a genuine and sensible interest in his relationship with Sarah. He was growing used to being married; not that he loved Sarah but he came to consider her like a good friend with whom he shared the same roof. She did her best preparing nice meals, taking good care of the house, placing her hand more than she needed to on her belly to make sure that her small bearer of hope had not vanished. Eli didn't come home late from the vineyard anymore and, at times, they talked and fell into a peaceful sleep after a kiss on the forehead. Lazarus, aware that the tension had relaxed, sought Sarah's affection. She, however, whose belly was distending a little more with each passing day, paid him no attention: however cute that little boy was, he wasn't hers. Lazarus didn't expect very much and was happy to listen to the lady sing. For now she was singing and the other lady with the shrill voice came over often and the two of them would talk a lot. The little boy was enjoying again the cheerful noises he had known before. He needed nothing else, just his father's love.

He was two years old when Joseph was born. In the dead of winter Sarah, exhausted, radiated with happiness each time she was shown the small red bundle who screamed at the top of his lungs. My son. Eli! It's a son! and she cried for joy, thanking God, kissing her mother who had just met a potent competitor to her vocal power.

Eli was excited at the news. God has given me two sons. They will play and grow up together. Give me your hand, Lazarus, you have a brother, you will help each other; if one of you is in danger, the other one will come to his aid. Like you, he'll be raised to respect the laws of Moses. God has given me two sons and I will teach you both how to grow wine and, like my father and his father before, you will, dear little Benavistas, make wine flow throughout the whole region.

Orpha, whose prayer had been answered, gave birth a month later to a girl she named Yael. Unable to hide his disappointment Avi, at first, refused this divine gift: he had wished for a son and could not accept that fate had not complied with his wishes just as everyone around him always did. Eli could have two sons but he, Avi, the leader of an empire got a girl! He locked himself in his room and steadfastly refused to see the baby. His wife pleaded and begged him to open the door and Sarah, a brand new mother herself, tried to comfort her. Even Isaac, upset at such display of disdain for the little girl he already loved, railed at him, in vain.

Avi waited a few hours before coming out morosely, his head held high. He walked across to the cradle with his entire curious family on his heels and, over the child, he declared: "I was expecting a son but was given a daughter. I had chosen a name for my lineage but I won't have the happiness of using it. I had dreamt of a successor for all our businesses and this too I am denied. But you are my blood and if the Lord wanted it so, I welcome you among us."

He took the child in his arms and kissed her,—to his family's relief.

There they were, David. Those insatiable infants, these babies that brought happiness into their homes. They were going to occupy the next century and shape your future through success and failure. There they were, the bearers of hope, the makers of tomorrow, —they were still so innocent. But that century tore asunder their hope, trampled under foot the future and mercilessly destroyed the innocence of the Justs.

Chapter 5

THE YEAR 1394

In 1394, the Council of Regents of Castilla sat don Henrique III on the throne of Spain. He was fifteen. All the kingdom churches and all the Cortes dignitaries celebrated the event. The king was so young that everyone, whether nobleman or mere knight, thought he could be easily influenced. And everyone hurriedly curtsied his way to the Court.

But the young man whose staid temperament made him somewhat circumspect, imposed himself as king and conceded nothing. No matter how Court's nobles tried to curry favors from him, he always thwarted their efforts. In spite of his young age, he understood that a king reigns, survives even, only if he surrounds himself with carefully selected and trustworthy counselors. During his youth he had taken the time to study the workings of his complex world, had noted attitudes, and had reflected on betrayals. Wise and studious, he succeeded in this incredible accomplishment: he affirmed his authority, took in hand the destiny of his kingdom, selected reliable counselors and reigned uncontested. He was just fifteen.

Thus, no one tried to oppose him when he surrounded himself with Christians and Jews. If one was given to make a remark, the little king answered back: "My kingdom is not inhabited by Christians only. Everyone has the duty to participate in the good functioning of Castilla, and I have criteria other than religious to find out my enemies." He accompanied that last sentence with a smile that left his detractors speechless and in a hurry to curtsy their way out.

The People of the Book felt as if they had been given back their souls. The fear that had lodged deep in their guts since the massacres of 1391 began to fade away. Let a peaceful, happy future in! A certain euphoria blew across the Jewish quarters of Castilla. For a while, Marranos thought that the time had come to renounce the religion imposed on them so stupidly. The king's powers, however, couldn't undo what the Church had commanded. He allowed converts to continue to live in Jewish quarters because he was aware that a hastily arranged baptism could not sever them from their past. All for the good of the kingdom.

From then on, a curious mode of life took shape in the Jewish quarters where brand new Christians assimilated into their ancestral tradition a few catholic precepts. They prayed to Jesus while crying for Jehovah, torn between the star and the cross, never knowing when to fast, unable to bring themselves to work on Saturday but yet resting on Sunday, celebrating some legendary characters called saints but still commemorating mythical events in the history of Israel. Some saw in that very ambiguity a double protection for, as Christians, they would never again be persecuted but, as Jews, they could go on to become rich; others were torn; many others resigned to their changed fate. And there would never be more massacres. Never again during the reign of such a good king.

After an intense period of reflection that lasted all three years, a few others, small in number, preferred to leave their *aljamas* for reasons usually more personal than religious. Their departure in 1394 was not prompted by fear or imminent danger and thus their decision was coolly acknowledged by the Jewish community. To betray one's people, to choose the enemy camp and have children who will one day turn against Israel was a thought much too painful for those who were going to continue, from one generation to the next and in the face of continued adversity, to live by the word of the Book. One less Jew was one more enemy.

This is what happened with Salomon Halevy, the rabbi of Burgos who was baptized during the troubles of 1391. He opted to fully assume the conversion he had been imposed. A man of faith and a theologian, he became progressively interested in the tenets of that new religion and then became so taken by it that he went to Paris to study Latin and Christ's teachings, hoping that upon his return he would be given an important position within the Spanish church. If his behavior distressed the Jewish community, the Church was quick to applaud, with some ostentation and a bit of consternation, a man who applied himself so hard to become a true Christian. Both sides used him as an example,—but they did not use the same adjectives.

Chapter 6

TOLEDO, 1492

Peace had returned for almost eight years now. The little king had matured and his authority was indisputable. Within the Jewish community, fear didn't hinder activity or breed suspicion anymore. Marranos who lived alongside their ex-correligionists had gotten used as best they could to an existence that was now free of persecutions.

Eli had become rich. The day-to-day routine had pushed the endless sadness of the beginning to the background. By making his vineyard his number one priority and by giving it his all, he had succeeded in making the product of his winery famous as far away as the distant Turkish world. Ahmed had become his representative in the Arab world but Samir had refused to leave the vineyard he considered his own domain. Business flourished, orders abounded. Eli felt the same fearlessness Isaac had felt some years before though he preferred to build and administer his enterprise rather than merely accumulate money. By observing Avi-the-authoritarian being seduced beyond reason by luxury, he was pleased to conclude that he, coming from the poor Jewish quarter, never had to deny his past.

Anyone in need could come knock on his door: with a smile on his face he would give help or advice to those in need. At times, a small but well-founded apprehension held him back: he feared that people would start considering him a Lord and would therefore flatter him to excess; he was also uncomfortable with the thought that people might talk about him the way they talked about the famous Isaac or Avi, his fearless son. Via gifts and his discreet deeds, he hoped to stay close to his own kind and to always be there to help.

When the evenings were pleasant, he liked to go to his old neighborhood to play with Moshe's or Myriam's children while reminiscing about the "good old days." Happiness was so simple then. He participated in it with all his heart. When Lazarus, the little boy or the young man, accompanied him, there was joy and laughter. Then it was time to go back.

His sons were two years apart but so much had happened during that span of time that they were profoundly different the one from the other. Eli felt a certain complicity with Lazarus. When he looked at him he couldn't help but thank God. Without Lazarus he would have died, gone mad or would have amounted to nothing.

Joseph had the same effect on his mother. She had entirely focused her attention on her son, smothering him with her love. He endured what his mother, the ill-loved one, had been deprived of because she suffered from Eli's indifference in an arranged marriage. But could one pass sentence on this man with a broken heart?

The baby grew up in the comfortable prison of his mother's love. Sarah's world shrunk to the size of the cradle. She would have died of sadness without Joseph. The handsome baby tortured his mother with the smallest tear, enthralled her with the slightest smile, and held her in awe with every little burp. Nothing else mattered and she could only sleep near him. In her own mind, Eli was losing his flesh and blood reality. He was becoming a mere shadow, duplicating that of his son, Lazarus.

Sarah was guilty and her son Joseph didn't have a chance. Even before he was born, he didn't have a chance. Thus, he grew up without a father: his mother's attitude made him an orphan. For no one could come near the prodigal son over whom she relentlessly watched; her heart broke each time the innocent child looked at someone or if he offered a tentative smile to Lazarus or the young maid. In the vise of daily life, he was quick to realize the power he held over his mother and just how far he could go. At one, he knew what screaming noise to make to make his mother come rushing to him; at four, he knew how to rudely push away his bowl to see sweets appear before him; at eight, he knew just what to say to be instantly forgiven for the foolish act he had just done. But he also realized that he would be nothing if he betrayed her by rejecting her hold over him.

The passionate osmosis between Sarah and Joseph grew more and more unhealthy with each passing day. Eli divided his time between his successful business and his son Lazarus; he paid scant attention to his younger son's education. He was delighted to have noticed his wife's improvement with their son's birth; their small universe became a little more stable. However, he was far from realizing how much attention he should have exercised to have taken Joseph away from his gilded jail. At ten years of age, Joseph only aspired to please his mother.

Less spoiled during his childhood but yet very confident of his father's love, Lazare knew neither hypocrisy nor fits of anger; the children and their parents lived the same misunderstanding; it was a status quo which permitted each of them to lead his own little existence. And so it was, as God had wanted it.

Chapter 7

That particular morning, the yeshivah teacher asked questions of only one student: Lazarus. The teacher kept on expanding on each question, testing Lazarus's memory and making him repeat over and over again. He so insisted that the lad became irritated. The teacher smiled.

"Poor Lazarus, you must be wondering why I am picking on you today!"

" Yes."

" I've heard that the Great Rabbi Meir Alguades will be in your home this evening. Right?"

The boy nodded again.

"Well, I wanted to test you; beside, you'll soon have your bar-mitzva and the Great Rabbi will most surely ascertain your knowledge. I must admit you're doing very well. You're a good student, Lazarus, you have it all on the tip of your tongue! As a reward, I'm excusing you from this afternoon class. You can go back home! Your brother, too!"

Happy at the opportunity, both children thanked their teacher and headed back home. When they weren't under the watch of adults, the two boys enjoyed playing like kids their age. Making blades of grass whistle and climbing small trees, they returned home leisurely. Sarah had invited the entire family to her home that evening in order to honor the Great Rabbi. The children knew that busy with all the preparations she would be in no mood to pay them any attention. As they had anticipated, she was rather upset when she saw them coming back so early. Between her pasta pots and her sauce pans, she panicked: "What are you doing here?"

They told her about the morning class and how they had been rewarded. Sarah kissed Joseph to congratulate him without Lazarus protesting. Sarah kissed Joseph to congratulate him under Lazarus's indifferent gaze, then she pushed them toward the garden. "Go and play outside, come on, go, go!"

They ran to it. Out of the window, she yelled: "Be careful! No silly stuff!" They went farther away toward the fountains; Sarah's voice dissipated in the wind.

Excited by the visit of the rabbi, Joseph wanted to show off what he was also capable of. He climbed on the ledge of the fountain and pretended to be a tight rope walker like the traveling entertainers he had once seen in town. Lazarus had barely had time to warn him when he was already falling into the water and hitting his head against the edge. Panicky, he began to scream at the top of his lungs and Sarah rushed to him right away.

The sight of the blood brought back the nightmare of Barcelona, the rivulet of blood streaming down the face of her son made her crazy; she began to scream right alongside him, caught him and squeezed him hard in her arms. The child, still dripping with water, quickly calmed down. Motionless, Lazarus watched his now almost hysterical mother with amazement. She was frantically kissing Joseph when all of a sudden she slapped Lazarus who, his eyes welling with tears, stammered: "Why, mommy…"

Concerned only with the sake of her own son, she blurted out: "Don't you call me mommy." Then, looking at him hard: "Don't you ever call me mommy, I'm not your mother!"

Lazarus stared at her, his mouth agape. Joseph stopped making any noise when he heard that strange utterance. Embarassed, Sarah led her son to the house and left Lazarus by the fountain. The child began to cry and locked himself in his room.

Eli came home earlier to be ready for the coming of the Great Rabbi. He could sense a great deal of uneasiness among all the activity in the house. When he asked Aviva the maid, he found out what had happened. He went up to his son's bedroom. Lazarus rushed to his embrace and, through tears, repeated the horrible sentence Sarah had said.

For a minute, Eli was struck dumb. How do you make up for such a blunder? Should he deny or play down the incident? Was Lazarus mature enough to learn the truth? Harm, at any rate, had been done. He explained everything to his son.

Before the Great Rabbi's arrival he led him by the hand, completely ignoring Sarah and Joseph's perplexed gaze, and they went to find Esther's grave. On the way, Lazare asked his father questions. He was answered gently: "Your mother is with the wise and pious one of the twelve tribes of Israel. In the immensity of the heavens, she watches over you, she protects you and will protect you all of your life."

Behind the El Transito synagogue built in 1357 by the great Samuel Halevy, was a small cemetery. Lazarus pictured a very soft face leaning toward him to kiss him, a very beautiful woman, his very own mother. Moved, Eli pointed to the grave: "Your mother is here."

They meditated silently over the tombstone, united by the same suffering. Lazarus's mind ran wild. Eli was reliving a past he thought he had buried. He told his son about Esther's blue eyes, her smile, her long hair, her sweetness. It was as if she was coming alive during his prayer over the small grave. But reality awaited them: Meir Alguades was probably at the house. They went back.

The Great Rabbi, physician to the king, was renowned in the entire kingdom. Very much sought after, he travelled the country and had not enough time to devote himself to those who solicited his expertise. He held Eli in great esteem: he had agreed to lead his son's bar mitzva service out of friendship.

That evening, in the beautiful Benavista's home, the day's drama faded to the background thanks to the rabbi's comforting presence. Lazarus, inspired by his perception of an ideal mother, answered every one of the rabbi's questions with a faith so pure, so strong, that everyone was moved. Even Sarah kept her head lowered because she could sense she had made definite her separation from her husband. Joseph was also able to feel a widening gap between himself and his brother, a gap that severed him even more from the world, that locked him in his mother's very restrictive universe.

From that day on, Lazarus began to regularly go to the cemetery. With each commemoration, whether happy or not, or for no reason at all, he would go to his mother's tomb by himself.

That event marked Lazarus's brutal entry in the adult world. He finally was able to realize why the one he called mommy had always been so cool to him. Yet, he was but twelve years old; he was at an age when one needs a lot of affection. He had to admit to this new reality, with his father as his only support.

Chapter 8

Late on a June afternoon in 1404, the humidity hung oppressively over the sleepy province. Only the cicadas could be heard. It was a scorcher of a day. A human form went by the Jewish cemetery of Toledo where a young man seated on a rock appeared to meditate. The man was lanky; he hesitated before coming nearer. He scrutinized the boy with eyes burning with mistrust. Then, already passing sentence upon the young lad, he thundered (accusingly): "Who are you?"

"My name is Lazarus Benavista, son of Eli Benavista," answered the young man, made ill at ease by that stranger who kept on staring at him.

"How old are you?"

"Fourteen."

"What are you doing here?"

"I'm praying over my mother's grave."

The man wasn't moved. He frowned: "When did she die?"

"In 1391. Killed by Christians," Lazarus answered in a muted voice.

His sorrow was genuine, his response without spite. Against all expectations, however, the man grew furious: "Killed, you say? No! She died because she didn't accept Jesus Christ, the savior of humanity. You are her killers, you, the Jews. That and that only is the Truth!"

Stunned, Lazarus stared at the man. "The savior, you say! The savior! What savior? He didn't come to my mother's rescue! He didn't save her!"

"Of course not! The Jews are too full of sins, they must pay. Your mother and the others have paid and all of you will pay! All of you! For all your sins!"

"But," responded an astounded Lazarus, "aren't Christians who kill babies, old people or women not sinners too? Then, why aren't they punished?"

"They are!" the man was wagging a finger threateningly while screaming, "and they'll pay for their sins just like you will pay for yours. God has decided to let you live scattered through all four corners of the world, but you'll live with your delusions and your anguish until you come to recognize your false ways and convert. That is your only salvation! Godless people that you are!"

In his frenzy, the man was preaching to the dead while wildly swinging his arms. But Lazarus didn't let go and, grinding his teeth before this pouring of hatred: "Then what are you doing here, you who speak with so much anger, in this cemetery where so many Jewish souls are observing you? Aren't you afraid of sullying your soul?"

"You are provoking me, kid! Do you know who you are talking to? But I'll know how to put you in the right path. Thanks to me, many Jews have already converted. You too, one day, will renounce your sinful ways and will stop rambling about our savior Jesus Christ."

Lazarus studied the stranger's face to etch his features into his memory.

"Who are you?" he asked him.

"My name is Vincent Ferrer".

In the span of a few seconds they had studied each other. Finally, the man drew his cape back to his shoulders, shook his head in Lazarus's direction, then in the direction of the graves and turned back while grumbling.

Lazarus followed with his eyes that figure foretelling new misfortunes to come. He knew nothing about Vincent Ferrer. A dominican priest from Valencia, he had been responsible, along with Hernando Martinez, of agitating mobs during the massacres of 1391. Inside her grave, Esther Benavista had met one of her murderers. Lazarus had just come across the one who, a few hundred miles away from Toledo, had destroyed his father's life and made him an orphan.

He asked his mother to please forgive the offensive exchange of words done over her tomb. On his way back, he understood why older people's eyes flickered with fear as well as their suspicion of allegedly pacific Christians. There was more danger in that one man than in all of nature. One single, solitary hissed word could do more harm than an arrow through one's heart; there existed in this world human beings capable of breeding hatred without ever feeling shame or remorse...

Fanatical to the end, Vincent Ferrer took his love of Christ quite far, convinced as he was that his mission on an earth peopled with godless men and women was to convert them or to get rid of them. He would appear on a village square, his feet bare and slashed by the rocks on the road. A crowd quickly formed around him. It was then that he proclaimed his faith loudly and, becoming entranced by his own discourse, he would bare his chest and would lash at himself until his body turned red with his own blood. Christ had suffered, he too would suffer. Through this display of humility he was able to transcend his own humanity and was so close to God that his violence erupted. In awe before this spectacle, the crowd, inspired by this saintly man who was sacrificing himself for the love of God, only needed a signal to descend upon the enemies of the Almighty. Then, Vincent Ferrer, proselyser of the word of God, a radiant masochist, bursting with hatred, led the mobs of men toward the nonbelievers.

In front of such powerful individuals who could stir mobs and destroy anything that stood in their way, what weight could the conciling words of peaceful rabbis carry?

Chapter 9

THE YEAR OF OUR LORD 1405

The Joseph Abu'Omar Ibn Shoshan synagogue of Toledo, built in the 13th century, was one of the most sacred places of castillian Judaism. A worthy successor of Salomon's temple, it was the pride and joy of an entire people.

Without a vaulted or plain ceiling it was still majestic with its simple wooden roof. Octagonal pillars in rows of seven, subdivided the interior into numerous small patios. These rows of pillars formed quite a remarkable nave. Delicately curved Moorish arches carved with graceful arabesques and fine rose-windows decorated the superior part of the nave. The stucco capitals of the columns were engraved with tree branches, leaves and garlands intermingling with pinecones. A frieze in relief surmounted the central nave which constituted the architectural jewel of the building.

In that hot summer day of 1405, like each year at the same time, Eli, Lazarus and many others had gathered in this sanctified site to honor the memory of those who died in 1391. Fourteen years after, that anniversary was still observed with devotion and sadness.

Lost in meditation and prayer, no one paid any attention to the distant din. But the uproar gained in strength and noises one could distinguish from afar became screams near-by, the pounding of steps grew like an echo from hell, and suddenly a crazed mob filled the temple. In a flash Lazarus recognized Vincent Ferrer as the ringleader: covered with blood and his clothes torn to shreds, he spewed his hatred as loud he could.

Entirely engaged in haranguing the crowd, Vincent Ferrer did not see the child from the cemetery. It is then that the diminutive rabbi Benmaiorque, that nothing would have predisposed to heroism, climbed on the tebah and in a faltering voice began to recite the Shema

Israel. The gang of attackers armed with their picks and their lances looked to Vincent Ferrer. He was eyeing the little man from head to toe. The Jews, looking straight into the Christians' eyes, joined their voices to the rabbi's: their solemn chant ascended toward the sky.

But they weren't able to complete their litany; a Christian climbed the altar, closed in on the frail rabbi who, white as a sheet, was still reciting his prayer, and put his hand over his mouth: "Enough, damned Jew," he said. Then, grabbing him by the waist he whirled him about and hurled him among sacred objects and books. Bloodied, the rabbi got up staggeringly, put his skullcap back shakingly and looked for his prayer shawl. But the brute was already upon him and, savage with anger, kicked him at least ten times in the head and body.

No one dared to interfere. Rabbi Benmaiorque died amid the hurrahs of his executioners, before his motionless coreligionists. His eyes turned toward the heavens, Vincent Ferrer thanked the Almighty for His help and let his throng of followers continue with their task.

When the bloodied body stopped moving, the mad monk drew a satisfied smile and, brandishing a finger toward the door, he ordered the Jews to vacate the premises with a simple nod of the head. They filed out slowly, not daring to register a complaint against their assailants. Hurrahs reverberated when they had emptied the synagogue.

"Leave and disappear, damned Jews!" Vincent Ferrer was screaming. Then, the murderous mob raised their pitchforks to scatter the frightened Jews. The maimed rabbi's body got thrown outside the synagogue. And everyone went home with his head lowered.

Inside the temple, Vincent Ferrer slashed ritual objects with the whip he used on himself, threw the tebah down and announced to the obedient crowd that such a sumptuous/majestic/luxurious place could only be used to honor the glory of Jesus: may it never again be sullied by the enemies of Christ! "You are a rock!" he intoned while spreading his arms out, and the Christians responded: "On that rock I will build my church." That is how that marvelous and sacred place became the church of Santa Maria la Blanca.

The great rabbi Alguades, chosen as the representative of the Jewish community of Toledo, tried to use his influence with the king to have the synagogue returned to its rightful owners. But no matter how brave this monarch was, he couldn't butt head with the Church. He declined the request. "Vincent Ferrer isn't the Church!" the rabbi challenged. The king sighed: "He is worse than the Church." Santa Maria la Blanca remained catholic.

The high catholic dignitaries had scant interest in the people. Close to princes and lords and other practiced intriguers, they let the whims of madmen like Vincent Ferrer or Archdeacon Martinez rule street mobs in the commission of any crime imaginable done in the name of God. If the results were bloody, they washed their hands of any responsibility. On the other hand, if the Church swelled with new converts or amazing new sites, they approved good-humoredly. In spite of himself the king was becoming a powerless accomplice to street antisemitism.

Preferring to play the incident down, too many Jews became unwilling or thoughtless accomplices: "There was no massacre this time!" "Rabbi Benmaiorque died because he provoked Christians!," "The temple was turned into a church? Well, then, our converted brethren will be at less of a loss when they come to pray to their new God in a place they have always known!", "The king is good and he likes the Jews, we are under his protection"… To deny danger was to begin to legitimize the fanatical violence of the Christians. But that they hadn't realized yet. To refuse to confront future exactions was to fuel Vincent Ferrer's desire to annihilate the Jews to the very last.

> *Thus, in that period's confusing plays for influence, each brought his own block to the building of despair. It would have been simplistic to have pointed to a single culprit. You're discovering the history of your family, dear little David lost at sea, but also that of man and his cowardice, his limitations but also his striving toward the sublime. Do not lose hope but do not forget the lesson drawn out of these mistakes. Be armed with that knowledge, be strengthened by it and carry as far as you can the memory of your people.*

Chapter 10

In 1406, twenty-six year old don Enrique III had been king for twelve years he was felled by illness. Already of a frail constitution, he now surrounded himself with a team of medical doctors. He was particularly fond of Meir Alguades who carefully tended to his care and who also held the king in deep esteem.

Lazarus Benavista was in his sixteenth year.

Uncle Avi held his breath when Lazarus shot his arrow. The makeshift target riddled with holes was hit almost dead center. Avi took a deep breath. Lazarus showed no emotion. But when his uncle slapped him on the back to congratulate him, the young man cracked a smile. Avi was complimenting him! Don Avi, the formidable merchant, was taking time away from his business to observe his progress in archery!

Avi cared for the stoic teen. The child had been raised in luxury in a sumptuous house but Sarah had never been a mother for him. Even priviledged, an orphan remains an orphan. He never complained and had poise and a sense of honor which amused and touched Avi-the-sly. From the top of his six foot frame, Lazarus already looked like a man whereas his brother, too sheltered by his mother, had a difficult time affirming himself.

Avi had an ulterior motive in his interest in Lazarus. His daughter Yael, with all the fragile grace of a fourteen year old, cast admiring eyes on him. Avi was amused by this. They were young, now, but one day they would certainly be married. Now they were just learning how to become adults. One last time, he cheered his nephew on to perfect his shooting and then left to survey the good workings of his empire.

Lazarus hit the bull's eye twice. He was flushed with pride. What an engrossing pastime. From the time he began observing the city's shooting-range from his window and the comings and goings of the Royal Guards who instructed the local peasants every Sunday, he fell in love with the sport. He built himself a small bow, placed a target in a far off corner of the garden and practiced every chance he got. Yael was constantly roaming these parts and her heartbeat quickened whenever she saw Lazarus's powerful figure come near.

A mischievous child, Yael enjoyed hiding to steal glimpses of Lazarus's endeavoring figure but, almost a woman, she was annoyed at not being able to compete with that stupid sport. Since Eli had given Lazarus a genuine bow, Lazarus spent all of his free time in that remote part of the garden. His progress had been remarkable but little Yael couldn't have cared less.

Late that afternoon, when all the family members invited by Sarah were gathered to savor her delicious pastries, Lazarus, in the garden, couldn't tear himself away from his practice. Everyone had found a place around Messod Hazan who was recounting his peregrinations. Cousins were busy playing and Joseph, near his mother, felt happy. No one noticed that Lazarus and Yael were absent. After a while, Yael finally let go of her frustration: "What can you possibly get out of that ridiculous pastime? Everyone is here celebrating and you are spending your time shooting arrows! Are you going to spend the rest of your life shooting these arrows?"

When, because of her boldness, she felt her cheeks burning and her heart beating faster, she suddenly understood that the word "love," of which she had but a vague notion up to now, could describe her feeling toward Lazarus. She began to stammer but Lazarus was already replying: "Why speak to me like this? I'm in nobody's way and I'm hitting the bull's eye more and more often and for me it's the best pastime there is!"

"Can't you spend time with me? But perhaps I'm not your type or maybe I'm less beautiful than your bow and arrow!" she retorted, staring him straight in the face. Lazarus, taken aback, was discovering that this was no longer a little girl, but a determined young woman who dared to boot conventions to declare her love.

"Yael!" he said.

Pouting, she lowered her eyes. He realized that she was beautiful with her long black hair. He stepped toward her with his hand out. She thought that he wanted to reprimand her. She quickly moved away. Still, he was able to catch her by the shoulder:

"Yael! Forgive me. Don't be angry with me. You are much more beautiful than my bow!"

Surprised at his words, she raised her eyes.

"I didn't think that... But you are only fourteen! I'm barely sixteen! I don't even have a profession! Perhaps later will we make a happy couple... But later..."

It was his turn to turn red. Yael bit her lip. They were looking at each other but no longer like children. They were surprised to discover each other. He leaned to kiss her on the cheek but their lips met. A stolen kiss. Then more passionate kisses. Their hearts in unison, they were entering the vast adult world hand in hand. Their eyes shut. Lazare, with his strong back, his blond curls and his blue eyes and Yael, the agile young animal with the dark mane, had distanced themselves from the celebration going on in the house, from Toledo bathed by the Tagus, from Spain and the rest of the universe to discover the simple pleasure of being together.

A FEW DAYS LATER

"Go away, let me be by myself!" Eli barked in the direction of his servant. "I look ridiculous!" he added. He paced the room with long nervous strides: he was worried at the perspective of appearing at court and of its protocol. Having to put on this suit unsettled him. Avi, however, had picked him a fine embroidered silk shirt and bright canvas breeches, a quilted vest, a wide coat and soft leather shoes he had made according to his own specifications. "What a costume!" he sighed again.

Sarah and Joseph were looking on, which didn't help matters. "I really don't like it." Sarah shrugged: "Your wine fills kings' cups and you can't make an effort?" Eli did not answer back. He knew he wasn't on his way to be tortured. On the contrary! Anyone else would have been tickled to death to be expected at the Alcazar. Also, to reassure him, Avi had agreed to accompany him.

But Eli remained annoyed. Avi had warned him: "Santa Ana, the Bishop of Burgos, will be in attendance during our meeting with the king." From that moment on, Eli felt very uneasy. Santa Maria, ex-

Salomon Halevy, ex-rabbi, the one Jews everywhere cursed each time they heard his name. The one who had so readily embraced the Catholic faith that he became Bishop. To be in the same room with him! How would he react? Before the king and the court how would he, the Jew, behave? Ah! to have to take leave of his habits, his house, his vineyards to enter a world full of traps... Just to sell his wine! He had barely slept and had badly eaten. Then it was time to go.

He stepped out into the garden, ready in his dress if not in his mind. He waved to Lazarus who, as he was bound to do, was practicing.

"I hit the bull's eye seven out of eight times and at a hundred and fifty feet away!"

This time Eli didn't reprimand his son for only thinking about entertaining himself. He grimaced a reluctant compliment, resuming his melancholic thoughts. Yael, who could always be found at the Benavista's house, appeared in front of him: coy, she stared at him with her large black eyes and then, in her strong voice, blurted: "He's really good!" Eli smiled. Avi was coming.

They decided to get to the Alcazar on foot. Jews could still afford this eccentricity that no Christian of noble extraction would have dared even consider. With a soft wind caressing their faces, they took the narrow path lined with tall trees and left the cigarrales to arrive near Toledo. They set foot on the Alcantara bridge. A flock of birds nose-dived toward the surface of the Tagus. Eli looked on their harmonious ballet and he flinched. Avi caught sight of it.

"Are you cold?"

"No," answered Eli somberly. "In a flash, I saw myself some fifteen years back crossing that bridge; I didn't know then what had just happened inside the Jewish quarter... I remember how deserted it was; how quiet everything was and the dread I felt, but also the desperate hope that nothing terrible had happened..."

Avi looked at him. "It's already been fifteen years, right? You are on your way to the royal court so don't think about it anymore. It's better to have all your wits about you in front of these people. Come back to the present."

Eli agreed reluctantly. After a heavy silence, he changed the subject: "Avi, I'm uncomfortable knowing that I'm going to meet Santa Maria."

"Don't worry, he only intercedes in church-related matters, and that's not our business. He'll be listening, that's about it. He might want to speak with you once the audience is over ... To convert you!" he added impishly.

"Cursed be he!"

Avi sighed. "Don't be so intolerant or so harsh. We are here to conduct a business deal among people who hold values different from ours. When we have concluded the best possible deal, then your day will be over and you'll be able to go back to your own world. In the meantime, Eli, loosen up a bit!"

Most of the houses in Toledo were built on ground level, one next to another. Streets were plain dirt paths where dust was heavy during the summer months and where, when it rained, mud made traffic quite difficult. But heading toward the citadel through the Jewish quarter, there were multi-levelled houses that stood alone and wide open spaces such as the Alcana, that incredible market where merchants and travelling performers, bourgeois and artists met around precious Persian jewels, elegant Cordoban leathers and spices from the far ends of the world.

They arrived at the foot of the Alcazar. On that particular day, the impressive rectangular fortress looked like an Oriental bazaar. A happy crowd was milling about. Itinerant merchants had set up shop in good locations inside the palace's courtyard while captains waited for their appointments. They paced the ground and looked suspiciously at each other while harboring the hope to be given a company's command or a pension. There were peasants who had come to look at the king dining. They were jostling and cursing each other as they vied for the best available seat, to later boast proudly: "I was there!"

The two men were led into the huge courtroom where four knights were waiting. The knights greeted them with a condescending smirk. Avi answered with a slight nod.

"Do you know them?" Eli asked in a low voice.

"No. Well, I have seen them a couple times. Etiquette requires that I salute them, and here at court you have to be courteous at all times.

These men all live above their means, they feast and bluster even though they don't own a red cent! They are here to offer their services in exchange for some settlement of debts. They are to be feared as dangerous, always living on the edge. What's more, they are typical of all the courtesans. They need our businesses and our gold and that's why they receive us. But be suspicious if they ignore you or if they smile at you. We have to be smarter and more resourceful than they."

Eli remained tense in that very hard world and after hearing Avi's advice he could hardly understand. "These people frighten me. I can't do it."

Avi was much more at ease in a world he knew well. He smiled paternally. "It's a question of habit. I was able to assert my authority here like my father before me. Some even fear me, you know? Look…"

Shortly, they were received by the advisor da Costa who told them that because of other commitments, Santa Maria would not be attending the meeting. Eli let out a sigh of relief. In one minute he regained his confidence and followed his brother-in-law more gingerly.

Shortly after the customary complicated cordialities, Avi came to the heart of the matter with his characteristic self-assurance: "My brother-in-law Eli Benavista owns one of Spain's best vineyards, as any nobleman can attest. To express our loyalty to our good king Henrique, we request we be allowed to label our export to the Orient with the following message: "Royal wine of the Crown of Castilla." Of course our monarchs' kindness will be duly rewarded in the form of a tithe proportional to the quantity of wine sold."

The king's advisor accepted the proposal and received, as was customary, a nice amount of money for himself. Eli watched this long rehearsed procedure: the smiles, the greetings, the high-sounding sentences, —a perfectly working, well-oiled mechanism. In his own mind, he thanked Avi to have accompanied him. Alone, he would probably have immediately failed to conclude the deal. He was ready to take his leave when the king's representative turned to him. perhaps to conclude the audience, perhaps to assess the enigmatic wine maker.

"So you are the one responsible for producing such a wonderful beverage! Congratulations! It is unusual for a Jew to succeed in that field!" He smiled broadly.

Very much annoyed, Eli replied shakily: "Yet, we have been winegrowers from father to son for several generations: I owe my ancestors all the secrets that give my wine its special sapor. That, and its renown!"

"I won't deny that you have the gift to excel in that domain but you're the exception rather than the rule among your people. Except for the study of ancient books and your retreat into prayer, I wonder what you and your people are able to undertake!... Ah! yes, of course! I was forgetting that you also know how to do business!" His grin grew wider. It was mockery he was after.

Avi did not interfere while the counselor plied his wit; later, the counselor would relate this feat to his friends. But for now, the merchant relished seeing his brother-in-law squirm clumsily. No one made fun of Avi. All deferred to him—hypocritically perhaps—and all addressed him as don Monsonego.

The man went on: "If memory serves me right, I do not believe that a single Jew was ever seen armed or ever distinguished himself in the martial arts in the whole history of Spain. You're scared of the sword!"

"Don't be so deceived," Eli answered as he attempted gamely to tangle with the deceitful counselor, many of us have helped the kings of Aragon and Castilla during the wars against the Moors.

"For sure, the Chancellor admitted, but it's been so long! Just a handful of old men would remember that. Today none of you would dare compete against our knights in a joust or a tournament. One can not be a merchant and be courageous at the same time!..." Thinking he had closed the audience, he was surprised by Eli's reply:

"Excuse me, sir, but my sixteen year old son Lazarus is a gifted archer who can hit the bull's eye with almost every shot."

"Is that so?" retorted the Chancellor in surprise. "There could thus be Jews able to fight? That's news to me! I'll be interested in seeing that phenomenon. You said it was your son..."

"Give me a time and a place and my son will surprise you," answered Eli piqued to the quick. Santa Maria's absence had liberated him and he was not about to tolerate that his son's gift be questioned so insolently.

Avi looked on with puzzlement, wondering where this exchange would lead.

"So be it, then. If your son is so skillful, let him show his skills... in front of the entire country! A tournament is scheduled four Sundays thence and the most gifted knights of Toledo and neighboring courts will test their archery skills against each other. Let your dear little genius attend!"

Roused, Eli shot back: "He'll be there!"

With a nod, he signaled Avi it was time to leave. The Chancellor eyed them from head to foot with a bemused, quizzical look. They took leave of each other without uttering a word and the two Jews left.

Avi had a hard time controlling himself past the palace gate. He exploded: "Are you mad? Have you gone mad?"

"You saw the arrogance and how he treated us! Lazarus is talented. Very talented. He'll show them!"

"That's not the point. He's going to make us pay for your insolence."

"Lazarus will win."

"What! You will have him compete? Do you know the skills of the nobles who will participate in the tournament? Lazarus will be no more than a distraction to them and you can be sure that they won't pass the opportunity to humiliate him. And us, too. You are acting irresponsibly, Eli!"

"Lazarus will win."

They stopped talking. Eli, moved by his faith, walked with his head held high. Avi began to wonder. Lazarus was skilled. Just the previous week he had observed him again and had been filled with admiration. But to imagine ... Then, he gave Eli a conspiratorial look. He smiled. What if! It is sheer folly but why not?

When taking leave of each other before going home, Avi addressed his brother-in-law one last time: "What you did is inconceivable. But for just a second I can imagine a little Jew beating all the Christians, all the Lords. And I want to believe it! Mazel tov, Eli!"

Eli went home feeling good. The children played in the garden. Yael and Joseph cooled themselves with water from the fountain while Lazarus, stretched out under an orange-tree, tried to escape the heat of the day. Eli kissed them all, without any word, then went to change, glad to relinquish his costume for a modest shirt. He hurried back down to the garden, more excited than he was willing to show.

" Listen to me, Lazarus…By the way, aren't you shooting, today?" he asked, letting his disappointment show.

Yael and Joseph clucked and Lazarus opened his eyes wide. "No!" he answered, fearing criticisms. Was his father about to stand in the way of his all-consuming passion, too?

"Could you hit the bull's eye with every shot?"

"I might! Why?"

"Could you remain level-headed if a crowd looked on?"

Lazarus glanced at Yael, his regular audience. It dawned on him and he began to smile: "Yes!"

"Well, then, I have a good news to announce to all of you. The King has organized a celebration in Toledo in a month's time and the country's best archers will compete against each other. It's an important tournament. I enrolled Lazarus!"

"An important tournament!" stammered Lazarus, stars dancing in his eyes.

"Bravo!" yelled Joseph clapping and Yael threw herself around her love's neck. But she quickly let go, blushing. Nobody noticed.

Sarah came closer and, frowning: "Are you mad? They'll make fun of your son!"

Forgoing an answer, Eli turned to his son: "There is still time to withdraw… I think!… I have faith in you, my son, but if you believe that this test is beyond your abilities…"

The teenager, his face cracking a wide smile, shook his head: "No! It's not too difficult. I can win!"

Father and son embraced. Yael batted her long eyelashes to hide her emotion and Joseph went to sit on the grass next to his mother to ask her to also believe in Lazarus's victory. At last, Sarah smiled and kissed her son. He was better skilled at loitering in the kitchen and dispensing advice to servants than he was at shooting a bow. But be it taste or skill, what difference did it make as long as one had a gift? Young Joseph, rounder than his brother, and looking insecure, ran to his father to join the festivities. Eli, however, focused his attention on Lazarus and paid none to Joseph, whose smile began to fade.

The news spread like wild fire. In the study halls, synagogues and in the Jewish areas, all the talk was about the tournament. A young Jew was going to vie against the Lords of the country. For all of them it was as if Israel was to be avenged; after centuries of humiliation, it was a matter of regaining one's honor and glory. Young Lazarus carried more than a plain bow across his shoulders, he carried the hope of an entire people.

For a whole month everyone recounted old legends excitedly. The one most often told was the story of David and Goliath; so much so that their names became confused: it was Lazarus, the famed archer, facing Goliath. If some elders, mumblingly expressed some doubts, they were cast withering glances. Lazarus-David would win, the stronger the enemy, the stronger the faith, the entire Spain-Goliath would not defeat the child, as sturdy, as resilient as the entire people of Israel...

Euphoria did not take hold among the nobles. "A Jew!" The word spread from salon to salon. "That's all we needed!" The king had already won his subjects' disapproval when he replaced the traditional jousting matches and the sword or lance fights with the much less spectacular sport of archery, but that was in honor of his guest the Prince Forest Vrys of Wales, himself a champion marksman. So be it, then. But a Jew! Many withdrew their participation, many more made rash pronouncements: "I shall not attend!", "Never!", "Over my dead body!" But the governing authorities relished the participation of the young Israelite: Christian morality will be safe, the boy would be beaten and his community again humiliated with him. With the spreading of this view, courtesans regained a sense of euphoria and forgot their grumbling. " Miss that spectacle? Ha! Never!", "I'll be there!"

Jugglers, singers and acrobats rushed the city's gates. The streets of Toledo teemed with a curious crowd a good two weeks before the tournament. People came from far away to attend the tournament, even if it meant having to sleep in the fields. Numerous Jews traveled to Toledo and found lodging in Talmud-Torah schools, in the courtyards of synagogues or at friends' homes. Young Benavista was at the center of all this activity and the focus of all the conversations.

Finally, the fated day came. A human sea stamped at the entrance to the Roman circus: it was in that impressive antique ruin with its large gardens that the competition was to take place. Everyone feared not securing a seat. That day, the bourgeois withstood the heat and the wait in their heavy colorful costumes. The masses, spread out in the streets of Toledo, waited patiently with the slim hope to catch something. Jews, arriving from all four corners of the country, could be seen praying supplicatingly.

When they were finally allowed in, they took their place in a sudden calm. Wealthy Christians, intent on showing off their station, glanced inquisitively in the direction of the Jews, over there, whose turn it now was to enter. Dressed much too warmly for the most part, they too wanted to show dignity and took their seats quietly, while trying to locate the Benavista family and the young hero. The king and queen took their place under the canopy above the wooden platform erected for their pleasure.

Uncle Avi had managed a few of the better seats. Both families were in attendance: Eli, Joseph, Sarah, Avi, his wife Orpha and their daughter Yael, as well as Isaac Monsonego, old but still with an alert eye, who had come out of his lair for the occasion. As a safe measure, senora Monsonego was assigned a seat next to her daughter, far away from her husband. Most of the Jews were not as well seated. They would not be able to see much, but for many decades to come they would talk about that tiny dot, over there, almost invisible, that was to be rent with an arrow.

First, there would be the qualifying rounds. Out of some thirty registered participants, only the best four would go on to the final round. Eli shuddered when he heard the rule: would Lazarus hold up that many hours, would he feel unsecure, and what about the sun? His son's powerful physique provided him some relief: his youth would be his trump card. He went to see him before the start of the contest. Father and son exchanged one last smile before Eli went back to his family who were anxiously waiting.

In honor of Prince Forest Vrys, the British rule would be observed by placing the targets two hundred yards away. The contestants would shoot two volleys of six arrows with goose feather fins. Most contestants had bows made out of yew; the Prince's had been carved out of walnut wood. Lazarus had never before shot from such a distance but it mattered little to him: he was sustained by an infallible faith.

Even though the protocol had not been followed, knights had asked that the colors of their houses fly atop wooden masts fixed above their tents, as if it were a traditional joust. The Benavista family had had some difficulties finding a suitable banner and a heated discussion had opposed several Jewish leaders inside the large Synagogue. Some wanted Lazarus to represent Toledan Jewry or even Spain's, with a large star of David embroidered on the acccompanying streamer. The possibillity of provoking the Christian crowd was judged too great. Finally, reason won out. A blue flag was constructed on which were written the plain words: "Citizen of Toledo."

Chapter 11

The competition began in a deafening silence. Even the wind died down. Lazarus was shooting in eighth position. He hit the target with each shot and each time a billowing hum rose from the crowd. His wrist was steady; during the pauses, he remained focused by looking at the ground. Each arrow that hit its target brought Yael closer to fainting. Joseph was slobbering; a firm hand stood ready to close on senora Monsonego's wrist when it looked as if she was about to let go a shout. Isaac was shaking his head; he never let go his gaze. Eli, Orpha and Sarah, were so anxious they did not make a move.

The preliminary rounds seemed interminable. The heat was becoming oppressive. The public was beginning to mutter, to break down the heavy silence. One last arrow was shot and missed its target; then trumpets rose on either side of the royal stand and the four winners were announced. "El caballero don Jimenez, el senor del Dongo, el prince Forest Vrys (who had a start when he heard his name pronounced thus), y el joven Lazaro Benavista." Music burst to mark the beginning of the first round of cheering; the public rose to its feet and everyone was applauding his favorite. This time, Lazarus lifted his head and looked for his family. He saw all of them, their eyes glittering, his father choking with emotion and Yael applauding and screaming all at once. Near him stood the magnificent red-haired prince of Wales, his eyebrows raised. They measured each other up. "It's between us," they seemed to be saying to themselves. "So, little Jew, you think you are about to beat me, me who has never before been defeated!" and: "You are very good but look yonder, it's for them that I will win, for my own people." Thus spoke their eyes.

The other two contestants were quickly eliminated. Deciding between the Welsh prince and the Jewish teenager was impossible. What was to be done? The prince was cursing. The intense heat of the sun was oppressive and Lazarus did all he could to keep his concentration. The targets were pushed back another thirty feet. One had to win.

Eli shut his eyes the span of a second to silently beg Esther: "Help your son, come to his aid and guide his arm, he needs you." Lazarus was far away from the spectators but at that very instant he found his father and their eyes met. Eli smiled. His prayer would be heard.

The two contestants would take turns shooting. A single mistake would make the other the winner. The crowd tensed up. Fate chose Lazarus to begin. He hit the target four times. Four times the British hit his, too. The competition had been going on for many hours now and Lazarus was showing fatigue. God, how difficult it was getting! He readied his bow, aimed and shot his fifth arrow… He missed his target… What a disaster! His father felt his throat tighten: the prince was almost victorious, victory was his. How could anyone have believed that the Hebrew would win? The would-be victor looked haughtily at the young Jew who had dared challenge him. This shook his confidence rather than ease up his anxiety for he shot and also missed. Everything was possible again.

Lazarus had the upper hand now. He decided he had to act quickly and did not pause to breathe or think; he shot by instinct with youthful thoughtlessness. He hit the bull's eye. For a split second the prince felt his knees buckle under him. He was also tired and now, his confidence shaken, he was furious at being kept at bay by a mere child. Much too proud not to accept the challenge, he readied his bow without pausing, shot and missed. He had lost.

The crowd couldn't believe its eyes. No one could believe the young Jew had won. The realization of his victory followed long silent seconds that Lazarus's joyous cries broke as he rushed toward his father to throw himself in his arms. Rabbis prayed, secure in the belief that the Almighty had guided the prodigy's hand; Jewish families exchanged congratulations; Joseph, Yael and Avi ran over each other to kiss their hero; then Avi pointed out the King standing in his stand and whispered: "Run, don't make the King wait." Lazarus, his face beaming with joy, nodded and proceeded toward the honor stand. There, he received a purse full of coins and a bronze vase engraved in honor of the winner.

"Here is your reward, young man," the king said. "Never before has anyone as young as you won such a contest. Your strength and your skills are amazing. Do not waste them and know how to put them in the service of the Crown."

A good sport, the prince Forest Vrys praised the victor in a sentence which, while uttered in Welsh, still managed to sound solemn. Lazarus bowed to him. The crowd of Christians did not take the prince's lead and the Roman arena emptied somberly. It was quite a different story in the Jewish section where spirited discussions were the order of the day. Lazarus felt as if he had shaken thousands of hands, had received hundreds of congratulatory taps; he was exhausted. All returned home.

But Lazarus had one more task to accomplish. He asked his parents to be left alone for one hour and then excused himself. Avi reminded him that he was throwing a party in his honor and Eli, guessing his son's motive, smiled to him as he left.

Lazarus covered his head and entered the Jewish cemetery, alone. He approached his mother's tomb where he meditated a few moments. He sobbed. During the tournament, he had felt in his waning strength a presence which had filled his heart with strength. He felt very close to the mother he had never known, and he remained but a mere child near the marble stele and, when he closed his eyes, he felt—was it the wind?— a caress on his head. He dedicated his victory to her, prayed to the Lord and, his heart at peace, he returned to his man's life.

Many were the celebrations in Jewish homes across Toledo. Many saw a sign of Jehovah in this victory, which gave this oft-humiliated people a sense of redress. In a flash, Lazarus had managed to lift all the insults heaped on his people for so long. His fame spread in all of the Iberian peninsula and people came from far away to congratulate him and to admire his trophy. The bow, that simple bow he had used during the tournament, became the stuff of legends; it was hung on a wall and for many years when Lazarus came to doubt himself, he could glance at it and recall his victory.

Avi took advantage of this suddden notoriety to find his way back to a Court which he had cautiously avoided before the contest. Without asking the young hero's advice, he garnered an invitation for the two of them. Willy-nilly, the nobles had to accept this victory even if they could not do without a modicum of condescension. Sarah insisted that her brother introduce Joseph, who had been quite neglected of late, along with Lazarus. Joseph was elated: to be introduced into the royal palace at fourteen was a momentous event. He listened avidly to his uncle and even his grand-father speak of the splendors of the Court and dreamt of occupying a position there one day. Like his father, Lazarus felt ill-at-ease at the thought of penetrating the gilded world of the courtesans. Joseph and his mother's wishes were followed and both nephews, dressed for the occasion, were shown to the palace by Avi.

"I want to show you a universe you'll have to deal with soon. I want you to meet Archdeacon Santa Maria, today. Like everyone else, the Archdeacon has heard of you, Lazarus, and he wants to have a private audience with you. You, Joseph, will listen and little by little you'll learn about the Court. One day you will take the helm of your father's business: your victory, Lazarus, is one excellent reason to have come here."

Lazarus shared his father's mistrust toward the converted rabbi. He grew upset at the prospect of meeting with him. Torn between his uneasiness and the curiosity he held for matters relating to the Court, he was apprehensive about the meeting. He smiled when he recalled that alone before his target he feared nothing and he began to relax a bit. Next to him, Joseph was clapping and grew so excited that Avi had to scold him.

On the way to town, Lazarus whispered to his brother: "Don't be so happy to enter this world. Father has told us many times how deceitful these people are, how hypocritical their smiles are. And even though you are a child, they won't spare you. We are Jews, don't you forget it, for they, you can be sure, will not."

Joseph, the plump child of fourteen, frowned and shook his head. "Why are you saying that? You, the winner, should be the last person to fear anything! You are about to be introduced to the Court. Do you realize what it means, Lazarus? The King's Court! It's quite an honor. You see, they do not turn their back on us because of our religion. They've invited us!"

"You listen to uncle Avi too much, poor Joseph. I believe in the teaching of our father."

"What are you children talking about?" Avi interrupted. "Lazarus, your father has never felt very much at ease in this place and that is why he describes it so bleakly. There is nothing to fear, you just have to show a little finesse and to keep your guard up."

"That's exactly what I'm saying," Lazarus replied, "one has to be on the defensive, always."

"Not at all," answered Joseph, "Uncle Avi just finished saying that there was nothing to be afraid of!"

"I am especially weary of Santa Maris. Uncle Avi, why did you wait for the last possible minute to tell us that he'll be there? And why does he want to speak with me? Does he think that I'll become a Christian, like those who killed my mother?"

"Calm down, Lazarus," Avi said. "Santa Maria is not a murderer. It is true that there are times he wants to bring young Jews closer to the Catholic faith because he is comfortable with his own conversion..., but he will never twist your arm. Perhaps he recalls his past faith and wants to thank the young Jew who accepted the challenge. He is a very secretive, don't judge him too hastily. If I let you know about the meeting at the last possible minute it is because your father would have been against it. We would have argued forever and in vain; that's why I decided not to let him know. But we are almost there. Stop talking, greet the people you see, smile and do not speak out of turn. Let's go!"

At first, the meeting with Santa Maria augured good things to come. The two young men and their uncle were asked to take a seat; the prelate soon joined them. He greeted Lazarus courteously. "So you're the young Benavista, the talk of the kingdom! Your feats are about to become legendary, let me congratulate you on your adroitness. You seem to also possess a keen mind rarely to be found in someone as young as you. Come visit me again. You'll talk about spiritual matters. I enjoy talking with men like you."

To Lazarus's ears each compliment went with the hiss of a veiled threat. As for Joseph, he seemed as if he were lulled by a divine melody. On the defensive, Lazarus answered: "I am not yet a man, I am just an adolescent. What do I know about either wisdom or faith?"

Santa Maria smiled. He was well aware that a sixteen year Jew knew the importance of the Holy Scriptures, but he was not about to be sharp with the young man. He thus tried to reassure him: "It is never too late to learn, young man. You are welcome into my home anytime, please come as often as you like."

Lazarus did not reply. At that moment, he would have liked to leave, never to see that man again. He didn't know how to reject the offer and simply lowered his head.

Against all expectations, Joseph began to speak with that rapturous look still on his face: " Could I accompany my brother? I would also like to benefit from your wisdom…"

Lazarus, Avi and Santa Maria turned to him in surprise.

"Who are you?…" The Bishop smiled. "Ah, you are the younger brother! Fine, then, fine, come also, you'll be welcome!"

Santa Maria caught Lazarus's ominously darting look to Joseph but did not take offense. He perceived in Lazarus a toughness, whereas in his younger brother he perceived a weakness that would make him malleable. The audience ended with a few proper banalities and the two boys took their leave while Avi stayed behind to conclude some other business deals.

Lazarus took his brother aside vehemently as soon as they were alone: "What game do you think you're playing? Your behavior is shameful! What are you trying to prove by conversing with this Salomon Halevy?"

A bit taken aback, Joseph answered: "His name is no longer Salomon Halevy!"

"True, he changed his name but to me he remains Salomon Halevy the apostate!"

"Not so fast. This is an important person and he has shown an interest in us!"

"You are forgetting his past! Do you want to know such a human being?"

Joseph was near tears. Without realizing it, he was seeking his mother's eyes but the brothers were alone. He shouted: "Think what you want, but let me do what I want. He said I was welcome!" Then, in a muted voice: "It does not happen to me very often… You are the hero, you won. If you want to make it a sport to despise powerful people because you let your victory go to your head, so be it! He spoke nicely to me and if I can, I'll go see him! Let's go back home."

They returned home. Eli was waiting.

"Well, how did the visit go?"

Joseph kept his head low. Lazarus was cautious: "The gardens and the palace are beautiful."

"What's going on? Why are you so quiet?"

"It's Lazarus's fault," said Joseph.

"It's Joseph's," said Lazarus.

Their tempers flared up at the same time: "You always want to be right! You have no pride! Who do you think you are? That man is evil!"

"What man?" asked Eli, frowning. He received no answer. "What man?"

"A renegade! An Archbishop. Salomon Halevy."

"You saw Salomon Halevy?" Eli screamed. "How is it possible? ... Avi must have a hand in this!"

"In any case, Joseph wants to go see him again."

"Not true!" Joseph caught a glimpse of his mother and ran to her.

Eli grabbed Lazarus by the shoulder: "What did happen?"

"Uncle Avi took us to Santa Maria. He knew he'd be there. The Archbishop had honeyed words for us but I kept my defense up. Joseph, however, caught me by surprise: he fell in Santa Maria's trap head first. Can you believe it? No matter how hard I try to tell him of the evil of that man, he won't budge. He wants to see him again."

Eli did not say anything else. He sighed and realized once again how much of the Monsonego's side he had inherited and how little of the Benavista's spirit.

Lazarus was happiest at the vineyard. "That's the one and only place where no one will talk about your victory," his father would say. At home, in town or when visiting, people were always congratulating him or calling him or pointing him out. That good-natured notoriety was slowly becoming stifling. At times, he wished he lived anonymously in his vineyard with a loving Yael, his father and Samir. The walks to the Jewish quarter had lost some of their charm: as soon as he set foot in the quarter, one cry went from house to house: "Our hero! Young David-Lazarus is here!" and people would gather in the streets. He could not bring himself to despise his ex-neighbors, the ones who had seen him born, but spending an afternoon with them was no small effort. Only Yael, whom he'd meet in the evening and who, with each passing day was becoming more and more beautiful, could relieve his boredom. There was also Samir who loved him and who taught Lazarus how to grow grapes while taking great pride in speaking of "his" land. Life could have gone on quietly, between love and wine making. Lazarus was sixteen years old, had wide shoulders and the Royal Court did not hold the attraction of his own small piece of land. When Yael came to meet him on the slopes, they talked about the future and were already thinking about names for their future children.

Yet there was a different life in store for Lazarus. One that would introduce him to intoxicating essences, to life's pomp and glitter, to the attraction of the flesh and the exhilaration of power broking. While shading himself from the sun under the shade of a willow and listening to Samir sing, Lazarus could never have suspected the decadent appeal that was to bewitch him within the city's walls covered with exquisite tapestries.

Chapter 12

A FEW DAYS LATER

The protocol section of the Alcazar has assigned me to hand deliver this sealed missive to senor Lazarus Benavista," said the King's messenger with great solemnity.

Amazed, Lazarus took the parchment and closed the heavy gate to the house. He opened the letter under the puzzled gaze of his brother and Yael. First, his face marked surprise, and then he began to laugh.

"What's going on? asked Joseph and Yael in unison.

— I've been invited to the ball given by the Queen in honor of Prince don Jose de Valencia, her guest!

— You won't be going, anyway!" said Yael while Joseph, his mouth agape, was examining the parchment.

"Ah! And why is that?" asked a piqued Lazarus.

"Because you'll be bored there and won't feel at ease."

"Perhaps so but I am the one who has to decide how to answer the Queen's invitations! Not you!"

He would have been happy not to attend the ball but Yael's reaction turned that around, he made an angry gesture and turned his back to her.

"Fine, since you…

Joseph stopped her: "Come on, Yael, Lazarus can not possibly refuse this invitation.

— If you are both against me, I'm leaving."

Her head high, she left, slamming the door behind her.

Lazarus thought about running after her but stopped on the threshold and, turning to Joseph, he said with a frown: "Really, what a bad temper girls have! At fourteen she would like to decide my fate! Believe me, Joseph, don't concede anything at the beginning if you don't want them to twist you round their little finger."

Impressed, Joseph eagerly nodded his agreement. Lazarus was repeating a few choice commonplace sentences he had heard around town. It made him feel mature, no longer a child but a famous "man" admired by his brother.

Joseph headed in the direction of his mother: "Mommy! mommy! Lazarus is invited to the Court's ball!" Sarah lengthened her step when she heard the news and all the servants came closer and a proud Lazarus held the invitation high.. Joseph went on: "Yael doesn't want him to go."

Sarah shook her head, a faint smile on her lips. "Yael is a sassy girl."

Eli came home around noon. Forewarned, he looked pensive. He did not favor the visit to the Court but decided against having his son be put on the Court's black list. So much set the Jews apart from Christians that it was hard to envision them sharing bread and wine together even if, in 1406, this type of meeting had not yet been forbidden by the Church.

Lazarus attempted to ease his father's fears: "I am not in awe of these people and you should not be worried about me. I will follow the rules of our faith and will not eat anything that is forbidden by our laws."

Eli assured his son that he trusted him. They left their house together after the midday meal. "It is time," said Eli, "that I talk to you about your future. I didn't think I would be doing it so soon but things are moving fast. You competed against men who will from now on consider you a full adult and will show you no mercy. My duty is to guide you toward a new life which I hope will be pleasant and tranquil. From now on you will help me with the vineyard, you will also oversee the workers and become familiar with the many vexing though necessary tasks that keep our operation successful. Then, once you will have mastered the workings of our business, you will assist me in the sales of our products. Later, your brother will join forces with you in this business which, I do hope, will be a source of wealth. May your entry into the world of adults never make you forget the religious teachings you have received. God put us on this earth to revere him and to act humbly; I ask you to think about this every time you run into difficulties. Our society is such that its temptations will be powerful and the agony of the soul is always a possibility, especially for us who have suffered so much and will continue to suffer. If by some misfortune you come to doubt, exert a tremendous effort upon yourself. Think of me and of your ancestors, and everything will be set right. May the Almighty bless you and protect you. Come, now, let's go to our fields."

Life was about to teach Lazarus that one cannot predict what is in store when one is barely sixteen, when the whole world lies within reach with its gifts and its surprises, especially when one holds but a vague notion of it. Life was about to teach Lazarus that the hopes raised in the heat of a Castillian afternoon, must meet reality and either merge or crumble.

The following day Lazarus grew concerned when Yael did not show at his house. A grimacing and gesticulating Joseph made him to understand that she was probably pouting in her room. Lazarus smiled and said to his brother: "Let's go to her house, I'll fix everything!" He knocked on the door but received no answer.

"Yael, open up, it's me!"

Finally, she screamed in her shrill voice (which she probably inherited from her grandmother): "I know full well it's you, so what? Why don't you go to the Court to say it's you! Go there crawling on your belly, senor Benavista!"

They argued through the door. "This is stupid, Yael. What do you care? Yes, I will go to the Court but I'll come back."

"Yeah! And I will patiently wait for your return so you can tell me everything."

"Where's the harm in that? You know I won't enjoy being there."

"Of course not! You go there to suffer!"

"Listen, Yael, if I have to stay home the rest of my life simply because you cannot stand being by yourself for just a few hours, I may as well tell you …"

She threw the door open so suddenly that Lazarus was startled.

"Finish your warning."

"I'm warning you that if you have to be so disagreable, I …"

"You, what?…"

"Nothing. You should not react like this."

"Are you saying that you won't marry me, is that it?"

"No! But be sensible, Yael!"

"I know why you are dying to go to that reception! You want to find an ideal woman there because little Yael doesn't interest el senor Benavista Lazarus anymore."

"Oh, you're so dumb."

"And you insult me, too!"

She slammed the door shut and Lazarus had to accept this turn of events and he left upset. Joseph, who had heard everything even though he had stayed below, bore a mocking expression which infuriated Lazarus.

"You think it's funny?"

Joseph suppressed a smile and shook his head vehemently. He did not abstain, however, to turn the knife some more. "Are you still going to that fete?"

"Of course, I am. Of course I'm still going."

The next day, a new message from the Alcazar announcing that the soiree will no longer be held in Toledo and that the Queen would not attend. Instead, it would take place at the hunting lodge belonging to the rich and powerful Lord don Martinez del Sancho, who had the great honor of representing the royal couple.

Lazarus did not hide the relief he felt. To have to attend the imposing palace in Toledo did not do anything for him; however, the idea of spending an entire afternoon in a country castle pleased him enormously. Of course, he would continue to ponder the very same questions—what to say, what to eat, how to act if the discussion centered on religion?—but the more relaxed ambiance of the castle appeased his fears somewhat. And, after all, wasn't he the country's current hero? Since noblemen seemed not to be concerned with his faith and did not mind inviting him, why fear anything?

His pride, wounded by Yael, found comfort in the invitation. That evening would be a success, he would come back rich and would show his fiancee that she had been a fool to have imagined anything else. He was not a man easily influenced by vain and superficial nobles. He was not a man whose conduct could be dictated by a young temperamental girl, he was not a man about to… But he wasn't quite a man, he was but sixteen… And since he chose to overlook that detail, life's ironic circomstances would make sure he would not forget it. The man was yet to be made.

The big day finally arrived. The carriage loaned by uncle Avi made the trip to the hunting relay in just about an hour. Gardens, fountains and century old trees spread as far as the eye could see. Half moorish and half gothic in its architecture, the manor had four large salons and several smaller boudoirs for private tete-a-tetes. Bedrooms were on the second floor.

After he had been ushered into the ballroom, Lazarus, feeling quite diminutive, withdrew to a corner of the room. His haughty self-assurance amounted to very little outside the walls of the cigarral and he felt the urge to run back to the carriage and escape. He regained some countenance when he saw Santa Maria, happy to recognize at least one person in this gilded entourage.

The prelate came toward him: "Lazarus Benavista! How happy I am to see you! I personally interceded in your favor with our King and Queen so that you'd be among us. You're a great-hearted and talented man!... (Leaning toward Lazarus, he added, sotfly:) Capable of infusing new life to this moribund and unimaginative court..."

Lazarus frowned. He would never have dared to utter that last sentence but Santa Maria who was in the service of the court had just said it! He now feared the bishop's gaze less: "Sir... My lord, while I am thankful for your sharing these thoughts with me please be reminded that I do not share your convictions... (He smiled.) At any rate, as far as faith is concerned, I'm afraid I'll be a great disappointment to you."

But inn spite of Lazarus, a complicity was emerging between them. Neither one cared for the courtesans' ploys, for an ambiance filled with suspicion and petty jealousies, for compliments often followed by insults muttered under one's breath. The Bishop reassured him: "Don't you worry about religion, young man. Your words are wise and I have no intention whatsoever to impose my personal views on you. But if, one day, you were to make them yours, it'll only be of your own volition. Today, I shall be happy, perhaps, to see in you the boy I used to be, in awe of the court, ignorant of the ways of the world but on the edge of making fabulous discoveries... Know that you have found in me an ally willing to offer you guidance for I, too, have known the old alliance before I came to accept Our Lord Jesus Christ."

Lazarus tensed up when he heard that last sentence. It was all about conversion, after all. How could he have let his guard down because of a few reassuring words? He shook his head, scowling. Santa Maria, however, smiled to him. "I shall now leave you or risk being labelled mannerless by my hosts. See you soon."

Lazarus chose an armchair in a remote corner and sat in it. If he was there it was because Santa Maria had wanted it, no one had come forward to greet the famous victor of the tournament. Yael was right after all... He yearned to be with her.

A perfume made him lift his head. and he saw a woman whose beauty letf him entranced. He blinked to clear his mind, but the young woman's gaze stopped him dead in his tracks. He began to blush, feeling suddenly very hot in his clothes and he lowered his eyes to resist the urge to look back at her. Time splintered away, voices melted into a great din and Lazarus, growing pale, remained motionless.

He was startled by a hand touching his shoulder. He turned round. It was Santa Maria. " Are you bored, young man?"

Lazarus sputtered, the bishop continued: "Listen, you are in a world you hardly know. Let me introduce you to a few people; that the way things are done in this type of an environment."

Lazarus stood up and followed the ecclesiastic who caught the burning look of the young adolescent in the direction of the dark beauty. He went directly to her and the conspiratorial smile they exchanged went undetected by the young and confused Lazarus.

"Lazarus Benavista, who doesn't need introductions anymore! Contessa Maria de Castro followed your victorious efforts with great interest during the tournament of Toledo. Her family converted to Christianity a long time ago; she will understand you better than anyone. Countess, take good care of this young man, he is bored... I leave you now."

At twenty-five, the countess was a widow. Her husband, who had been dead for three years already, had left her a huge fortune. Men sought her favors but, as aware of her beauty as of her wealth, she was in no hurry to remarry. She had a better time crying over her dead husband. But the Prince Charming revealed himself in the person of naive Lazarus. She was stirred by the way he blushed, by his long batting eyelashes and his hesitant demeanor. She liked his broad shoulders and his obvious innocence. She fancied she would seduce him. She mercilessly deployed the entire array of her spells to bewitch the shy adolescent. Her victory came easily.

Completely at her mercy, Lazarus could hardly hear the contessa's questions and only gave vague answers. He was already drunk with her voice, and blinded by the whiteness of her naked skin. He would willingly have sold his soul just to touch it. The contessa would probably have offered a modicum of polite resistance. Lazarus could not see anything else at the reception, his mind became so confused that he was unable to think any simple thought. He suffered that divine torture ecstatically.

It was getting late and the ever-smiling contessa accompanied him to his carriage. It was then that she dealt him the final blow: "My gardens are delicious, my property huge. Come lose yourself in it. I'll wait for you. Good night, lad." With a sign to the driver, the carriage took off and she waved a quick good-bye. When the carriage was no longer visible, she let out a long sigh and bit her lips. "Hurry," she muttered to her coach.

On the way back home, Lazarus only could hear a deafening buzz in his ears: "Come lose yourself in it. I'll wait for you… My gardens are delicious. My home is huge. Come. I'll wait for you!… Oh God!…"

When he stepped out of the carriage, his legs weak, he looked at his house as if he had landed in unknown territory. He had never before noticed that certain branch or that particular mosaic nor, for that matter, had he ever noticed the sheer hugeness of the central building. He did not recognize the color the full moon created on the facade and he was aware of the noise of his steps on the gravel. So this is where he had been raised… All of a sudden, he hit himself on the forehead: "Yael!" He had completely forgotten about her. Yael! His little sister. Well, his playmate during their children's games. A nice friend. Weren't they supposed to get married, later?

To be married! A little girl! The contessa. Her very dark eyes, her hair masterfully braided that could turn into a flowing black river when a man undid it… A man. Come lose yourself in it. Oh God!

He tried to regain some degree of lucidity before facing his family. He forced himself to smile and, taking in a last breath of the outside air, he went in.

Sarah was already asleep but Joseph and Eli were waiting for him; they welcomed him like a brave hero returning from an expedition. So? How were they? Did they recognize you? Did you meet anyone? Was the hunting castle beautiful? Whom did you speak with? Lazarus smiled, making a sweeping gesture at every new question.

"I'm tired! I was a bit tensed throughout the entire afternoon. Phew! It was exhausting! Santa Maria was there."

"Santa Maria! So?"

"So… Nothing. Well, yes! He did confide in me that this society was quite boring. Then he talked to me about conversion again, but in a roundabout way."

"Who was there?" Joseph asked. "Were there princes and noblemen?"

"Oh yeah! Quite a lot. But don't be so taken by these people. They are only good at squandering their money on brocaded clothes and luxurious carriages. They have nothing interesting to say. Talking to them is a waste of time. They are superficial. But I am really very tired. Let me go to bed."

"Of course, my son. I am happy to see that this world doesn't impress you. Come, Joseph, everybody in bed!"

Lazarus resisted his urge to run toward his room. Once alone, his back against the door, he bit his lips and began to undress but ran into trouble with his shoes and his belt and then threw himself on his bed and closed his eyes…

He relived his afternoon experience dozens of times; each sentence, each look, each smile; he made himself sick reliving the rush of images. Sleep finally bested him, late in the dead of night.

Chapter 13

Day broke. Lazarus, who usually rose early, remained in bed a long time. He didn't want to believe in this blue sky nor did he want to believe that yesterday had happened. He was anxious at the thought he'd have to face Yael and, more than anything else, he was consumed by indecision. Torn between his desire to visit the Contessa and the fear to appear ridiculous, torn by shame and the fraternal tenderness he felt for Yael, he stayed under the fine cotton sheets to struggle with his emotions. Sarah decided his heavy sleep was due to profound fatigue.

Avi, Orpha and Yael had been invited for lunch and Lazarus was still in his bedroom. Is Lazarus still asleep? What can be so tiring in frequenting the Court? Even Yael who had come ready to give him the cold shoulder, became worried. Had he had a dispute? Was he wounded? Sick? The old and faithful maid Aviva was sent to knock on his bedroom door: "Lazarus, are you coming to lunch? We're waiting for you! —Not hungry," he shot back and in that second he realized that his delaying would give rise to unwelcome conjectures. Controlling his voice, he shouted: "I'm coming! Tell them that I'm coming!" The maid nodded and descended the stairs to bear the news.

He dressed quickly, studied his face in the reflection of the tepid water in the bowl and took a deep breath. "As soon as the meal is over, I'm riding a horse over there." He tamed his wild hair. "I won't go there." He opened the door. "What will I tell her first?" He came down. "She was toying with me. I won't fall in her trap."

When he entered the large room, he smiled to everyone gathered around the table but, meeting a majority of frowns, he desperately groped for words to fit the occasion … but to no avail. "Well, Lazarus?" It was Orpha who, noticing her daughter's anxiety, broke the silence.

"Please, excuse me. I … Perhaps I had too much wine!" That plausible explanation brought a sigh a relief from everyone. "Well, you know, I usually don't drink! Just two glasses, lots of talking and the return ride in the carriage upset my stomach … But I didn't want you to be worried!

I'm just a bit out of it!" And while he was making his little speech, his mind kept on chiding him: "Liar, you're a shameless liar, Lazarus. What are you becoming?"

A silly little smirk accompanied his explanations. He was still very careful not to look in Yael's direction. To ease the tension, he went on: "And it was the wine from our winery. How could I refuse it?" Sarah smiled proudly and Joseph was once again very much taken by his brother who now even drank. Reassured, Orpha looked at Yael who had not looked up. The young girl in love could not imagine Lazarus drinking and, intuitively, she saw through his lies. The great love of her life, the one without whom life was not worth living, her Lazarus, was lying; he must been keeping an important secret from her. Lost in her thoughts, she absentmindedly pounded her fist against the table. Silence fell around her and Lazarus blushed. With tears in her eyes, she stood up, excused herself faintly and left.

Orpha tried to remind her daughter of her table manners but in vain. She turned to Lazarus. "What's gotten into her?" Everyone shrugged. Whatever it is, it's no reason for impoliteness." The mother went after her daughter. Joseph was already bombarding his brother with a myriad questions: Lazarus almost betrayed himself several times. Sarah, her lips pinched, listened to all the honors she had dreamt for her own son but which had been given to her stepson. Later, a balance would be struck, nobody would pay any attention to Lazarus, whose fame could only be temporary. People would soon realize how smart, refined and insightful her own son was: how much a Monsenego he was! Like Avi and like Isaac the keen-eyed patriarch, he would one day dominate the business world! True, Lazarus had won the tournament, but he completely lacked the acumen for public relations and for business. Acumen that had been bestowed on his younger brother, in spite of his young age. Thus thought Sarah, brimming with maternal love.

Orpha returned without her daughter, a puzzled look on her face. "Poor girl, she's crying. She didn't want to tell me why. I reminded her that her behavior was …"

"Oh, forget it, she's still so young …"

Lazarus knew he was a liar and a coward. He stayed outside the conversations, unable to sort out his ideas. Luckily, his father was having lunch at the vineyard and thus he did not have to meet his gaze. Joseph drank his words, the mothers chattered among themselves. When lunch ended, they all returned to their tasks. Lazarus announced that he was meeting his father, bid everyone farewell and left on foot in the cool, early spring countryside.

As he walked, he laid in the grass, picked berries, and strolled along the riverbank. He would have liked to behold her; he would have kissed her lips, held her hand … The previous day's conversation played again in his mind. "So you are going to be a wine-grower, Lazarus … But where did you learn to shoot a bow … All by yourself! What a feat!" Lazarus smiled, conversed with the clouds, shrugged. "Alas, I lost my husband three years ago … Poor man, he died at fifty-eight. But he lived a full life. This is a comfort to me …" Fifty-eight years old … Lazarus shuddered. This so perfect a face, those silky shoulders had belonged to an old man of fifty-eight! "Yes, I do know many people here. But, frankly, they bore me." Lazarus blushed; he was not a bore to her … But was she anything more than a coquette? … No, she rejected the favors of bewigged men and had chosen him, the young and shy adolescent … But perhaps she was at this very moment in the embrace of another man! No, that couldn't be! Hadn't she said to him: "I'll wait for you!"?

She was a Christian, a Christian of a Jewish origin, but a Christian nonetheless… So beautiful. And Lazarus shuddered. His father would never forgive him… But then he didn't have to know about her! Likewise, Yael. But Yael knew. Her hurried departure from the dining table was proof that she knew. So what? He wanted that woman. Neither fear nor shame nor hosts of unanswered questions mattered anymore, and soon he would come riding at full speed to find refuge in her arms.

He arrived at the vineyard, greeted Samir and found a little rest. They had just received news from Ahmed from far away Turkey; Ahmed recounted the splendors of Constantinople and the Sultan's warm welcome. With the wondrous descriptions of the Oriental palace, Lazarus's anxiety subsided a bit. Eli joined them later and the day ended agreeably. But when he laid in his bed that second evening,

Lazarus was traveling with his love to far-away Turkey where he covered her with gems and gold. Sleep, once again, eluded him.

The next day, he endeavored to avoid Yael. In just a few days their break became irreversible. It was a break Yael felt so deeply that it broke her heart. She lost her appetite and zest for life. Lazarus, his back squarely turned to what had been important to him until now, made up his mind to meet his beautiful lady. More lies helped him to saddle the fastest horse and leave without arousing suspicion. Yael was the only one to see him from her window: Lazarus was riding the galloping black stallion. She understood then that she had lost him.

Less than a hour later his presence was announced to the Contessa.

She appeared with a flighty smile on her lips, and in a dark dress that made her skin shine. In her eyes, Lazarus saw a burning passion. It consumed him. Once again he shuddered and could only utter dumb things. Little could he fathom that his shyness was charming to the Contessa. She was quick to make him comfortable. He regained his voice and more self-assured gestures. Smiling generously, the Contessa complimented the change but added to Lazarus's confusion when she sent her servants away. They were alone, very close to each other, left to relish the imminence of what they had dreamed about for the last two days. Lazarus felt awkward but the Contessa, experienced in these matters, came so close she was almost touching him and Lazarus drowned in the sweet perfume exhaling from her skin so white. When he put his lips on her breast, he thought he would die. Then, when he realized he was still alive, he surrendered to the charms of the young woman.

That is how panic and shame traded places with pleasure and that is how he knew that all the Edens and all the glories could not rival the moments he had spent that afternoon in March.

In the cold moonlit fog, he took leave of a dishevelled and breathless Contessa, still more beautiful than she ever was in his eyes. He would have wanted to spend a whole eternity near her but realized, his legs weak, that eternity needed some rest. He arrived home very late. His concerned father had been waiting for him on the threshold. He stammered some meaningless excuses before going up to his bedroom. That night he had no difficulty falling asleep.

The next day, he had not qualms about embelishing his lies, and conjured up quite an amiable nobleman, although he was a Christian: he was passionately interested in the cultivation of the grape and was so fond of conversing that he would spend several days at a time engaged in that activity. "We spoke the entire afternoon at the ball; he is but twenty-five years old but manages his estate quite successfully. His father died leaving him a huge inheritance. Perhaps will we do business together; at any rate he quite enjoys my company."

Eli was unfamiliar with lying and he never grew suspicious of his son. The Monsenego clan offered no resistance because they smelled new business opportunities. Once again, Lazarus took the south road, riding the black stallion that was becoming his mute accomplice. A nervous gallop brought him quickly to the gates of the Castro's property where, his shyness now gone, he asked for the Contessa. Relishing the discoveries she had made the night before, the Contessa smiled without malice when she saw her lover coming toward her.

They talked about inconsequential things while drinking fruit juices, then the Contessa played the zither and her voice drifted toward the thin white clouds while Lazarus gazed at her greedily. When they had grown tense with expectation, they joined together passionately. If the Contessa furthered the education of the young man, she found in him a gifted student who needed only a few lessons to become adept and expert in the art. Student and teacher rejoined in a physical celebration that seemed to go on forever.

The feast lasted all spring long. Seeing Lazarus mount his black horse had become such a customary event that no one paid it any attention. A single day without her caused his heart to ache, his horse to rear up, and his nights to seem endless. A day with her, and their silent dance continued its intoxication. They did not relent before the vastness of the property and visited its every bush, hallway, salon, bedroom, shed and meadow.

The feast lasted all summer long in suffocating heat, the dampness of the sheets and the cool water of the fountains.

The feast lasted all autumn long and grapes rolled from cleavage to slip waiting to be devoured. When winter came, the two lovers were still not weary.

During more serene afternoons, Lazarus met visiting nobles or courtesans who helped him become versed in the arts of conversation, elegance and deception.

When he finally obtained advice and then contracts, his absences became meaningful and the names he would drop to satisfy Avi's curiosity did ring the bell of truth. At sixteen, he became the official Benavista spokesman to the Royal Court. His life became organized between corsets and business, between curtsies and sex. When, in his barely male voice, he made sarcastic comments about the oppressiveness of gilded prisons, the ever-present Maria, always a lively and witty presence in salon conversations, encouraged him with a look or a witticism.

At the beginning of their relations, Lazarus used to worry about the consequences of being discovered but she reassured him with these words: "Dear lover, you are not aware of the laws that govern this world! We don't even need to hide, we can proclaim loud and clear a friendship so pure and they'll take our word for it. Of course, they know very well that we're lovers and they have no qualms discussing us among themselves. It excites them. Believe me, they are jealous of you; however, if we respect conventions while proclaiming our innocence, we'll be able to play our little games much longer. Come, unlace my corset." Lazarus soon realized that the Contessa knew what she was talking about.

Chapter 14

On the first day of January of the year of our Lord 1407, the good king Henry III of Castilla died peacefully. Rumor had it that Rabbi Meir Alguades, the king's physician and confidant, had poisoned him. After a mock trial, the saintly man was condemned to be torn to pieces on the public square. Catherine of Lancaster was given the reins of the kingdom since Juan II was too young to reign.

Soon, Lazarus was leading a life that had nothing in common with the life he had led just a year before. Yael rarely visited the Benavistas now and spent her time with her grandfather whose strength she found comforting. She cried often, spoke rarely, spent time embroidering under the weeping willows while looking at the Tagus. Avi and his wife were powerless witnesses to their daughter's languishing and were at a loss as to what to do to rekindle her spirit. She was only fifteen but the future loomed uncertain and dark. When she saw Lazarus, even though she managed her best to avoid him, she could read in his smile, in his gestures and his supple gait, how he had blossomed and that the famous Christian nobleman could only be a woman with experience. He was happy… on account of another woman against whom she was powerless. She often thought about killing herself but her love for her family kept her from putting her thoughts into action.

When her grandmother fell ill, she stayed with her day and night. Old Isaac himself was touched and, along with his granddaughter, attended to his wife in her last days. Her famed screaming had turned to gasps. Tenderly, he told her of his lifelong sufferings and how he'd hated her shrill voice and why, because of her, he had decided to go in quest of Africa in 1372. In the winter of 1407, the couple reunited and the grandmother died holding her old husband's hand. Yael cried long in her grandfather's arms.

During the funeral, Lazarus was able to forget the life of the courtesan and was stirred to rediscover his family. He innocently looked in Yael's direction and was shocked by her great sadness. He noted her hollow cheeks and her tired eyes and her skin so pale. He was moved and smiled faintly. It broke the young girl's heart. She dropped to the ground crying uncontrollably. Silence fell around her and Lazarus. Like a reassuring big brother, he took her in his arms. She spent a long time sobbing in the arms of the one she loved.

It was the grandfather who, firmly, separated them. The accusatory look he gave Lazarus was plain enough. He took Yael by the shoulders and whispered in her ear. The last few days she had spent in her grandmother's bedroom had brought the old man nearer to his granddaughter. Isaac had seen through her misfortune and he was not about to probe Lazarus's heart. Isaac could not bear to see the boy's past cowardice be so easily forgotten. He made no disparaging remarks, however, and the day ended quietly, with prayers.

Isaac's gesture had not been caught by Eli-the-righteous who had not paid any attention to what was going on. He had total faith in his son. True, Lazarus was always on the go and had taken some liberties but wasn't he also successful in running the business? Innuendos concerning his lustful escapades had not reached his ears. Sarah, though, would address them with her brother but he could find nothing distasteful in the whole affair. Avi was chagrined by his daughter's sadness but was that enough for him to steer his nephew back on a right path that he might abandon again at the first opportunity... No, better a Yael all alone than a Yael married and cuckolded and much unhappier then.

From that day on, the relationship between Yael and Lazarus took a new turn. He looked at her warmly and they did not avoid each other any more. Even if this was a poor substitute for the love they had shared before, Yael began to hope again. Joseph found his cousin more accessible, Orpha was comfortable with the Benavistas again, and life returned to normal. But Lazarus still rode his black stallion in quest of secret pleasures.

Out of boredom or fatigue, Isaac died the following year. Once again, Lazarus comforted Yael, but only as a cousin would. He was too entranced by the beautiful Contessa to realize, even for an instant, where his duty lay.

Chapter 15

YEAR OF OUR LORD 1411

Joseph had just turned eighteen. Uncomfortable with himself, he felt clumsy and was beginning to resent having to depend on his family's wealth to impress young girls. If the times were kinder to plain but rich heirs than they were to penniless beauties, Joseph could not help but dislike his brother for all his successes. His brother, a perennial yardstick: the victor of tournaments, the seducer of Contessas and littles cousin girls. God knows how beautiful Yael was… If only she had cast her gaze in his direction; if only she would look at him… But that couldn't be. She was in love with Lazarus.

Avi had noticed long ago that Joseph lacked masculine authority. His sister had always protected him and unwillingly, perhaps, she had undermined his development and had driven a wedge between her son and his father. He witnessed Joseph growing up in the shadow of a taller, handsomer and stronger brother. He alone was aware of his nephew's secret crush for Yael. When the nature of his meetings allowed it, he would take Joseph along to introduce him to influential people and to the workings of the business world. He quickly realized how apt Joseph was at seizing forces at work, interests at play and all the pain that made up that world. But because he was rather aloof, Avi could not express toward Joseph the firm affection his own father could have shown him.

Joseph at eighteen was a successful businessman but was diminished by life and it showed in his deportment. He was not bitter, however, and held his brother in deep esteem and would look toward his father with sadness in his eyes. At times, he grew upset at his mother when she treated him as a child but he owed her respect and often found solace near her. Life might have been bearable, enjoyable even, had not this impossible and secret love for Yael existed. It grew bigger and soon it possessed him. Yael was in love with Lazarus and Joseph loved Yael... Yael, moreover, was patiently waiting for Lazarus, weaving and unraveling her web.

Lazarus frequented his lover assiduously although their rapport had evolved from stage to stage: they went from passion to complicity and then to friendship. She was as fond of pleasure as she was fond of her personal freedom. In the four years they had been lovers, he had matured, had acquired manly manners and was no longer slave to his senses or fears. At twenty, he was on his way to discovering the best life had to offer. Not even Avi was privy to this scope of experiences, for even though he had brilliantly succeeded in business, he had never known overwhelming erotic harmony. The same could be said for Eli; he and his wife had loved each other tenderly, but at present, he preferred the serenity of the vineyard. Lazarus, on the other hand, was master of the universe at twenty.

Eli was finally made aware of his son's life; he felt much shame and was deeply pained. His son frequented Christians! His son lived in sin with an apostate, turned away from the teachings of his youth! Lazarus, the blue-eyed baby, Esther's living memory, the young adult with the sturdy wrist, had fallen to debauchery... Eli had never wanted this. His life had once before fallen apart that day in August in 1391 and he had never been at ease in his remarriage. He also often felt that he had been bought by the Monsenegos, whose values went counter to the simple life he had wanted to lead. He felt exhausted and spent. His long silences were more noticeable and his solitary walks in the countryside more frequent. Ahmed had died during a tempest at sea. Only Samir was left to understand the aging man and to attempt to restore some strength/vigor.

The Amoyal family always received Eli with the same amiability in their house in the Jewish Quarter but he feared the customary query: "And how is Lazarus?..." He would shrug and mutter: "Fine, fine..." He did not realize that his ex-neighbors knew of the son's escapades and had forgiven him. In their minds, the blue-eyed baby could never do any harm. Even if he happened to break religious law!

Once in a while father and son would meet, as they used to, on a walk. Lazarus could not see how hurt his father was by what he took as indifference. He was hurt and tired. He did not see Eli's stooping shoulders, his head lowered or how he babbled about the future, commerce, organization. A tired Eli would let him speak his fill. He still very much loved his son but also wished to be proud of him.

Chapter 16

The four-year relationship between Lazarus and the Contessa entered a new phase when don Alonso proposed marriage to dona Maria to unite, as he was fond of saying, "beauty to gold." A courtesan in his sixties, he had been a widower for the last nine years and often met the voluptuous dark beauty with the dazzling eyes in the hallways of the Alcazar. He knew she was a convert yet, as months went by, the Contessa loomed increasingly larger in his most intimate thoughts. He proposed with the typical grace of an aging Castilian aristocrat. A beaming Contessa withheld her reply and begged, instead, to think it over.

At first, Lazarus didn't pay any mind to his lover's tittle-tattle: a woman of rank, forever a widow, a charming breath of fresh air among polite and wealthy courtesans. The mourning period for her husband had now ended… The social demands of her lifestyle… He sensed something ominous but was unable to read between the lines, until the day when, his face a frown, he lost his temper: "Won't you please tell me what this is all about?"

So, Maria explained to her dumbfounded lover that she was ready to wed don Alonso, a most respectable party.

"What about me?"

"We will do as we did before! We'll have to be a little more discreet, that's all!"

Lazarus felt slighted. Would he, from now on, have to sneak through the small door to regale the schemer with his youth and vigor? Ought he to become a cheat to sate her with the sinful pleasures they had shared recklessly? What need did she have to add pearls to her dresses when he gave her the best life had to offer?

The relationship between the two lovers suffered. The Contessa interpreted Lazarus's scowling looks as mere childish poutings and became more determined to marry don Alonso as if to punish him for not giving in to her wishes readily.

Lazarus needed time to reflect. Therefore, he was glad to have to travel to Valencia. There, some distant cousins on his father's side, the Gozlans, manned the Aragonese counter. While auditing their revenue sheets, Lazarus became disturbed by the unimpressive figures. Eli attempted a weak defense. Perhaps a lax set-up…"Father, they are robbing us blind! They are not lax! We ought to receive twice as much money!"

"Son, they have been working for me for so long! Even if what you're saying is true, I could never fire them…"

These were the words spoken by a tired man to his son. Lazarus noticed it and pressed his father's arm in his. He promised to investigate the matter discreetly and not to fire the culprits—even if he found guilt, and to straighten out the situation as best he could.

"Father, he went on, as if to justify himself, I have been neglectful of our affairs lately. I want to make it up to you."

Eli smiled and nodded. He sensed a change in his son and seized the opportunity to address a series of objections he had kept to himself for a long time: his inconsiderate behavior so contrary to his education, his offhandedness vis-a-vis Yael, his uncompromising attitude with his own family. He talked about his first wife and the life they would have led if the Toledo massacres had not put an abrupt end to it all. He described the simple life he longed for: strong children, a house, the vineyard..

"Go, my son, go to Valencia and may God bless you."

Lazarus left at day break, still dwelling on his father's words. He sent a message to the Contessa letting her know that he had to go on a short trip. "This will give us the opportunity to reevaluate our present situation before thinking of our future together."

A convoy of mules, horses and of two heavily armed servants to fend off any potential danger on the roads, began its journey slowly. The sky was as grey as the mules' backs. The uneventful road that wound its way to Madrid offered nothing but a long stretch of hills, withered shrubs and parched soil. Lazarus reflected and reached conclusions in the rhythmic gait of the animals. Scales fell from his eyes: he remembered the day a nobleman, whose name he had forgotten, had looked at him with contempt. And also the Contessa's patronizing bursts of laughter! And what was she whispering in those old bores' ears while observing him from the corners of her eyes... And the mysteriously prophetic sentence spoken by Santa Maria: "Have fun or, rather, entertain them," echoed in his mind. His father! All at once, he could see his stooped back, his slow step and his tired face, so deeply tired... And all he could think about was himself...

Shrubs replaced shrubs. Yael! He had stopped caring about her for so long now. What could she be doing? Was she being courted? Was she about to be married, too? Why she, too? If she was to marry it would only be for love and not because of mundane reasons, like Maria. Yael was innocent. An overwhelming feeling of guilt assailed him.

Madrid came to sight late in the evening. After he settled the animals in the stable, he gently rapped on the door of the Zafrans, his father's old friends. The oldest son, Simeon, opened the door on a tired Lazarus. He let out a joyous scream when he recognized him and, taking him by the shoulders, invited him in. His parents were asleep and the house was quiet. This was the time he set aside to read. He fetched a drink and something to eat and invited his guest to share his bedroom.

Lazarus had a difficult time falling asleep: he kept his eyes wide open in the dark, his father's words kept haunting him. That dream of a united family living in the Jewish quarter of Toledo that he had never known; and here, in Madrid, the very example of a simple life, lived in tranquility. He grew melancholy and gently slipped into sleep.

And thus he travelled: sleeping at friends' or at other Jews' homes. No enmity, no contemptuous looks, instead warm smiles and heartfelt welcomes. He thanked his hosts as simply he could, not forcing himself as he would be bound to do at the Alcazar. What a difference between the life of the court, although he had come to love that life! As the mule prodded along, he volunteered answers to the questions he was asking himself: true, entering the world of the powerful and being honored had been a rewarding experience, enough to be seduced by it, but the process had matured him, and he came to realize that archery champions no longer impressed people. "Have a good time or, rather, entertain them." That cruel but accurate sentence spoken by Santa Maria aptly summed up his youthful years of dissipated living. Without any bitterness, he was transiting to a different type a life simply because in two or three nights he had enjoyed being home, among his own kind. Being a Jew among Jews, away from hurtful looks, away from a tense environment where the slightest gesture could be misinterpreted because protocol codified everything to excess… Among his own, their way of life, the genuine life.

Chapter 17

The road to Valencia went through Motilla, where La Mancha gave ground to the mountains and the soil was greener. Lazarus and his men proceeded cautiously and remained on the alert because they feared an attack of highway robbers. But nothing happened on that late afternoon. However, some twenty-five miles away, Motilla was hosting a very strange personage.

The sun tore through the clouds. On the threshold of their home, Joseph and Ibn Molina were conversing and enjoying the sun's warmth when they suddenly saw a group of children running toward them. "An old man, all dirty and with a big staff. He wants to meet Jews!" Ibn and Joseph Molina exchanged a puzzled look and followed the children. Soon they came upon an old and exhausted man seated on the ledge of a fountain. He was peering out of his small eyes at the adjacent streets. Ibn Molina took pity.

"Who are you, stranger?"

"My name is Salomon Sprung, and I come from Cologne."

"More people were now milling around the fountain. Cologne? Up in the northern kingdom where men are blond? Cologne?"

"I have crossed many countries on foot, and I am exhausted, but God has helped me. He gave me the strength to continue the road to you."

Ibn Molina had pointed to his house and invited the old man to find rest there when ten other Jews, alerted by the children, showed up on the square.

"I've been walking for months. I spent a winter crossing snow-covered mountains, then the green plains of France and endless vineyards, and again other mountains, the most difficult ones in Navarra. Now I follow the coastline heading south to relate what I have seen. If God chose to spare me, it is because He has chosen me as His messenger. He has placed on my way kind people and small Jewish communities where I could tell my story. At times, even in all—Christian villages, peasants took me in.

"I am originally from Coblenz; we were a few families living in perfect harmony with Christians. We made ourselves inconspicuous, and life went on trouble-free. One day we heard of violent acts perpetrated against Jews in some northern regions of our country. Ought we to be worried? The news came from so far away. But the rumor became more specific. Still, we didn't see anything at our front door. But then two, then three survivors showed up in our village and told us about the attack launched by fanatical gangs. We were at a loss. Unfortunately, before we had time to protect ourselves, they were there by the hundreds. Filled with a mad fury and brandishing sticks and pitchforks, they kept screaming: "Death to the killers of Jesus!" They entered homes, destroyed everything, and killed… I was hit violently on the head and lost consciousness, which is why I am alive today. When I came to, there was nothing but destruction and blood. I was the only one to survive."

The small group that had gathered in Ibn Molina's house was quiet. Old Sadoun nodded and recounted to Salomon Sprung the sprees of bloody violence that had befallen the Jewish communities of Castilla many years before without reason. "Anyway, what reasons do they need? It is as if Christians accept Jews so that they can release their violence."

Salomon agreed. "I escaped from my village and headed for Cologne, where I found out what had fed this murderous frenzy: We were accused of committing ritual murders."

"Of committing what?"

"Christians became convinced—God only knows how this rumor came to be—that our religion demanded human sacrifices."

The entire group let out the same stunned cry.

"That slander spread like wildfire. Even the Church authorities came to denounce the incredible lie, but it only takes one fanatic to yell 'They killed Jesus!' for the frenzy to resume. I came to understand that a dry spell or an unjust decree is all peasants need to start looking for scapegoats.

"The Church points them in our direction when it accuses us of killing its God, and it lets the people vent their anger at us. When reason returns, the harm is done, and we are the victims. I swore on my relatives' tombstones that I would travel across the entire world to bear witness to these atrocities. Before I resume my trek I will, with your permission, stay a few days among you."

Lazarus and his two manservants neared the outskirts of Motilla. When he entered the Jewish quarter Lazarus was surprised not to find the usual ambiance, children running toward him or men talking on the stoops of their houses. The Soustiels' home, where he had stayed when traveling with his father, was empty. Close by he saw a group come out of Ibn Molina's house and heard a voice whose seriousness made even the children keep silent.

He dismounted, came closer and heard the end of the story told by the old traveler. Then he made his presence known.

Ephraim Soustiel recognized him, greeted him, and introduced him to the community: "Lazarus Benavista, the hero of Toledo."

Lazarus cut in and, while observing Salomon Sprung, said: "Please, don't exaggerate."

Salomon greeted him with a nod. "Lazarus Benavista? Oh, yes, the story of your deeds reached us in Coblenz."

They only exchanged a few words, but it troubled Lazarus more than he was willing to admit.

The group broke up slowly. Ephraim took Lazarus in and spent the whole evening talking about life's hardships, personal problems, but especially about the old man, so close to death yet so full of hope. He rekindled the spirit of the Motilla community with a few sentences. Lazarus was listening intently. He was moved.

Noticing the intense interest his guest seemed to have in the old man, Ephraim asked if he wouldn't mind taking the old man along to Valencia. "Your strength and your traveling party would provide him security." Lazarus agreed, but his sleep was disturbed. He was haunted during the night by the old man's face. He felt ill at ease. He, the grandees' equal, was touched by these simple people.

The next day he quickly settled the affair that brought him to town. Then the entire community gathered to treat both visitors to an unforgettable day. Lazarus was no longer the cocksure young hero who frequented the important people of Toledo. He felt strong, but he drew his strength from his people, its history and its struggles. Early the following day, as he prepared to leave, his mind was clear; the sky, as if to match the change in him, cleared up, and a cool breeze began to blow, much to the travelers' delight.

Salomon had a sweeping vision of the destiny of the Jewish people. What he had lived through and the countries he had crossed had enriched his experience. Lazarus questioned him about everything. Should the Jews still accept their roles as scapegoats? Salomon was against the idea of reciprocal violence but spoke about a form of resistance in the mind: making one's people aware that fatality could be challenged.

The Jewish people had survived for centuries in spite of adversity. The aim was to prevent oneself from being destroyed, to continue the work of the Almighty, and to carry His word. Lazarus felt guilty about his thoughtless escapades at the Alcazar and his intimate rendezvous with the Condesa. He felt guilty about the way he had neglected his father and Yael in foolish, youthful fashion. He confided in Salomon, and the trip went on in the excitement their discussion generated. They were getting closer to Valencia. Then, they were there.

After winding their way around the city they entered the Jewish quarter at the Xares gate. Once they got to the entrance to the beautiful synagogue of Abraham Morvan they realized that word of their arrival had preceded them; a large and enthusiastic crowd awaited them.

Salomon pressed Lazarus against him. "This is where our paths split. Accept yourself fully and there will be nothing for you to be ashamed of at the Last Judgment. May God bless you."

The worshipers surrounded the old man and led him inside the temple. Lazarus remained motionless a long time, then turned his tear-filled eyes away and, with his manservants, pushed on.

The Gozlans, whom he did not know well, were a small family, but their kindness was touching. Lazarus, who had assured his father that he would settle the problem tactfully, realized how he would have hated himself had he acted harshly. He watched his words carefully so as not to offend the branch's overseers; the least offensive remark was wont to scare them. Going from mindless questions to precise addition, he soon realized that he was not dealing with unscrupulous people.

With much concern he understood that his father's own neglect was the source of all the accounting errors. Old Eli had become so tired that he neglected his business affairs! Lazarus felt guilty to have been suspicious of these decent people but also to have been a poor partner to his father; upon his return to Toledo, he promised himself, he would regain control over all the affairs. He felt reinvigorated and would have liked to have been giving orders on the vineyard, innovating, advising. He made the Valencia branch a viable business enterprise again. The Gozlans, having found in this determined young man an ally, were happy to promise him full satisfaction.

Lazarus was impatient; he would leave the next day for Toledo. The road would be long, but his work would take even longer. Before leaving town he took a solitary walk in the sea breeze of the harbor. The setting sun painted the calm waters; boats swung majestically; the wind carried the odors to the open seas. A ship was slowly leaving the pier, its sails snapping, victorious. What a regal pace! Where was it going?

He heard a shrill scream from the bridge. There, among the passengers, a dispirited young girl was staring at him. She resembled Yael. He called out, but the ship was already moving away. A strange feeling overwhelmed him. It was as if the ship carried a part of him away. He called again, perhaps to cover the din of his heart's frantic pulsing. He saw the sad young girl wave, but she did not answer him.

The ship took its secret toward the horizon. He was torn with doubt. Please tell me, sad young girl, he though, that you are not Yael. Tell me that she is still in Toledo, that I will be able to kiss her when I return. Lazarus asked around. Where was this ship going? To Italy, was the answer, to Italy…

It was still nighttime when Lazarus and his men started out on the road. He had slept little and kept waiting for the day to break to load the animals. The sun rose high enough to make the shadows on the ground disappear. He saw the ship leaving the harbor a thousand times. He saw Yael entering her adolescence, blushing, in love. He had given her up for the diabolical Condesa. Today he knew that if by chance she was still in

Toledo, he would fall on his knees and would ask for forgiveness. And if she was willing to forgive him, he would ask her to marry him. "Let the Condesa marry. Let her go back to her gilded world. Let her seduce other young men who will come to her in secret until the time when, an aging woman, she will cool her heels and assume at last a more respectable conduct."

Lazarus arrived home four days later. In spite of his fatigue, he jumped off his horse and came rushing into his house. He ran into Nathan, the old servant, who, looking somber, said snappingly: "Go to the second floor, your father is very ill." The earth shook under Lazarus's feet. In his worn-out voice Nathan went on: "He was found lying in a field, unable to move. He kept asking for you, but his condition has worsened since this morning; he has not made a sound since."

His heart pounding, Lazarus rushed to his father's bedside and took his hand. "I am here, Father. Everything is going to change. I have a million things to tell you. Father, can you hear me?" Emotion strained his voice.

Sarah came out of the darkness and said coldly, "He cannot hear you and he cannot speak. Don't tire him more."

Joseph now spoke: "We tried everything. It's useless."

"He has to answer me. He must. Father, if you can hear me, try to move your hand. Please, try!" He waited, poised at the edge of the bed, expecting a miracle.

"It's useless. You won't get anywhere." Sarah repeated.

But Lazarus let out a scream. "He's moving his fingers, he understands, thank God! Father, I met a man on the way, a wise man from the north who has made me understand so much. He rekindled hope in me. Father, you are going to recover, and I am going to stay close to you to help you and Joseph, too. Hold on, Father, for the sake of God!"

Joseph left the room. He was hurt, and once more he could feel how much his father preferred Lazarus. He realized that even in agony his father had held on until his brother returned. Would he have shown the same strength if he, Joseph, had gone to Valencia?

His mother came out looking vexed. "He seems to be doing better." She could not accept how little she mattered to her husband. She retreated behind a mean exterior to hide her resentment at having been nothing more than an accidental event in the life of the Benavistas.

Lazarus spent a long time at his father's bedside. He recounted his trip, his wonderful meeting with Salomon Sprung, his projects, and Yael, whom he thought he'd seen in Valencia.

Later he left Eli in Sarah's company. He went downstairs and learned from Nathan that Yael was indeed traveling to Italy.

From his crouching position in the hallway Joseph had heard his brother say to their father, "I will marry Yael." That sentence stunned him. A few days prior to their cousin's departure he had let her in on his intentions. "I would rather die," she had replied, "than belong to another man." She kept the secret hope that Lazarus would come back to her one day. Joseph was chewing on those harsh prospects when his distraught brother came to him.

"I just covered hundreds of miles only to find misfortune upon my return. My father is dying and Yael is gone. Why?"

"She wasn't too keen to travel but my father, who had hosted cousins from Genoa, wanted her to see new things. She is to stay a few months there, before she makes up her mind. For when she returns we are to be married," he lied.

"Get married! But I intend to marry her!"

"You! Lazarus Benavista, the hero of Toledo—you have ignored her for so long that she finally realized that you were not meant for her! You needed converted Condesas, courtiers, not your simple cousin Yael! I was able to console her, pay attention to her, and she realized that I did exist."

Carried away by his dream, Joseph found the right words to confuse his brother. Lazarus didn't answer. He worried about his father's failing health and decided to table this most disagreeable discussion for a later date. Joseph, in a gentler voice, asked: "What have you decided about the business?"

"I reflected long and hard during the trip. Since you are enthralled with the court, you will be in charge of the markets, of buying and selling. I will oversee the operations in the fields and the harvest and control the quality and supervise the casking of the wine."

Joseph's eyes shone: "Hadn't you thought of doing the opposite?"

"I told you I gave it a great deal of thought. I have had enough of the pleasures of the court these last few years to realize that I was no more than a distraction to those people. My relations with the Condesa, which was a secret from no one, did unlock a few doors for me, but I feel it's time to close them; I want to go back to nature, lead a simple life, and wait for Yael. I can't believe she could have forgotten me."

"Yes!" Joseph yelled, "she did forget you! Wait for her? Don't be ridiculous. She'll laugh in your face. Why don't you resume your affair with that doña María instead?"

"During my stay in Valencia I understood that my feelings for Yael hadn't changed and that the Condesa meant nothing to me."

Raising his voice, Joseph kept up his lying: "You are nothing but selfish, and you have no right to her. She is engaged to me, and I will marry her."

"It will be up to her to decide when she returns," a confident Lazarus concluded.

Joseph was devastated. He could still recall Yael's parting words: "I would rather die than belong to another man." He would have liked to put a spell on his brother so that he'd become the Condesa's lover again. By an ironic twist of fate Lazarus was now thinking about Yael more than ever before. Powerlessness, bitterness and rage were gnawing at Joseph. How unjust life was! A bastard would have been luckier. If he had been a bit more adventurous he would have left this town, where he was always overshadowed by his brother. Like his grandfather Isaac, he would have gone to the Orient, where slaves would have kissed his hands, whispering, "You are the greatest." But he was afraid of the sea, of the unknown, of savages; he belonged in Toledo.

Thus they became rivals. Both brothers kept silent and went to their father's bedside. They weren't fortunate enough to find him alive. Sarah and Nathan were in the room. His voice broken by his crying, the old servant related Eli's last moments: "I brought damp cloths for his forehead. After a sudden jolt he opened his eyes, smiled at me, and said, 'Esther, Lazarus.' Then, he was gone."

Sarah was crying. She held Joseph in her arms and repeated bitterly, "Esther, Lazarus! Til the very end, until his very last breath." Lazarus tried to console Joseph, but in vain. A despondent Joseph turned around violently and stormed out of the room with his mother on his heels. He could not stop repeating those cruel words: "Esther, Lazarus!"

Lazarus, between tears, promised his father that he would remain true to his faith, would lead a simple and pious life and would never again bring shame upon the Benavista name. He held him in his arms one last time and looked at him a long time to etch his features in his memory forever.

To be without support, thought Lazarus, to know that no one stands behind you anymore to prevent you from falling, is this what becoming a man is? Lazarus's wealth was his future. He had to take the reins of the vineyard, be determined. Both brothers worked conscientiously: they poured all their energies into their work, which helped them deal with their sorrow but not bridge the schism between them.

They organized their work to fit their personalities. Joseph's main concern was to be introduced to the court to meet rich merchants and negotiate deals. Lazarus had to groom him; he had to curb his impatience, correct his errors, give him some pointers, all of which Lazarus did obligingly. He introduced his younger brother to some members of the court, who greeted him curtly. Merchants could not help but sneer at this new representative. Joseph, who cut a less impressive figure than his brother, had not yet figured out how to show off his salesmanship.

He railed at them in his mind: "Just wait, people. One day you'll show me respect. And even if I do not have Lazarus's presence, I will become so powerful that no one will resist me. I will marry Yael, I swear it. You, Lazarus, will not steal from me the one I love, you cannot..." Joseph stared into the darkness at the end of a long and exhausting day of work.

As for Lazarus, he quickly realized that he could not go on ignoring the Condesa's numerous inquisitive letters announcing her upcoming marriage to don Alonzo. One afternoon he saddled his horse and galloped in the direction of her estate. He reached it quickly and had his visit announced from the large entry gate.

When he saw her, a little out of breath, he could not help but admire her. What a beautiful woman, and how he had loved every curve and valley of her body, her breathing, her gestures... but that was then. Her beauty no longer excited him. What strange spells can love cast, what extraordinary and harmful sorcery can a dying love conjure. He kissed her hand; she shivered. Any mistress would have noticed the change in Lazarus; the man standing before her was poised, self-assured. She knew he no longer belonged to her, and for a few seconds her sensuous nature was swept up in her irrepressible passion. Her rational self quickly regained control. If only he would be willing to convert, she thought, she would readily marry him, but—oh, despised religion!—he would never accept. War was declared.

She reminded him of all she had given him, and the acquaintances he had made through her, and of his station in society that, with a snap of her fingers, she could take away. Lazarus, embarrassed by such petty babble, made up a lie to placate the Condesa. He told her that, in order to fulfill his father's last wishes, he had to go to Constantinople to manage his family's outpost for a year. "Not to fulfill his wishes would be a sacrilege. Go ahead, then, marry don Alonso and be happy. I will be thinking about you under the skies of the Orient that are said to be as perfect a blue as your eyes."

He was determined to go to the Orient for at least a year—in Yael's company, of course. The beautiful but dangerous schemer would likely be offended and seek revenge. It was better to put distance between them, to let time cool passions.

He left a despondent María, in spite of her own efforts to keep up her dignity. He rode his horse back slowly. With the Easter season fast approaching, the countryside was green. Soon the heat on that route that he would never again travel would be unbearable. Lazarus reflected on his lost years with relief and sadness. Adieu, Condesa, adieu, youth. Future, what have you in store for me?

With the help of rabbis he managed to have his father buried next to his mother. A raving Sarah kept cursing him: "You are taking my husband's body from me, and you want to take Yael away from my son. Stop your evil deeds!"

The harshness of her words stunned Lazarus. And, although he knew there was no point in arguing the matter, he refuted her exaggerated charges, repeated his father's last words, and reminded her of her lack of feeling toward him even though she could have been his second mother. He also reminded her of the injustices he had suffered during his childhood. As for Yael, it would be up to her to choose between the two brothers.

Finally, he told them that he was leaving a home where he was unloved, to live among his people in the Jewish quarter. Sarah rejoiced at his decision. She ordered her servants to place a large trunk that had belonged to Eli on the stoop and then fled without a good-bye.

The spoken word has sown dissension, but everything was so much clearer now! Exhausted by so much confrontation, Lazarus ordered his belongings to be gathered. He wanted only to take what he really needed. He locked himself up with the dust-covered trunk and opened it as one would open a treasure chest. With much apprehension he found a beautifully embroidered dress, an infant's outfit, a piece of jewelry, and a dried flower that fell apart when he touched it. When his father left the Jewish quarter he could not part with everything that linked him to his previous existence.

There were also carefully wrapped parchments that seemed to originate from time immemorial. "You shall write," had said the rabbi who had made them his gift to him when he was born. In his unsteady handwriting his father had authored some of the parchments. There he recounted the tragedy of the Jewish quarter, Esther's death and the demands the Christians had exacted. "Father, you did not want to forget, and you did not want me to forget. Your wish will be granted. It's up to me now."

Lazarus spent many hours writing. Completely focused on the past, he could feel his love for Yael grow stronger as he wrote about her. He could almost see her as he described her and was suddenly seized by a mad urge to hold her in his arms. "Come back to me, Yael."

When he put his quill down night was quietly surrendering to the silence of the crickets. He let the ink dry before carefully rolling his parchments around his father's and putting them back into their container. Then he held the embroidered dress that had probably belonged to his mother close to his chest and fell asleep.

It is that parchment roll that you are holding close to you, dear little David, almost a hundred years later, aboard that boat that is taking you far away from Spain. It contains the memory of your ancestors, your memory. May your children inherit it, may this story never be forgotten.

Chapter 18

Lazarus began to get used to his new life. He did away with servants, fine clothes and wordly vanities. The intimate ties that had once drawn him close to his brother had now evolved into a formal business partnership.

He settled in the middle of the Jewish quarter, reclaiming ownership of his father's house, a stone's throw away from the house where he was born. He avoided going to town, preferring to spend his time in his vineyards or in the company of his friends, especially the Amoyals, who had welcomed him warmly. He felt comfortable here; his father would have loved this life, so close to what his temperament had yearned for.

Seemingly absentminded, Lazarus was coming back from a day's work in the vineyards. The afternoon was receding into evening. His mule made way slowly, and the sun lavished a radiant softness. He felt somewhat uneasy on his way back home, but, deep in thought, he shrugged off his feelings. But the more distance he covered, the more uncomfortable he felt. Suddenly it dawned on him: There was not a soul around. No children playing, no noise. The Jewish quarter was eerily calm for a weekday. He hurried his pace and soon neared the Alcana. Joseph came running toward him; he looked panicked.

"Hurry! Quick... Christians have gathered not far from the Alcazar. They are about to attack us!"

Lazarus followed his brother to the Illouz synagogue, which served as the neighborhood meeting place for the men to hold council. He asked that everyone be silent, and then he began to speak. "My name is Lazarus Benavista. Twenty years ago Christians came and slaughtered us. They killed my mother and many of our brethren. Today they intend to go on another rampage, but we shall not let them. We will defend our street. Many years ago I proved that I could do great deeds. So listen to me, and you shall live."

Impressed by such talk, the men raised their arms and cheered.

"Bring out the tables and the pieces of furniture you have at home and erect a barricade on either side of our street. Hurry! Have every able body armed as well possible. Women and children, make sure that you are out of harm's way and do not make noise. Protect yourselves and wait."

Joseph was getting nervous. "Can you hear them, Lazarus? Do you hear them? They're coming at us!" Lazarus rushed his men, giving orders. He was no longer paying attention to his brother, who, too shaken, had left to be with his mother; he went south around the Jewish quarter, found his horse and galloped toward the cigarral, where he collapsed, relieved and shamed all at once.

The rumor was becoming more ominous in the Jewish quarter. Elders who had witnessed the massacres of 1391 prayed fearfully, but Lazarus succeeded in inspiring courage in them. Shouts could now be heard from the adjacent street: "Death to the Jews! Death to the killers of Jesus!" Lazarus focused on the old man he had met on the road to Valencia and imagined him fighting to the death, his head held high. "We must purify!" the Christians were now shouting very close by. Abruptly, and mindless of the risk to which he was exposing himself, Lazarus climbed to the top of the first barricade and addressed the gang of fanatics.

"What are you looking for?" he shouted.

"Is that you, the Benavista Jew? Do you think you're still scaring us with your bow?"

Ten men reached the top of the barricade behind Lazarus. They held axes and sticks. That was not the answer the Christians had expected. Lazarus boomed: "Have you come to commit evil deeds?"

"Assassins! Christ's killers!" the leading priest screamed back.

"You will kill no one here today. For you'll have to kill all of us first!"

Taken aback by such audacity, the Christians hesitated. They had not counted on meeting any resistance. Besides, those Jewish scoundrels looked quite determined. The priest resumed his talk, but a bit less belligerently: "Renounce your filthy religion and convert. Come into Jesus, who will forgive you as He has forgiven all who have trespassed. Baptism will be your redemption!"

"Leave now!" Lazarus answered. "Take back your pitchforks and go home. We are staying right here."

Visibly impressed, the priest commanded his party to turn around. His men had killed enough for one day; they took the hint and started home. Lazarus had won.

When they knew for sure that the band of fanatics had left the Jewish quarter, Lazarus and his men dismantled a barricade to look into adjacent streets. What they saw was horrible. They came upon many wounded, many young women who had been raped and whose bellies had then been ripped open, many dead elders. All in all, however, there were not many victims. Instead, many men and women had been forced to convert.

That murderous hatred had spread throughout much of Castilla, afflicting many unfortunates who had not had the luck to have a Lazarus as leader. Who had given the order to attack? What unpopular new tax had been levied that could arouse the populace to raid Jewish quarters?

This was no ordinary decree. The Church had launched a covert but determined conversion campaign. These renewed acts of violence paled in comparison to those of 1391; they killed fewer Jews, opting instead to goad frightened families toward their churches with pitchforks and sticks. Once there, three drops of holy water made them new Christians.

Jews had to leave their quarters at once, follow religious rites that were unfamiliar to them, take on new names, lose their identity. They became contemptuously known as "marranos." Caught between two religions, they were condemned to live like outcasts. With the passage of time some of them made the best of their situation while others always resisted and, at the risk of forfeiting their lives, clung to their ancestral traditions. The Church kept a keen eye on their activities and waited for the slightest breach of the words of Jesus Christ—who, many centuries before, had preached tolerance and love.

Jews found solace in prayer and exhibited a total and profound indifference to the tauntings and the contempt of Christians. Their culture extolled respect for others and nonviolence, and they followed to the letter the laws of the Old Testament that called for complete submission to

God. That was the proper response to aggression. Rather than rebel against precepts that worked to their disadvantage, they expected God to come to their rescue.

Lazarus had his own interpretation and was not about to accept this fate. In his own mind he felt the equal of the most powerful and would, when the time came, know how to fight and lead his men into battle.

His uncle Avi helped him in his purpose. With age Avi had renewed the faith of his ancestors he had ignored because of his social status. The indifferent moderation he once preached had given way to a genuine concern for his coreligionists' welfare. Lazarus and Avi were thus responsible for sending messengers to the most important Jewish communities in Castilla. They invited them to a secret meeting where they would discuss the means to defend one's community in case of renewed attacks.

Every community agreed to send a representative.

The meeting would take place in the modest Isaac-Karsenty synagogue in the heart of the Jewish quarter. It was connected to the community hospital, where representatives from all four corners of the country would stay. When evening came it would be easy for them to get access to the adjacent temple through a hidden passage door. Caution was a must. Several Marranos decided against attending because Christians were spying on their every move.

Twenty representatives from the largest Jewish communities in the kingdom were expected to attend. They were greeted at the gates to the city by community youth, who took them to the Jewish quarter. Within a few days they were all in attendance, and the meeting opened.

Moshe Hamon climbed to the pulpit and asked for silence. "As rabbi of this synagogue I am happy to welcome all of you and am thankful to all of you for choosing this holy place for your meeting. I congratulate Lazarus Benavista on his courageous initiative because it has allowed all of you, the respected members of our community, to get together for the very first time. May the Almighty protect him, and may He continue to guide him toward good. Before this meeting begins, let us observe a minute of silent meditation for the victims of the latest rampages. May God spare their souls, and may they be included in our prayers."

An emotionally charged silence followed. Then the representative from Zaragoza, a gray-haired, impressive-looking man, began to address the gathering, and the walls of the synagogue resounded with his deep voice.

"Dear brethren," he began, "my soul is stirred when I think about all the dead, and what I saw frightened me. Even though the persecutions we have just suffered were not as deadly as those of 1391, they show us that it had become increasingly difficult to live in Castilla. I fear for our children and see but one way out: self-imposed exile. Some of our brothers have sought refuge on the African coast and in the Moorish kingdom of Andalusía. I think it is time that we followed suit, that we organize our exile en masse."

Tempers flared. History would prove him right, but his wise counsel came too soon in that century. Moshe Aziza the Elder lashed out with the words everyone was waiting for: "Exile, you say? But our ancestors have resided in this country for over a thousand years, well before Visigoths or Christians! So why should we leave this land that is ours? Why don't we, instead, think of ways to stop the persecutions?"

Everyone felt vindicated. Jacob Sourek, the rich Toledo merchant, added, "Yes, let us buy our safety! I know that we are all burdened by taxes and levies, but we are still well-off. I propose that we offer a large amount of money to the powerful heads of our kingdom in exchange for our safety. They are not likely to turn us down, since they need money badly. On the other hand, let us not exaggerate the impact of all this. Last week's troubles could have been predicted."

A furious Isaac Maryam interrupted abruptly. "I cannot stand to listen to such talk! So there were fewer dead than in 1391! But didn't the Christians force thousands of our brethren to convert? They hold us in contempt and feel only hatred for us. There is no dialogue possible with them. I am mortified that so many of us haven't come to realize this! You say, "Let us buy our safety." I say to you: That is not the right solution, because it won't prevent more persecution in the future. If they renew their attacks, let's defend ourselves. Let us organize a Jewish army!"

Again tempers erupted. Most of the representatives were older men who had spent the greater part of their lives in a state of meek acceptance of violence. And then, out of nowhere, a fanatic among them was preaching resistance. That was more than they could accept. The great rabbi of Toledo almost lost his composure in his effort to restore order. "Young Maryam, your youth is taking you astray. Our Holy Scriptures, as you know well, forbid us to fight. God doesn't condone it even if our lives are at stake."

A spirited Maryam waved off that argument. "This is your interpretation of the Scriptures. It is not mine. In the Holy Land our ancestors often confronted similar situations, and God never once forbade them to wage battle to defend themselves."

Lazarus, who had kept quiet, seized the opportunity to intervene.

"Honorable representatives, I side with young Maryam. We can no longer afford to remain passive and wait for the Christians to annihilate in a few moments what has taken us tens of years to build. Organizing ourselves is not an impossible task. Look! People on my street offered them resistance, and we did not shed a drop of blood. It only took a bit of conviction and a few weapons for the Christians to defer to us. Resistance is definitely possible."

There was a long silence. Avi took advantage of the lull to lend Lazarus a decisive hand.

"Friends and brothers, the speech you've just heard is the speech of the new generation. I trust my nephew. He may be young, but he can inspire our community to act. Remember how proud you felt when Lazarus Benavista, a young Jew, won the impossible tournament of Toledo? He was just seventeen. This pride is ours. The whip has stooped our shoulders for too long. It is time we hold our heads high."

The commanding tone this well-respected man used unsettled the audience.

"I am concerned," said Moshe Hamon, "with the determination displayed by our young leaders. I, for one, will go on preaching caution and restraint." "But," he added in the direction of Lazarus, "since your fiery ideas are those of the new generation, tell us what you have in mind."

"I have the good fortune," Lazarus answered, to be on good terms with Santa María. I am aware that this ex-rabbi who converted to

Christianity is a disgrace to all of you, but we have to go through him. He will listen to me. I will tell him about the massacres, about the forced conversions and the means we intend to take to protect ourselves, and I will also ask him to stop forced conversions."

"He will never accept that!" Hamon responded

"Then we'll have to organize to stop them ourselves. Let us learn how to defend ourselves. Our survival is at stake."

After intense reflection the assembly of wise men agreed. For the first time in recent history Jews were ready to act, just as in Judea, some fourteen centuries earlier, the Maccabees had revolted against the invading Roman army. Lazarus had the build and the confidence of a leader. He was elected to meet with Santa María alongside Avi; Joseph, who had stayed outside the heated debate, volunteered to join them. His motion was granted but everyone heard the comment young Maryam made under his breath: "That's the one who did not stay around when the Christians attacked us."

The meeting was adjourned. Everyone swore not to reveal any of what had transpired. They planned to meet again within a few days.

Two days later Santa María greeted Lazarus, Joseph and their uncle in one of the private salons of the Alcazar.

"You requested that you be granted an official audience as soon as possible, and I went through some trouble to comply with your request. Let me hear you."

This did not bode well. Avi pointed to Lazarus, and Lazarus began speaking in a curt tone.

"My lord, we requested this meeting to ask, on behalf of our community, for your protection and reparation for the serious incidents that have taken place in Castilla."

"Lazarus, I condemn what took place, and I promise that in the future we'll do our best to prevent the repetition of such events."

Lazarus became flustered. Santa María's friendly but somewhat condescending tone was directed at the Condesa's lover, not at the newly elected leader of the Jewish quarter. Avi and Joseph were silent. Lazarus attempted to consolidate his request.

"If you could go after and punish the responsible parties, we would know that you mean what you say."

Santa María's eyes opened wide Avi tightened his fists, and Joseph held his breath.

Lazarus continued with his plea: "We also want every one of our brethren who had to convert to be allowed to rejoin Judaism."

A pale Santa María looked at the three spokesmen and spoke emphatically: "You want, you demand, and I have to prove to you my good faith? If you weren't Avi Monsonego's nephew, I would have you thrown in jail. Your insolence goes far beyond the limits of propriety."

Lazarus kept quiet. Avi spoke. "We have lived through tears and blood. We have been persecuted, humiliated and massacred. Please, my lord, excuse my nephew. His honor, our honor, is too often disrespected. The same goes for those forced to convert. You voluntarily chose Christianity, and so you can understand why others would want to go back to their true religion."

Somewhat mollified, Santa María remained implacable nonetheless. "No one can undo a baptism, so let's not discuss that anymore. As for your protection, let me think the matter over. But please excuse me I have many things to attend to."

The three visitors got up, bid their to Santa María, and left the room. They could never have anticipated such a failure.

On the steps of the palace Joseph, who had not uttered a word up to then, let his temper get the best of him. "You spent four years in the king's antechamber for naught! Do you realize that your behavior may cost us dearly?"

"I failed, but I held my head high. Would you have preferred to beg and get the same results? I will report this to our wise elders. And since you have granted yourself the authority to judge me, you'll be in a position to relay your criticisms."

Avi stayed out of the exchange. He had caught the remark made about Joseph's desertion during the attack. Joseph blushed and did not belabor the point. Lazarus bid his uncle good-bye, turned away from his brother and left.

Joseph felt slighted. Avi was torn between contradictory feelings. Lazarus had let his pride speak. Well, so be it, he thought. His pride was justifiable, and he might be right to point out that deference would have gotten him nothing different. But if this were true, the encounter was doomed from the start. Avi, who had followed the brothers' development since birth, felt both tenderness and pity for Joseph. He knew that Lazarus had broken with the Condesa for Yael's sake. If he was unaware of Joseph's lying about his upcoming wedding, he did easily anticipate the younger brother's despair upon his rival's return. Tenderness mixed with compassion. Lazarus had organized the Jewish quarter's resistance, and Joseph had fled. But who had ever thought about teaching him the meaning of courage? Sarah? She mothered him too much in the misguided hope so many mothers have, to keep a son a child forever. Eli? Peace be upon his soul, but Eli had never cared much for his second son. Who, then, ever took the time to teach him courage? He took his nephew by the shoulder, and they walked together. Joseph was shaking with rage. Then they went their separate ways.

Chapter 19

Joseph was seething. He ranted and raved as he roved the hallways of the Alcazar. He had no intention of going back home to have to answer his mother's questioning looks. Once more Lazarus had imposed his views, and it had become unbearable. His brother was nothing but a boor; if it had been him, he would have found the perfect word to stroke Santa María's ego. Why wasn't he ever taken seriously?

He was so absorbed by his thoughts that he had a start when he heard his name. It was Eduardo Funchal, a young Christian he had met on business, who was calling him. He was accompanied by a very beautiful dark lady who became quite surprised when she heard his name. "Say! Are you the young Benavista?"

Happy at being recognized, a smiling Joseph stopped.

"Yes, I am." Then, regaining his composure, he asked, "What can I do for you?"

"The lady looked startled. "I am doña María. We've met on two or three occasions!"

"Yes, of course," answered Joseph, feeling embarrassed at his faux pas. God almighty, what a beauty she was! Lazarus had given her up to steal Yael away from him. Breathless, he greeted her very humbly.

Eduardo Funchal said in a casual voice, "Joseph Benavista, I might need your advice on a wine shipment to my uncle up north." Then, realizing he was not needed, he said to the Condesa, "Perhaps I should leave?" The Contessa did not answer; he kissed her hand, and the young man left.

Joseph didn't have to search through his racing mind for a topic of conversation, for doña María staightaway said, "I finally meet you. Lazarus told me about you on some occasions. I learned, your father ... May God protect him."

May God protect him. Lazarus also told me about you and ... I... he never said how…" His glowing eyes completed his sentence.

"Really? The Condesa was now playing her favorite game. "Tell me, are there just the two of you to take over for your father, and Lazarus has to be away?"

"Well, he leaves me in charge of the commercial aspects of our business; he prefers staying at the vineyard to overlook the productivity of our fields."

"But ... and ... his departure for Constantinople?"

"What departure? I don't know anything about it."

"Well, then, what about the outpost you have there? Lazarus has to..."

"We do not have a branch in the Orient!"

The Condesa felt a cold chill run down her spine. She managed to hide her anger and tried to smile instead. "Of course, at the vineyard, not in the Orient, not in the Orient..."

Joseph frowned. "Is Lazarus so ashamed of our small wine business that he has to invent faraway branches?"

His question reinforced doña María's bitterness. "Yes, maybe he was ashamed... Then he is not going anywhere.."

"He left the house. He went back to the Jewish quarter. Not any farther."

"Perhaps there is a woman?" The Condesa clenched her teeth. Getting answers out of this young man was no challenge, but the answers he gave were devastating.

"A woman! Yes! The one that was promised to me. He wants to wait for her return in order to steal her away from me..."

Crushed, doña María hid her rage by quickly looking for another topic of conversation. "Tell me, why are you at the Alcazar?"

"Well... We came to meet with Santa María to... on business."

"Was Lazarus there?"

"Yes, unfortunately. He became so arrogant that all our best hopes vanished. If only he had shown himself humble and had let me speak!"

"I might be in a position to help you. As it was, I was on my way to see Santa María. Joseph, why not come along?"

Falling in step behind her, Joseph felt himself sliding down an abyss. But he did nothing to prevent his fall. How, he wondered, can anyone resist so much charm?

The Condesa was flying, buoyed by her desire for revenge. What would she do? Would she seduce his naïve younger brother? Would she plot his destruction? Well, she would certainly know how to make him pay. Right then and there she would have been happy to tear Lazarus to pieces and throw his body to the pigs!

Santa María had retreated to the Alcazar chapel to calm his anger; Lazarus's arrogance had deeply disturbed him. When the Condesa's visit was announced, his mood began to change, and he came to greet her in the patio. When he caught sight of Joseph he hesitated, and then a sly smile ran across his lips. Santa María was a clever diplomat; he didn't let his surprise show. He made himself a most accommodating host and waited.

Joseph never saw through the ploy and let his bitterness flow: Lazarus, the plotter, the organizer of the Jewish resistance movement. Lazarus, the proud Lazarus... The Condesa kept pressing for more information, and Santa María wanted more details, and Joseph kept on telling; in less than an hour, Lazarus's fate was sealed.

Santa María thanked Joseph very warmly for his help and promised to reward him. The Condesa, relieved and composed, took leave of the bishop and left in Joseph's company. Before leaving the Alcazar she looked directly into the young man's eyes and said, "It will be our own little secret, do you agree, Joseph?" God! that sentence seemed to promise so many pleasant moments ... Joseph went back home extremely confused.

Because Lazarus was organizing an uprising, Santa María's first impulse was to have the plotters arrested at their next meeting. He thought it over: If the leader was made a martyr, his followers would rally around his memory, and breaking the uprising movement would be impossible. It might be better to discredit Lazarus in the eyes of the Jews. The bishop came up with a plan as perfect as it was evil.

Transformed into a church a few years back, the Santa María la Blanca synagogue held a vast quantity of sacred objects that had belonged to the previous religion. The Jewish community had never come to terms with their seizure. The Jews had often requested that these objects be returned to them, but always in vain. Santa María would find a way to have Lazarus found guilty of having entered the ex-temple to steal gold ritual objects. His own willful and vindictive behavior could only make this accusation more plausible. All Santa María needed to do was enter Lazarus's home unseen and hide the evidence of his evil deed. Then a search would turn up the evidence necessary to arrest him. Juan Lopez, the man assigned to carry out Santa María's most vile tasks, was instructed to accomplish this mission with two of his trusted henchmen.

Chapter 20

Betrayed by the hero of her nights, the Condesa was foaming with hate. Her beauty lost some of its brilliance in the process. Happiness emanates from a strange alchemy; a common material, almost vile when it is in our possession, it evaporates one day, and nothing can ever make it whole again. She was going to marry don Alonzo; she loved Lazarus, but Lazarus no longer loved her.

She understood too late that the bitter game she'd played with Joseph and Santa María would lead to her lover's death. The plan unfolded flawlessly; Lazarus had been arrested, and he would soon be executed. Thus had decreed the authorities in order to secure the kingdom. The Condesa collapsed. She might as well die, too. Her life would be nothing but a long nightmare from now on. She was taken to Santa María's and, with tears flowing down her cheeks, threw herself at his feet. The bishop understood immediately her visit's purpose.

He got her up gently and confessed that he was not in agreement with the death penalty for Lazarus. For the last few years he had taken a liking to the young man and had anchored it in his hope that he would bring Lazarus to Catholicism, patiently, persuasively. He promised he would do all he could to spare Lazarus's life. He might rot in jail, but he would be alive. Doña María thanked him by kissing his hands. She knew how much influence he had at court: she knew Lazarus would be spared.

The next day don Alonzo died in the fencing gallery as he was preparing for his wedding day. The Condesa was free but alone.

Lazarus was thrown in a dungeon at the Alcazar. The night guard made his imprisonment bearable. His name was Antonio Camino, and he was married to a new convert who told him about Lazarus, the young champion who brought back pride to the Jews of Castilla. Very much in love, he had lent a receptive ear to his wife's stories. Lazarus Benavista was under his supervision! He was neither a thief nor a murderer. He sweetened Lazarus's day-to-day life in many small ways and kept him apprised of what was going on on the outside. "No, there hadn't been any attacks against the Jewish quarter," "They say you will not be killed," "They say that you'll spend the rest of your life in jail," "They mention a church dignitary that intervened in you favor," "They say that your uncle came to the palace." "They say that you are about to have a visitor…"

One morning, in the dark space of his underground prison, Lazarus got the shock of his life when he saw the Condesa. Dressed in black, her face hidden by a veil, she came forward, greatly agitated, her eyes fixed on the small window of the cell door. A gold coin to the guard was all it took for the cell door to open. She went in.

A dirty and bearded Lazarus got up, his throat tight. She thought she was about to faint when she realized the results of her deeds.

"What do you want from me?"

"I came to save you, Lazarus," she answered fervently.

"I have already been spared."

"Thanks to me! I begged Santa María, and he was able to sway the judges. You can be set free, Lazarus."

Lazarus did not respond.

"Lazarus, my wedding is cancelled. Don Alonzo is dead. I am free. I can save you. If you convert, if you marry me, you—"

"How little you do know me, poor María! Do you think even for a second that I would agree to renounce my faith?"

"But you must live, Lazarus, you must get out, you weren't meant for this."

"In this cell I remain faithful to myself. You are asking me to commit the worst crime. You know I am innocent. Who betrayed me? Tell me who."

"I… I don't know. Lazarus, I beg you, leave with me!"

"Don't insist."

"Lazarus, I love you!"

Tears were streaming down doña María's cheeks. Lazarus lowered his head and whispered, "I will never convert."

The Condesa let her tears dry. She couldn't utter anything; she had played, and she had lost! It was too late. Had she ever expected such a sordid unraveling? Finally she pounded on the door to call the guard's attention. He came, and with his keys clanging he locked the heavy door of hell on Lazarus.

A demon lived inside Joseph, robbing him of any peaceful moment, keeping him awake when sleep was finally upon him. His face began to show the changes. His wrinkles became more pronounced, his gait more awkward. He was lost in his lying and his shame. He was all alone.

But he was successful in all his enterprises. As he had promised, Santa María expressed his appreciation generously. By talking up the quality of the Benavista vineyard, Santa María gave Joseph means to make his entreprise more successful. Santa María put him in touch with wealthy buyers, and orders abounded. Joseph began to count on Samir and made him responsible for the productivity, and he hired many workers to perform quality work.

That was how he was able to focus on Yael's return. He had dresses made and had a court painter paint the nuptial bedroom. He could only think of the "yes" she would say. But his brother's shadow was weighing him down.

When he found out that Lazarus would not be put to death he felt relieved. The weight of his death would have been too much to bear. He could now wash his hands of any guilt. Wasn't it Santa María who had pulled his confessions out of him? His own brother was a thief: he would never have believed it. He smiled weakly. The hero of Toledo was an arrogant boor who didn't resist the temptation of gold. Yael would come to believe it. He would know how to convince her.

No one ever suspected Joseph except Avi. Avi had taken leave of Joseph on the steps of the palace, and two days later they apprehended Lazarus. Avi could not bring himself to admit that Joseph could be guilty of such a crime. He would have liked to talk to Lazarus, but the authorities had ruled against any visits. Thus he tried to gather the representatives of the Jewish quarters one last time in order to convince them that a conspiracy had ruined their hopes; but they had already started on their way home when they learned of Lazarus's arrest. They only wanted to go back to their routine, even if their backs were stooping a little more.

Was Joseph to blame for that failure? Isaac's grandson, Eli's son? Never. Yet..

He summoned Joseph and spoke to him. "I've noticed that you are in Santa María's good graces. I am quite surprised, since so few of us were ever able to gain his trust. Allow me, however, to utter a word of caution and to remind you that if it is exciting to be honored, to benefit from the niceties of life, it is more difficult to remain faithful to oneself and not give into the Devil's temptation.

"The Church holds us in contempt and accuses us of all possible sins. It seeks our conversion, forcefully if need be, and sends demented hordes to murder those who resist its faith, in blatant contradiction of the teachings of Christ."

"Yet Jesus was of our blood and respected our laws and customs. He died on the cross, but he never said, 'I will send into exile and annihilate those among my people who do not accept me.' It is his disciples and those who succeeded them who debased his teachings when they created a new religion."

"Dear nephew, if I address these concerns, it is because you seem to enjoy more than you should the company of people who have caused a great deal of harm to our community. You must keep a safe distance from these people and observe their new alliance with suspicion, for it only will result in unhappiness and despair for us."

"I might have given you the impression that I am different from my people. We do live far away from the Jewish quarter, and I do frequent the court, but know that my faith is whole. We belong to a people that has its own values. Don't ever forget it; be proud of it, be worthy of it. That is all I wanted to share with you, and it is what your own father would have told you if he were still alive. Now go and find happiness."

Joseph listened to these words ecstatically. Yes, he would make up for his sins by becoming a good son of Israel. God might even absolve him if he prayed. Before taking his leave he asked, "Uncle, any news from Yael?"

"She will be here in two weeks."

Chapter 21

Yael came back. Joseph had counted the days and, torn between joy and doubt, had elaborated a thousand arguments.

Avi gave his daughter a warm welcome. He didn't know, however, how to broach Eli's death, the attacks from the Christians or Lazarus's imprisonment. She talked briefly about her voyage before inquiring about Lazarus. "How is he?"

Avi stalled, but Yael kept pressuring him, her eyes lost in a gaze. "In Valencia, when the ship was leaving the pier, I thought I saw him. I yelled, he answered, but the ship was already far away. This vision of him kept me going. Maybe he will come back to me. Where is he?"

"He is far away," Avi whispered back.

"He left again?" She thought she was about to faint. As gently he could, Avi related the apprehension and imprisonment of the man she loved.

"He is innocent, he is innocent! Who could ever believe he was guilty?" she cried angerly.

"Everyone ... Except me, Yael. Like you, I don't believe it. But one thing remains: He is lost to us. We will probably never see him again. The Christians fear him. They were about to kill him, but someone from the court asked that his life be spared. Yael, you must forget him. It was not meant to be. Go ahead and cry, dear daughter of mine, cry. Your mother and I are here to comfort and protect you."

Avi visited Joseph the following day. "Yael is in shock and is resting. Come by the house this evening."

Joseph agreed and went to synagogue, entertaining the desperate hope that with a few anxiety-ridden prayers he would be cleansed of his sin. Rabbi Hamon listened to him and then told him about the Bible and how Lazarus's excessive pride might have displeased the Almighty. In a low voice, Joseph asked him what the Bible said about love. "Love, Joseph? Here, take this to a secluded area and read the Song of Songs."

A very emotional Joseph entered the Monsonego's residence. The atmosphere, however, tensed up immediately. When Yael saw him she began to cry. No matter how obliging he was or that he never mentioned the wedding, she remained cold as ice.

"Your eyes are like doves behind your veil, and every look steals my heart," said the Song of Songs. Joseph returned home late, his heart filled with sadness. Uncle Avi had advised patience. But no matter how much he devoted himself to his work, no matter how many rich potential Christian customers Santa María introduced him to, he could not help but think about Yael. Patience, for how much longer?

Yael refused to give into fate. She resolved to see Lazarus no matter what. Passion fueled her courage. She found out that the Condesa went to the Alcazar regularly on Sundays. She took advantage of a splendid afternoon to go to town and found herself in the hallways of the Alcazar. Everyone noticed the air of mischief and pertness that trailed behind her. Her young beauty spared her inquisitive looks. A man asked her what she wanted.

"I'm looking for Condesa doña María," she replied, flashing her prettiest smile.

The man pointed out a courtyard. The Condesa... She was probably that dark-haired woman in black who fanned herself so languidly. She raised her eyes and blasted Yael balefully. Without ever having met, each woman had recognized the other.

Shyly, Yael came closer. "You are doña María?" When the woman nodded, Yael fell to her knees. "Help me, I beg you, to see Lazarus. I am Avi Monsonego's daughter.I am begging you."

"You are behaving like a madwoman. Get up. People are looking. There is nothing I can do for you or Lazarus. He is not allowed visitors."

"Do you have any news? Is he fine? How is he treated?"

"I have no news, and I want you to leave me alone now. This man is a traitor, and no one should care about his well-being. His arrogance got the best of him, and now it is too late, He is paying for it."

Yael looked at the woman who had been in love with Lazarus. Suddenly she began to doubt. What if it was true? What if he had stolen? In that case, he would have rejected her upon her return from Italy. The condesa was so beautiful. But Yael could tell that her own beauty was punishment for the condesa. So it was for that soft-gazed young woman that Lazarus had deserted her. In a curt tone and with carefully chosen words the condesa began an implacable denunciation of Lazarus. Yael left, her face ashen; doña María resumed contemplating the water. Nothing mattered anymore.

Lazarus's pride! Certainly, in spite of the elusive sight in Valencia that had rekindled Yael's hope, he would have rejected her. Without realizing it, she was following her father's advice; she was painfully letting go of her past. She agreed to consider Joseph as someone other than her cousin. He offered her a small art piece, a carved sandalwood box.

She could see love glowing in his eyes and lacked the heart to refuse his present. Spurred on, he told her about the dresses he had had embroidered, the bedroom he had had repainted, and how his business was prospering. He touched Yael's soul.

A month later she agreed to marry him. She didn't love him, but she would know how to be a good wife and a good mother.

Joseph's happiness lasted a few weeks.

Lazarus was visited by the condesa on two occasions. She had to see him, and her court status gave her that privilege. Strangely, she was resigned to her fate and only lived for the few minutes she spent in his company, talking about a world that was beginning to fade for Lazarus. She related her meeting with Yael with impish relish. Lazarus's head filled instantly with a thousand pictures. Yael! She had thrown herself at doña María's knees! She still loved him. When the condesa left him, he lay down and stared at the ceiling dripping with humidity, and he surrounded himself with his memories. He composed a letter in which he swore his innocence to his beloved.

He was taking a terrific risk. Antonio, his good jail guard, went to the Benavistas' vineyard to deliver the scrawled note to Samir, who promised to place it discreetly in Yael's hands.

Yael's new life collapsed. Lazarus was no traitor, Lazarus loved her.

Joseph never understood why, one evening, the woman who had finally opened her heart to him closed it to him forever.

In concert, Antonio and Samir had agreed to hide Yael's marriage from Lazarus; it would be better not to add to his despair. Life went on. But between him and her, who was most a prisoner?

The years 1412, 1413 and 1414 were dark ones in the history of Spanish Judaism. During that period a series of events altered its structure and its physiognomy completely.

The attitude of the country's authorities was shaped by a single aim: the total disappearance of the Jewish religion.

Chapter 22

In 1407, when King Henry III of Castilla died, the Regency Council did little to hide its resentment of the people of the Book. At first only a small part of the population was affected by acts of discrimination. It was in 1412 that full-fledged persecutions began.

That year, Regent doña Catalina made public a twenty-four-article edict meant to make life impossible for Jews. It required them to live apart from Christians, inside selected fenced-in neighborhoods with a single entrance, and it forbade them to sell anything to Christians. They were not to set up tents or shops; they could not practice any of the following professions: veterinarian, physician, carpenter, tailor, shoemaker, butcher, stocking maker, shearer, furrier, rag-picker; they could not engage in any other commercial activity; nor could they have a hand in the trading of honey, rice, oil or other merchandises; nor occupy a public position; nor wear expensive materials or valuable braodcloths; nor move into a new home; nor cut their beards and hair. Finally, it made it mandatory for Jews to wear the Jewish star and made it a crime for Christians to open their homes to Jews.

These new laws were enacted unevenly, depending on the city. They succeeded, however, in maintaining a state of moral despair among Jews. The authorities in place assigned them to special neighborhoods; they had to move within eight days. Their comings and goings were under surveillance. Everything about their physical being was to inspire contempt and disgust—the wearing of the beard, of long hair, of thick black woollen clothes and of the felt circle, that small piece of yellow cloth sewn on clothes at chest level. The aim was to strip them of hope and to show them that there could be no salvation outside Christianity.

It was against this background of misery and turmoil that Vincent Ferrer delivered his most virulent speeches. He kept repeating fervently what he had preached for so many years: conversion, conversion, conversion.

The mesmerized crowd only needed a command to fall on the enemies of the Almighty. They showed up at synagogues with crucifixes and Bibles held high, bent on accomplishing their work of purification. "We have come in the name of the Lord to save you. Tomorrow will be too late, tomorrow you shall die. Repent, accept salvation!"

For the first time in her history Israel gave in en masse. Contrary to what had taken place in 1391 and in 1411, there were no killings this time, but entire streets and neighborhoods submitted to a new faith. Led by the wisest among them, tens of thousands of Jews converted because they had no other choice. In 1412 alone two hundred thousand Jews changed their faith.

Humiliation and shame reached their highest point during the conference of Tortosa. There, during the course of many months, the Church organized a public debate in order to prove that Jesus was the long-awaited Messiah, since he had fulfilled all the prophecies. Thus the "lost children of the house of Israel" had to recognize him as such and dispose of their Torah. The most respected rabbis of Spain, Zekharia Ha Levi of Zaragoza, Moshe Ibn Abez, and Joseph Albo took part in the numerous discussions that took place in the ciy of Tortosa.

The Church rejoiced, for it was triumphant. Many of the followers of the Mosaic law who witnessed the partisan and dishonest argumentation and the confusion of entrapped rabbis renounced their faith. Similar scenes took place all over Spain. Village after village, city after city, conversion spread, eroding the Jewish community. Many thought they were witnessing the fall of Judaism.

But Israel resisted. In spite of a critical hemorrhage, the "final solution" failed because it clashed against an insurmountable wall of faith. Nonetheless, the Hebrews, who had been the majority at the beginning of the Christian era, became a minority after repeated massacres and forced mass conversions. Thus, at the beginning of the fifteenth century, Judaism underwent a complete mutation. On one hand, hundreds of small communities had hardly been affected at all; on the other, and in greater numbers, new Christians felt forlorn. If a few among them accepted their new condition philosophically, most of them rejected it and, in secret, practiced their ancient rites. Later on they would fuel the stakes of the Inquisition.

Chapter 23

Yael had been married two years when she separated from Joseph. Lazarus had always been in her thoughts. Through Antonio and Samir she had succeeded in keeping up an intense correspondence with him.

Lazarus was kept apprised of the political and religious upheavals in Castilla. He despaired when he found out about these edicts that sought to annihilate his people. There he was, powerless, unable to assist his own people. His messages found a receptive ear in Yael, for whom remaining Jewish was a sole priority. She proclaimed her faith each time a little louder.

She enjoyed spending long evenings at her parents'. Avi, who refused to perjure himself, was happy with his daughter's behavior and had, little by little, come to lose his affection for Joseph. Their relationship had evolved into indifference. The young man had matured and become arrogant, but, for unknown reasons, he had been unable to make the best of his only chance at conjugal bliss.

Contrary to everyone's expectations, Joseph had become self-assured and haughty in the span of two years. His meteoric success, however, could be brought into question at any time; a mood swing in one of his protectors would be all it would take to make his life difficult. Because he cared too much for honors to risk losing it all, conversion loomed as an acceptable solution.

He had, moreover, lost his wife altogether. He suspected that she knew he was the one who had betrayed his brother. She had given him neither love nor children. The perspective of a tranquil and happy life had been replaced first with bitterness, then with muted hatred. But as he climbed the ladder of power and money Joseph became less concerned with his personal failure. He no longer attended synagogue; he had other priorities. Did he have to stand to lose everything for a faith that had become foreign to him, or ought he to correct the fate that had made him Jewish with a drop of their ridiculous holy water? He pondered this question just long enough to wonder if his spouse would follow in his footsteps.

He went to the church. Santa María was officiating, goodwill showing in his eyes. The service lasted but a few minutes. Joseph could not help but think that a Christian who wanted to become a Jew would have had to undergo many years of study and challenges. The Church seemed more interested in numbers than in the sincerity of faith. All in all, what a dismal joke conversion was!

Sarah, his mother, took the news with some bewilderment, but she had gotten accustomed to the niceties of an easy life, far away from the Jewish quarter or the bustle of the city. Her son was well-known and respected; he must have made a wise decision. He was all she had, and she would have followed him to the end of the earth if necessary. She would convert in the course of that week. She went to bed, leaving him to wait for Yael, who was visiting her parents.

He revealed his baptism as soon as she came in. ""Do as I did," he said, "if you want to go on living with me."

"Since you committed this sacrilege," Yael answered contemptuously, "I am now released from my obligations to you. I thank the Lord that He has not to have given me children. I neither love nor value you enough to kill myself. You no longer exist for me; you never were anything in my life. Lazarus, whom I always cherished, would never have done what you did. You lack his strength of character and his generosity."

These words filled Joseph with rage.

"Our marriage is null and void. Leave this house and never come back."

She measured him up contemptuously before taking refuge at her parents'.

"That was to be expected," a bitter Joseph said to himself. "Ah! If only she had tried to love me…"

The next day Avi came to his house looking for answers.

"My past is dead," Joseph said to him, a hostile tone in his voice. "From now on I'm turned to the future."

"You didn't have to convert. Here we are protected, our station at court—"

"Your station at court is eroding every day a little more. Soon you'll be nothing but a pariah. Your obstinacy will be your ruin."

"My heart is at peace. Yours, Joseph, is lost. You have greatly disappointed me. I was closer to you than you might have realized. I witnessed your love for Yael, and I understood your loneliness. When Lazarus was apprehended I encouraged my daughter to marry you. I was never your enemy. You have now turned into a stranger to me. Stay your course, and may God forgive you."

Avi, the reasonable uncle, the strong Avi of Monsonego, turned on his heels and left. He was able to hear his nephew yell, "You'll see, it will turn out bad!" Joseph slammed the table with his fist; hatred replaced despair and shame. He was all alone. Almost. From the top of the stairs Sarah was calling him.

Chapter 24

Joseph didn't have to connive to take revenge on his uncle. As he had rightly predicted, the atmosphere at court had been corrupted, and a few indebted noblemen seized the opportunity created by the decrees enacted against Jews to forget to repay Avi. Avi, who had placed his entire fortune in different loans, found himself ruined from one day to the next as one indebted nobleman passed the word to another. He was forced to sell his property on the bank of the Tagus to live among his people in the Jewish quarter. Joseph became the new owner of the magnificent Monsonego cigarral.

His influence at court spread. His personal wealth opened the doors to most of the grand families of Castilla, and he was introduced to many young women. Still hurting from Yael's attitude, he avoided eligible women converts, even if they held a high rank. When he was introduced to Isabel da Silva he found her so unappealing and ordinary that he decided to marry her. Her parents held an impressive title, although their personal fortune was in disarray. They rejoiced that their daughter had been chosen. She was sixteen, with an unpleasant face, and was reserved and seemingly obedient. Joseph was no longer the inferior; he had found a mate he could easily dominate.

Avi, his wife and his daughter took refuge in an almost-forgotten home in the Jewish quarter. The destitute life he led among a few tenacious Jews who would not give up and the repeated cruelties and humiliations he suffered sapped his strength. His wife, exhausted by a terrible illness, died first. Yael cried over her a long time. She attempted to comfort her father, revealing to him her correspondence with Lazarus, and describing the will that kept him alive in his sordid cell. She begged her father not to leave her. But Avi was tired; he no longer had the will to fight, and with winter coming, he passed away. The Jewish community of Toledo paid him its last respects.

Against her father's advice Yael decided not to leave Toledo to go live with one of her mother's uncles in the north. She found her will to live in the proximity of Lazarus, of whom she had received no news for almost four months. She began looking for Antonio, the good prison guard. She knew nothing about him except that he was married to the most wonderful woman in the world, a young convert named Deborah. Buoyed by her passion, she was able to enter the hallways of the cell block; there she asked to speak to Antonio. She was told that he had died, stabbed mysteriously at that very spot, a couple months before. She panicked, and demanded news of Lazarus Benavista when she was grabbed by two men who pushed her outside.

Panic-stricken, she ran to the Alcazar to find the condessa. She went directly to her, and without any ado she asked: "Lazarus?"

The Condesa frowned. That Jewess again! What insolence! "Lazarus? What?"

"Lazarus! What had happened to him? Where is he?"

"Lazarus! He is ... he's dead."

Yael screamed and then fainted on the stone slabs. The condessa looked at the young woman and called some people to attend to her.

Doña María still visited Lazarus; he had become accustomed to it. She brought him news from the outside, and she also let him vent his hatred. It was only his hope to avenge himself one day that made him resist the degradation of jail.

She was surprised to learn from Santa María that Lazarus kept agitating for rebellion from his prison cell, thanks to a night guard named Antonio. The king's entourage would have wanted nothing less than a dead Lazarus, but Santa María kept opposing them. The guard, however, had been taken care of, and that decidedly bothersome prisoner was moved to a distant fort. There, isolated from everything, he would be spared but would no longer be in a position to rally Jews to revolt.

"Dear condesa, I went to visit your protégé. I wanted to bring him into the fold of our faith. We had a long conversation. His intelligence and his impetuosity are impressive. But he conceded me nothing. He was not even interested in the Gospels. I find his stubbornness vexing. Let him go, then. I do not know where that forsaken jail is located."

The condesa reflected; elaborated stratagems. But Santa María forewarned her: "It's all over. He's already far away. Sorry, doña María."

When, three weeks later, she saw young Yael in the languid silence of the palace, she lied to her spontaneously. To her it was just half a lie; Lazarus could be considered dead. He would never be seen again.

"Lazarus? He is ... dead."

When Yael came to, doña María shed light on what had happened; she simply changed Antonio's murder into a double murder. She let a distraught Yael go home, feeling a tinge of pity for her, before resuming her dreary affairs. She thought about entering a convent. This was not suicide but a life tailored to her situation. Life without Lazarus was devoid of any interest.

A ghostly Yael crossed Toledo. She could hear beggars mocking her, but she could not see the children running nor feel the young rascals' hands flicker at her cheek. She went as far as Lazarus's vineyard under a pallid February sun. There she saw Lazarus and herself in their youth and saw the hills where they had walked holding hands. She found the tree under which they had sat. A few memories from childhood came back, some remenbrances of happiness... and there was Samir, the only human left in the world who cared for her. Yes, Samir was there; he had just finished telling his workers what tasks had to be performed and had settled in the sun to do some accounting work.

She collapsed in front of the small house. Samir found her and picked her up. He brought her inside and laid her down. She had lost weight, her teeth were chattering, and tears ran down her hollow cheeks. She told him about her mother's death, her father's and Lazarus'. Her story deeply sorrowed the man.

Yael found some peace at the vineyard. Samir did all he could to comfort her. Then, through one of his friends, he contacted a group of travelers going north and entrusted Yael to them. One fall morning she left to meet a distant uncle of her mother's. "Insh'Allah, may God protect you," he whispered to the frail silhouette melting into the fog.

He said nothing to Joseph the next time he saw him. Yael had taken along with her the last vestiges of a life that no longer existed.

Jostled every which way, tied up, taken at night to an unknown destination and then thrown into a dark cell without ever having seen the face of his guards, Lazarus collapsed on the ground.

He fell into an uneasy sleep. He had been locked away in an isolated tower close to Soria. In his cell his garret window let through the light of dawn. He went toward the winter light as if in a trance. The light hurt his eyes; he had not seen the sun for so many years, and then, suddenly, he could look at the sky! He would be able to look out of the heavily barred window at the clouds dancing along the rhythm of the seasons, and see the end of the earth getting green and then brown, and see leaves wither before being born again. A mad, primordial hope got the best of him. Life pulsated on the outside. He, too, would live. God would not abandon him; his time had not yet come. One day he would find a place in the outside world. One day perhaps. In spite of the cold, his hunger, and especially his loneliness, he was determined to hold on.

Two months later, in Soria, a group of travelers took leave of a melancholy young woman. Yael found the Bachrach family rather easily and showed up at their home. Surprised, the Bachrachs listened to her sad story and offered her their hospitality. She began another life episode, unaware that a few miles away Lazarus looked up at the same sky.

Chapter 25

In 1416 Joseph Benavista became a happy man. His wife Isabel had a son; they named him Joachim. At the reception organized to celebrate this event Joseph realized how hated he was among nobles. All the ladies praised the child's strength, if all the gentlemen congratulated Isabel, but the father remained ignored. His wealth had not opened all doors and the respectability he had gained was only a hollow façade. One did not so easily enter good Christian society. He now had the answer to the question he had pondered the day he converted; it was an easy act, and no proof of faith was required, simply because he would never be a Christian. That was all the Church was after: "Prove to us that you will betray your own and we will allow you to live. But nothing else. You are not and never will you be one of us."

That evening people chatted in Joseph's beautiful salons to the sound of violins. "His fortune was ill-gotten," "He converted only out of self-interest." "His son must be raised as a true Christian." "You can never trust these people, you know." These people… Joseph would have liked to scream loud and clear that he had sacrificed everything to cease being of "these people." Such pressures had been brought to bear on the Jewish people that it had become nearly impossible not to convert. Did he convert out of self-interest? Staying alive had been his only interest.

He ordered that the music be played louder in an effort to drown the talk. He also swore to himself to amass an even greater fortune and to strengthen his power in order to convince all these right-thinking people with the only argument they could understand: money.

This is when he began to understand, while flashing a gracious smile to his guests, why Lazarus had been able to relinquish his pampered status as a young hero to go live in the Jewish quarter, to return to simplicity, to faith. But Lazarus was now dead, killed in his cell.

His sturdy and fat bawling baby son was there. In that child's eyes he would never be the mediocre little brother of the great Lazarus. To him, he would never be a traitor or a coward. He would become the powerful, good and generous person he had dreamt about during his nocturnal ponderings.

Isabel's parents were delighted to entertain little Joachim in their home as often as possible. With many a smile Señora da Silva would take the baby in her arms, humming a melody, and then take him to her private quarters with Isabel in tow. At first, Joseph offered no resistance, though he was somewhat upset. He did realize that in all good faith the child "should be raised as a good Christian" and that "one never knows, with these people." He also realized that his in-laws very much appreciated their son-in-law's wealth because it allowed them to regain a comfortable living, although, in their eyes he would remain for ever and ever a Jew who converted. They did not mean ill. They simply never doubted their moral superiority. With the help of God and with a sanctified Catholic education they would be able to eradicate in the child his regrettable Jewish origin. These were good people, full of goodwill.

Joseph did not know what to do. His son was being taken away from him. He worked long hours and could not spend days at home to take care of him. And there were so many little games being played! Cruel was the world of duplicity, of hypocrisy. Joseph was afraid of nothing in business. But this had to do with his own son! Not just a signature at the bottom of a page!

A wall was erected around Joachim. Months went by. Joseph saw him grow outside his embrace. He was saddened and bitter. He had reached the bottom of his loneliness when his mother, one spring afternoon, passed on. To whom would he turn, in whom would he now confide? The day of the funeral he went by the Jewish cemetery where his father was buried. "Why did you never love me, Father? The woman to whom we are giving a Christian burial was your wife. She will not rest next to you. What have we done to you to have become such strangers to you?"

That afternoon, he paid a visit to Samir, the only person left he could confide in.

"Why do they hate me?"

"Why?"

"Yes, people are only interested in my money. My own wife remains a stranger to me."

"My poor Joseph, you are nothing but an impostor to them. You sought to be one of them but you were wasting your time. They reject you, so you use the only weapon you have at your disposal: money. They have a hard time accepting that a convert can be more powerful than a Christian."

"This is frightening, Samir. I perjured myself for nothing. I betrayed Lazarus and Yael for nothing."

"Joseph, Have you ever wondered what did become of Yael?"

"Yes, at times. Do you have any news?"

"Two or three years ago she came here in a wretched state. Her mother and father were dead. Then she went north, I don't remember the name of the city. You won't ever be able to undo the evil you have done, but maybe you can prevent the evil to come. Think about it, Joseph. You still have a full life ahead of you."

He remained silent a while, then he left, burdened by deep despair. The sky heralded summer and was a resplendent blue.

During that time, dear little David, Lazarus, in his cell, awaited death, but death was not yet ready to take him. Although he was emaciated and always an object of derision, his heart remained steadfast; the hand of God was upon him and protected him.

Chapter 26

Joachim turned two, Joachim turned three. From the top of his little frame he was a bit afraid of his stolid father, who seemed given to unreasonable fits of anger. His ire was often directed at mommy Isabel, the well-intentioned if somewhat simple spouse who could not stay put three hours without rushing off to her mother's. The child had a choice between the squalling, gluttonous women who surrounded him and the melancholy man who tried unsuccessfully to make him laugh after a day's work. The gap was widening between them. Life was unbearable. Bitterness slowly gnawed at their hearts. In 1419 Vincent Ferrer, the great destroyer of Judaism, died. The state decreed several days of mourning, and official ceremonies blessed his memory. Joseph attended the funeral in the cathedral in to which the dark corner to which he had been assigned to. Once again he felt that familiar surge of bitterness. The mere name of Vincent Ferrer, as far he could remember, had always been synonymous with terror and death. This man who had destroyed so many lives was now considered almost a saint. And it was he, Joseph, the ex-Jew, that they were looking at and whispering about.

A papal bull arrived at the same time to confirm the edicts promulgated in 1412 by the regent doña Catalina. In the name of Jesus, the Christ of love and tolerance, permission was granted to the persecutors, to the assassins, to resume their work of purification. But with the death of Vincent Ferrer his followers, deprived of his warring fervor, gave up on his methods; pressures against the people of the Book lessened, and calm once again settled in. And it was a good harvest year; the country fell indolent in the transition between two regimes. There was no need to go after the perennial scapegoats.

The critical change occurred in 1422, when Juan II took the reins of the kingdom of Castilla. A weak, generous king, he, along with his advisor Alvaro de Luna, gave a new breath of life to Spanish Judaism. The papal edicts against Israel were canceled.

The Jews who had never wanted to give in began to hope again, and new babies brought life back to abandoned Jewish quarters. Among converts, joy mixed with bitterness; their old religion was respectable again, but not for them. Joseph did not escape this sentiment. Strangely it was Santa María who stilled his anxiety.

"Do not regret the past. What did your Jewishness do for you? I know what you feel when Christians stare at you, but were your old correligionists more tolerant? Do not lose faith. You're still young; you will find your place. Let time do its work."

Joachim turned ten in 1426. He was a quiet, poised child who already displayed a haughty attitude. Doña da Silva and Isabel were always praising him. Joseph observed him pensively, torn between his pride at having fathered a boy of such cold beauty and his sadness at being but a stranger to him. His son did not despise him; the da Silvas had taught him to respect money. His father was rich, and he was always greeted sincerely, if not warmly.

Near Soria, Lazarus was into his fourteenth year of imprisonment.

Chapter 27

YEAR OF OUR LORD 1426

Piercing screams! Hurried footsteps, objects thrown upside down! Lazarus got a start and shook off his stupor. Was his mind playing tricks on him? He listened. No, he wasn't dreaming. An acrid odor teased his nostrils. "Oh, God! Fire!" he said out loud. With his fists he hit the heavy door that kept him prisoner and screamed at the top of his lungs. Was he going to burn without attracting anyone's attention? Had he clung to life a whole eternity so that he might die in this hole?

He regained his wits quickly. After all, it was better this way; the Lord had finally decided to call him back and end his misery. His hope to be free one day had faded with the passage of time. He never received visitors or messages. Once in a while his guards would open his prison cell to let him stretch. He went to the heavily barred small window and settled into a deep contemplative mood. Outside the countryside radiated the joyous spring. He directed a fervent prayer to the heavens, begging God to let him suffer little.

His cell door swung open. "Come on, get out," said a soldier. Lazarus thanked the Almighty and followed the man. He had a difficult time climbing down the endless staircase filled with black smoke. Suddenly they heard a terror-stricken scream. Raising his head, Lazarus saw a large portion of the roof collapsing above the man's head. Struck with fear, he felt his his legs fail him, and he fell to the ground.

He shut his eyes, expecting the worst. But it was not his time yet. He got up with great effort, looked behind him, and saw the unfortunate guard buried under debris. He pulled himself out as best he could and walked into the open air. No one was around. Soldiers were busy at the other end of the fortress and were too preoccupied with saving their own lives. Here was his chance. He caught sight of a thicket nearby and jumped into it. He hid long enough to catch his breath before rushing off toward the forest. He never looked back.

Earth! He could finally touch the earth he had never tired of looking at from his cell. He was free; he was alive! He went east. Would he be able to run on his atrophied legs? He kept on falling, but he kept on trying, bathed in sunlight, inhaling as much of the fragrant air he could.

Once inside the forest he slowed his pace. Everything looked so miraculous. He ate berries as red as blood and drank the water of a babbling brook. The sun climbed to its zenith over tree branches, and its rays diffused a divine light. God's presence was such that he forgot about his filth, his rags, his long beard. Walking, going forward, breathing. His legs tired quickly because he had been inactive so long. The sun pursued its course toward the west. He came near an isolated farmhouse, but, not certain as to what he ought to do, he sat down on top of a knoll and watched. The day was coming to a close when he saw a woman in her forties and her two young children. When night fell he decided to come closer; he must have looked terrifying with his beard and his blackened cheeks and hands. God, however, had helped him thus far. Why would He abandon him now?

As soon as she saw him the woman began to scream. With much awkwardness, she grabbed a big stick to chase him off. He begged her to listen to him, and he began to tell her about the nightmare that had been his recent life, about the years spent in jail that had carved his terrifying figure. He was neither a thief nor an assassin, just a man dying of hunger. The farm woman took pity on him and offered him hospitality.

She was an Arab named Zorra. Close to six hundred of her people had lived here once in good harmony with their Christian neighbors. Then relations between the two communities deteriorated; the Moors, some ten years earlier, had preferred to join their brothers in the kingdom of Granada. Only Soliman el-Mustapha had stayed behind. A bad decision, as it turned out: he was to die, crushed by his own cart, leaving a destitute widow and two orphaned girls.

Lazarus asked a million questions relating to the country's present situation. He asked the name of the new king and how Jews fared. He received few answers; Zorra had little contact with the outside world and rarely traveled to the nearest village, located some sixteen miles away. But she knew that Jews were no longer persecuted. That single piece of news made Lazarus happy.

Under Zorra's good care and with her children's affection he regained some of his strength. Soon he stopped worrying about being recognized by soldiers who might be on his tracks; he gained weight, his body became stronger, he shaved off his beard, cut his hair and dressed in Soliman's clothes. Working the farm with Zorra was a real delight. Her children adored him, and Zorra beamed; that dirty, raggedy visitor had been a gift from Allah.

Often, at night, as he sat directly on the ground to feel its warmth, his mind wandered toward his past, toward Yael. Zorra would then watch him silently, and at times she would cry. "You want to go?"

"I don't want to, Zorra, I must. If I stayed here I would never find happiness or peace of mind. I have to know what happened to my people. I might come back." But Zorra knew that if he took to the road he would never be back.

He worked all summer long, repaired all the tools, strengthened the walls and the roof, erected a sturdy fence around the house, told a thousand stories to the children and showered the generous woman with myriad expressions of gratitude. He left in the early part of September. Zorra gave him one of the three donkeys she owned and some food for the road. They parted silently. Each treasured in his heart the memory of the other.

Lazarus crossed several villages without any incidents; he identified himself as a peddler. It was hot. He slept under the stars and thought he would never tire of feeling under his body the soil whose contact he had sorely missed.

As he came near Toledo he became feverish. His heart began to pound as soon as he recognized the outline of a young woman. Of course, it was not Yael; Yael had gotten older; and she was no longer the frail young girl with the large brown eyes of his memories. How are you doing, Yael? he mused. Will I have a hard time recognizing you? Will I ever see you again?

The road had a familiar scent: that of his youth; perhaps the berry bushes were the same ones, or maybe the small trees lining the road were the same. The donkey did not travel at the same pace his old black stallion had, so many years ago. The future stretched as far as eternity.

Finally he came to Toledo. Prudently, he opted against entering the city and decided instead to take a solitary path leading to the vineyard. Did it still exist? He saw Samir's house in the distance. Nothing looked different. Was he still alive? He knocked on the front gate. An old man came to open the gate.

"What do you want, stranger?"

"S-Samir? Don't you recognize me?" Lazarus asked, his voice choking with emotion.

The old man stared at him. Suddenly his eyes wrinkled and filled with tears.

"Lazarus! You are alive! Blessed be the Lord!"

"Did you think that I was dead?"

"Yes, I thought you had been killed in the Toledo jail a long time ago! What did happen, then?"

Lazarus told his story and then asked for news. News of Yael, Avi and Joseph. What he found out threw him in a panic. He had a few times toyed with the possibility that his own brother had betrayed him, but to have destroyed Yael's life was more than he would ever accept. Joseph had to pay.

"He must die," he said ragingly. "Where is he? At the cigarral? I am going to strangle him with my own hands. I—"

"Don't, Lazarus, it's too risky. Everyone thinks that you are dead. Take advantage of it. Leave this city and never come back. I will give you money and the few belongings that are still yours."

"What about Yael? Where is she now?"

"Up north, I believe. I do not recall the name of the city but it was there, somewhere in the north... Lazarus, you are alive. In memory of your father and for me, I beg you not to try anything against Joseph. He is too powerful. Try to live instead, Lazarus. As you can see, I am about to meet with death, my back aches, my sight is poor, yet each morning I thank God to still be alive...especially this morning."

Samir talked about happiness and hope forever. He spoke about a young and spirited Eli, about the small vineyard they had seen expand, about the union between the Benavistas and the Monsonegos. He also tried to paint a fair picture of Joseph. Times were hard; Joseph had survived, but he had also paid for his mistakes. And if, as he was prone to do on Friday evenings, Joseph came by, Lazarus would have a chance to listen to him from a hiding place. He would thus get a true gauge of his brother's character and could then decide on appropriate retribution.

For two days Lazarus waited inside the small house; his temper cooled down, and he began to think rationally. He locked himself inside a small closet as Joseph arrived in a big cloud of dust. Samir, who had been waiting for him on the threshold, was greeted effusively. Joseph, a sparkle in his eyes, pointed to the other horse, ridden by a young man. "Samir, this is my son Joachim. His mother leaves him in my care so rarely."

Samir had seen the child only once in the last ten years. He was thunderstruck when he saw the demeanor of the young lad on his horse.

"He's an excellent horseman! He's very much in demand at court. Joachim," he said to the child, "here's the man who knew my father, as well as my father's father, and without whom this vineyard would not exist!"

Samir returned the greeting with a smile. Keeping his reserve, the child never said a word. Samir invited them in and offered them a drink. The weather was perfect that weekend; the air was pleasant, and a cool wind blew across the vineyard.

Joseph began to recite his son's exploits. These were far from extraordinary, but Samir was touched and said nothing. He was thinking about Lazarus, who, locked in the closet, was probably fighting the urge to confront his brother. Then, as he did each Friday, Joseph addressed the ongoing business deals. Joachim was allowed to stroll in the nearby areas, and then Joseph related how difficult it had been to take his son along and told the latest foolish things his wife and mother-in-law had done. But this Sunday he was going to avenge himself; he had invited a poet very much sought-after at court who could spout his works for hours at a time and whose pedantry put his listeners in awe. "This is how my power serves me, Samir!"

The closet door opened a little. Joseph frowned. The sudden apparition of a tanned stranger was curious. Joseph felt his legs give out under him, and he fell to his knees. "Lazarus!"

Lazarus said nothing. If truth be told, what he had heard on the other side of the door had irritated and surprised him. He was facing a Joseph who had matured and put on weight, and who was now on his knees, and whose eyes were filling with tears. Should he kill that man? Samir was right; it wasn't worth it.

"Lazarus, blessed be God, you're alive! Forgive me, Lazarus, please forgive me!"

Lazarus could not find any adequate words. He shook his head while Joseph continued to relieve his conscience.

"How much you must hate me. I am so sorry. Ah! If you only knew! When I fully realized the consequences of my action, I thought I would go crazy. I could never have anticipated it would go that far."

Lazarus sat on a chair and waited for his brother to get up. "Joseph, I intended to kill you. Not just for what you did to me, but for the way you treated Yael and Uncle Avi. The desire to take revenge is the only thing that kept me alive in jail. Today I am no longer interested because I can see that you're paying for everything. But what you committed against that innocent child and our uncle is unforgivable."

"I was in love with her, Lazarus. I was so much in love! When she agreed to marry me I thought I would finally find happiness. But then she turned quiet, mean, cold. My life became a living hell. I loved her so very much, Lazarus…"

"You betrayed me, you left Yael, and you let Avi die, and then you converted."

"I had to. Avi did not want to give in. If he died, it's on account of his stubbornness …"

"He didn't want to betray his people!"

"But Lazarus, many thousands of us converted! Life had become a living nightmare! Since then, though, Christians have made us pay dearly for our conversion. Even if I am rich today, they still despise me. They do me no harm, but they have never accepted me. But my son, perhaps..."

Lazarus stood up, opened the door halfway and searched for the svelte figure. He saw the child striding up and down among the grape plants. "I didn't hear him speak."

"He's cold, reserved, but he's a good child. His mother and grandmother have kept me from taking care of him. You see, they want to make a good Christian out of him. My own son is a stranger to me, but if you knew how proud of him I am... He is going to come back, he must not see you, he might talk. I want to help you. Tell me what I can do to redeem myself."

"Nothing, Joseph. I am going to search for Yael. Go back to your world and do not reveal a thing, although I will already be very far away by the time you turn me in."

"Turn you in! Never, I swear on our father's memory!"

"Joseph, please. You're a Christian, I'm a Jew."

"But I remain your brother."

"You're Cain. I forgive you. I will go my way, Joseph. Pursue yours. Adieu."

Joseph lowered his eyes, took his hat and left.

A troupe of gypsies was performing in Toledo. They went from city to city and put on spectacles greatly appreciated by the populace. Samir reminded Lazarus that he had been a formidable archer and that the troupe would probably hire him on the spot. By traveling up and down the country he might, with God's help, find Yael. Lazarus liked the idea. But was he still a talented archer? Samir smiled and disappeared for a few minutes. He came back with an object Lazarus knew quite well: the bow with which he had won the tournament.

"One day your brother brought me a chest containing parchments, clothes and this bow."

Lazarus was moved to tears. He grabbed the bow, closed his eyes, aimed. His arms had not forgotten the gestures, his wrists were still strong; he delighted again in the pleasure archery gave him. He took some arrows and went outside. He came back an hour later, a huge smile across his face. "Yes, I can do it."

Samir showed him the forgotten trunk at the other end of the room. It was the one Sarah, Joseph's mother, had given him the day he left the cigarral. Lazarus choked with emotion. The rolled parchments had been waiting for him; he began to read the neat handwriting. Fourteen years had gone up in smoke. As he waited for the gypsies to leave Toledo he consigned the story of his years of living hell.

When the parting day came he took as his sole baggage the precious parchments, along with his magical bow. A tearful Samir took leave of Lazarus on the same road Yael had taken twelve years earlier, in the stillness of the morning. "May God join one day these two beings that life keeps apart," he prayed.

Chapter 28

Lazarus met his companions. Two Moors, Ali and Omar, gyrated to a frenetic beat as they juggled sabers. Children loved their act. A man with an olive complexion and his nimble mute wife were the snake charmers. They came from a faraway country and had names no one could pronounce. They fascinated their companions. Lazarus often stopped what he was doing just to watch them.

Vaslic, a man with an enormous mustache, had taken a liking to Lazarus. The little Spanish he spoke was heavily accented, but that did not stop him from making long speeches, which he punctuated with loud slaps on his thighs. He came from the east, where the forests are thick, and gave the impression of having been born on horseback. With him around the troupe feared nothing and no one. Lazarus was fond of this rock-solid man, who had had his share of personal defeats: His family had been killed on the whim of some noblemen who had decided to entertain himself by using peasants as hunting prey. Vaslic had miraculously survived. He went west to escape the pall of gloom that hung over the forests. He made it to Spain, where he joined the adoptive troupe. Draga, his rambunctious little black horse, was the other half of a riding act duo that delighted crowds. Women found Vlasic attractive, especially Rita.

Rita and her sister Lola had been saved by Ali and Omar just as their father was about to mutilate the two twelve-year-old girls to sell them to some itinerant jesters. Valsic had perfected an act especially for them. With its simple choreography and pretty costumes, their mirrored dance was a hit. They grew up fast, and their skeletal frames took on rounder, more feminine forms. Rita was mad about Valsic and wanted him to notice her. The magnificent rider, however, saw in her only a child to protect. Lola fell for Lazarus the moment she set eyes on him. At night, under their woollen blanket, the two sisters shared secrets.

There was also a man, blond to the tip of his eyebrows, who hailed from frigid Wales. He was a killer on the lam. He was not noted for his amiability but was known as a hunting expert. He was not made a member of the "small family" because he had announced he would leave at the first opportunity. But when he grilled a fragrant piece of meat everyone was quick to forgive his aloofness.

This was the eclectic troupe. Never before had Lazarus suspected that such people existed, although as a child he had attended shows put on by jesters, colorful creatures from another world. He was now one of them, an outlaw. The populace would applaud them one moment before banishing them the next. These remarkably caring but odd people had no god or master nor family or country. Free as the air, they could vanish from one day to the next without arousing anyone's concern.

They went from village to village, and their audiences were never the same. They were reserved in Galicia, serious and surly in Navarra, happy and playful around Valencia. During the winter they traveled to the Mediterranean coast for its warmer winds. By the spring of 1427 they had gone to fifty different towns. At each stop Lazarus would meet with the local Jewish community. He only had to speak Hebrew for hearts to open up to him; he then began to relate his quest, grasping at the smallest bit of information that could set him on Yael's tracks. People were willing to lend a hand, but they weren't able to help. They had never heard of a Yael Monsonego. On the other hand, they entrusted him with messages for family members living up north or in the hills; sometimes he would be recognized. He was always touched by the warmth and the trust he encountered; still, he could not find Yael. In spite of the romantic-minded little twin girls' efforts to raise his spirits and be at his beck and call, Lazarus was beginning to lose heart.

With the start of the nice weather the troupe traveled north, toward Soria. Would being so close to the fortress less than a year later be a good idea? he wondered. Some forty miles outside the city Lazarus made it known that it would be risky for him to participate in the spectacle. Even if the tanned and muscled man he had become bore no resemblance to the emaciated prisoner he had once been, it was better to remain cautious.

When the traveling troupe set up the tent for the evening's spectacle Lazarus watched the wagons and the animals.

When evening came he left to meet with fellow Jews. The Jewish quarter was desolate. He knocked on doors, but few opened their shutters. Most of the abandoned homes were beginning to crumble. "Yael Monsonego? Ask Salomon the elder, he'll know."

Lazarus found the old man. He was able to give him the information he had hoped for for so long: "Sure, I remember. She arrived in our village right after the death of her father, but that's quite some time ago already. She was very beautiful. Cousins of hers, the Bachrachs, took her in. Few people got to know her. She was very self-effacing, very depressed. Then, about a year later, the Bachrachs gathered their belongings and left for the Arab-controlled town of Granada to find a better life. They took the girl with them."

"Was she married by then?"

"You know, there were few able-bodied men left. Most of them had already converted. Look around you and you'll be able to measure how much has happened in this neighborhood. I still remember it when it teemed with life. We have suffered greatly. But no, she wasn't married."

Lazarus was crying. He felt joy and disappointment all at once.

"Who are you?" the old man asked.

Lazarus told him his story, told him about the fortress close to Soria and about the love that kept eluding him. But he would go to Granada, would travel to the end of the world to find her. The old man gave him his blessing and wished him luck.

Lazarus told the news to his companions. Would they go south with him? The troupe gathered to decide what to do. The male snake charmer had a curious reaction: He slashed the tip of one of his fingers and deposited a drop of blood inside Lazarus's left palm. A surprised Lazarus looked around at his companions for an explanation. Lola smiled and said, "He wants you to know that he's going along with you in your search and that you can count on his friendship." The man said a few words in his strange tongue, and his wife approved with a smile.

"He knows what I am looking for?" Lazarus did not know that the couple understood Spanish.

The man straightened up and said "Yael?" while pointing to his heart. Moved by the unusual but genuine expression of empathy, Lazarus took the man's hand and held it in his.

"Well," Omar said, "Ravadmalala has spoken. We will go south with you, but we'll have to leave you at the border of Moorish territory. Ali and I are... not welcome among our brothers. But I have family in Granada; they might be able to help you."

The twin girls were glad. Even Lola had resigned herself to losing Lazarus as long as he would find happiness. As for Vaslic, he drank more good Castillian wine than he was used to and prodded his good friend to join him. They opted to stay one more day in Soria, where they had received a warm welcome. Then they took the road to Granada.

#

They traveled peacefully for a good two months. Then it was time to go their separate ways. Even the Welshman had lightened up during this trek; Lazarus had taught him how to shoot arrows so that he could take his place. Rita and Lola were in tears, and Vaslic swore they would see each other again. He gave Lazarus a small flute, as was the custom in his faraway country. Omar gave him his parents' addresss in Granada and a few presents to give them if he reached them. Ali thanked him, and Ravadmalala and his wife bade him farewell and tried not to let their emotions show. Lazarus stroked Draga's mane, and to Vaslic he discreetly whispered, "Rita would be so happy to be your wife." Then he parted ways with his wandering friends.

A strip of dry and desolate land served as a border. There were no crossing guards, not a soldier around. Only people who had business interests would travel there. After walking a few hours he came upon the first houses. He was in Moorish territory. The outline of minarets replaced that of churches. He experienced a strange sensation: The air was ... sweeter. He shrugged off the thought, yet he could have sworn that the air was easier to breathe. On the outskirts of the first village he met fellow Jews who welcomed him with open arms. Yes, there were many of them in the Islamic land, and Arabs proved to be tolerant, although it was better not to challenge them on religious matters; Islam accepted no contradiction to its tenets. Here life was livable. He pushed on with some fresh bits of advice and some new food. He was always asking about Yael, even when he was miles away from Granada. Maybe he would glean another clue, as he had in Soria.

In the small village of Zarbib el-Kebir he got his first answer. A man remembered the starving trio to whom he had given hospitality.

"I remember the Bachrachs. There was the father, the mother and... no, the young and beautiful doe-eyed girl who never said a word. She wasn't their daughter."

"Yael!"

"Yes, that was her name, Yael. You know, it has been just about ten years already. They were saving whatever little money they had to go to Morocco. They had lost everything to robbers on their way here. That was a shame. They wanted to get to Granada, and I gave them the address of friends who could help them.

"I am on my way to Granada. Perhaps I could visit your friends and get more information." The man was happy to oblige and wished him luck.

Lazarus took to the road again. He reached Granada around the middle of May. Before looking for Omar's family he showed up at the address the man from Zarbib el-Kebir had given him. Ephraim el-Kabach, a round and pleasant man in his fifties, welcomed him amicably. "You were sent by our good friend Jacob! Please feel at home and give us the most recent news."

Lazarus was relieved. He felt that at the end of this road blessed by God he was going to find Yael, trembling with anticipation at seeing him again, yet ready to finally enjoy her well-deserved happiness. Everything seemed so perfect....

He was mistaken.

Good-natured Ephraim and his wife remembered the Bachrachs and the sad-eyed girl. "They came here. They had had their share of misfortune. They had only one thought in their heads, especially the woman: Morocco. They had crossed the country hoping to find a better life. The young woman's eyes showed a profound melancholy. She looked as if she was leaving Spain reluctantly. Once in a while she attempted to say something, but the woman ignored her and always talked about Fez as a paradise. Her mind was made up…but they lacked money to board a boat."

"That's how this woman, may God put a curse on her, came up with an evil solution. She had found out that sheik El-Moktar would pay a dear sum for such a beautiful and fair-skinned young woman. She sold Yael to him and told her husband only when the deal was done. He boiled with rage, but it was too late. She got rid of her niece as she would of cheap merchandise for a handful of gold. They boarded a ship and left for Morocco. The sheik took the young woman to his harem, and she became his second wife. We don't know anything more…God! Rachel! He fainted!"

Ephraim and his wife rushed to Lazarus. When he opened his eyes he was on the verge of crying, to his hosts' utter dismay. They helped him up and tried to comfort him. Then Lazarus told them his story. The couple looked at each other quietly.

"I know!" volunteered Rachel el-Kabach. "Ephraim, do you remember Rebecca Cherki? You know, her husband sells fabrics and perfumes. Each year she goes to the sheik's property with trunks full of wonders. The women at the harem wait for her with great anticipation, and the sheik himself is greatly appreciative of her visits—it is his way of showing his generosity to his wives. Rebecca gets along well with everyone. I'll go talk to her and maybe she can fill me in more. Don't lose heart, Lazarus. Stay with us a few more days."

It took Lazarus a few minutes to understand; he began to feel hopeful again. He thanked his hosts profusely.

"You see, we are a united couple, we have a beautiful home, and our daughters have given us beautiful grandchildren, but we never had a son. God showed us His kindness when you came knocking on our door. Helping you is our opportunity to share our happiness."

#

Rachel met with the merchant lady and brought back wonderful news. Rebecca Cherki knew Yael very well. Yael impatiently waited for her visits in order to speak Hebrew and keep alive the memory of the man she loved.

"She thinks you are dead. According to Rebecca, she should be eased into the news that you're alive; the shock could be too strong. But she can tell you all of this better than I can. Go see her. I think she may have a plan."

Lazarus did not waste any time. As soon as she saw him Rebecca took him in her arms. "My son! How handsome you are! Yael told me so much about you—you are exactly as she described you!"

"Rachel said that you might have a plan."

"Yes, my son, but we have to be extremely careful, for it could be very dangerous."

"Does it involve meeting with Yael?"

"Yes, but you have to be better informed about life at the harem. The women there aren't unhappy, but they are forbidden to leave. They are more or less lifetime prisoners. They are allowed visitors and can organize their own activities, but it must be exclusively with other women. The only man they are allowed to see is their husband. The sheik is a refined and learned man, and he follows the laws of Islam to the letter. Any man arrested on harem ground would meet instant death. That's the reason why, my proud and virtuous Lazarus, you'll have to dress as a woman. You're tall; you'll have to stoop. You will come with me at the next fair, a month from now. That day is a day of festivity at the harem, and all the women there are anxious. The excitement will be such that you'll blend in more easily. As for me, I'll tell Yael that you're alive to give her time to get used to it. One last piece of advice: To maximize our safety, do not talk to anyone about this plan. It will all go well, my son. You'll see Yael again."

How was he going to kill that month? The El-Kabachs were happy to open their home to Lazarus, but Lazarus insisted on performing some useful tasks. David, one of their sons-in-law, owned a tile factory. He produced the porcelain tiles that adorned the walls of southern cities. Lazarus learned the baking and painting and calibrating processes; a short time later two neighborhood houses were displaying his work. This meticulous work captured his hands and his concentration, if not his mind. While painting ochre or blue arabesques he thought about Yael. Rebecca informed him that Yael had been told. The shock had been great, but her perennially sad eyed had sparkled.

The long-awaited day arrived. Rebecca met Lazarus at her warehouse at dawn, before her workers showed up for work. She made him up, covered his head and wrapped him in veils, Arab style. To cut down his size she gave him the figure of a bent old woman. Only his eyes could be seen; the rest of his face disappeared under layers of fabric. Rebecca waited for her salesladies to arrive and watched their reaction. There wasn't any; they didn't even notice the tall Muslim woman. The small party began the journey to the sheik's property, delighting in the prospect of the great sales they were about to make. Lazarus's heart beat so hard that he thought he would faint with every step he took. Fortunately, Rebecca was there to help him along; she talked to him and sang ancestral melodies, joined by the other Jewish women.

They finally passed through the gates and the edenic gardens that surrounded the residence of sheik El-Moktar. The women were led to the harem and their precious trunks set in a room lined with mosaic tapestries. There, they waited for the sheik's wives. Lazarus crouched to hide his height. He felt a pinch in his heart when he saw a merry group of veiled women come in his direction; Yael was probably among them. This one—no, too short. That one or the next … no …

He didn't have to wonder long. When Yael came in he knew immediately it was her. Their eyes locked as if they were magnets. Lazarus had tears in his eyes. A disconcerted Yael frowned, then shook her head slowly. She glanced furtively about her. The trunks were open, precious fabrics were spread out, everyone delirious, excited, but nobody paid them any mind. She moved in the direction of a hallway with marble walls. He followed.

They caught up with each other in a small empty room. Yael closed the door, locked it, and finally dared to turn around. Lazarus took off his veil, and they rushed into each other's arms. In that moment they had an entire life to catch up on. In the intimacy of their embrace they forgot the world and its dangers, they overcame their obstacles; at last, rewarded for their pains, they were holding each other. They satisfied the desire repressed for so many years with the kind of despair felt by those who have nothing to lose. They would never stop. Guards could kill them; they had taken back what fate had robbed of them.

Then came the moment to talk, to evoke the dark years.

"Lazarus, my love, not a day has passed that I didn't think of you. In Toledo, when I learned you were dead, and then when my parents also left me, my life lost its meaning. I was waiting for death to take me. So I began to speak with you, I began to make you live inside me."

"The sheik was kind to me after he bought me because he was very proud to have me as his wife. But I kept spurning him because I had decided to resist him to my death. Do you realize that I had been sold? Sold! Well, he never forced me into anything; he kept saying, 'I shall wait until you're ready.' He was extremely considerate and gratified my every whim. The women in the harem could not understand my sadness. 'You don't know how lucky you are. You're his favorite!'"

"I was helpless. The sheik let me speak, listened to me, inspired me to trust him. He consoled me without ever being sharp with me. One day I quit fighting. I have resigned myself to my new life. Even if he has taken other, younger women, I remain his favorite. My role is that of a confidante, especially since the death of his mother. His love is genuine. I now speak Arabic and, all things considered, their customs are not so removed from ours. The prince loves me for my temperament. He says I am proud and rebellious and that he would not ever want me to resemble any of his other wives. You see, my prison is very comfortable."

"Yael, my love, I came to find you, and we are never going to be apart again."

"Alas! Lazarus... Alas! I have two children. I cannot abandon them."

She began to cry. Lazarus had just been dealt another blow. He took her in his arms and kissed her on the forehead. She dried her tears and stood up.

"We have to leave each other now. The sale is almost over. Let me dress you back up. Oh! Lazarus, I know you're alive. That's already a blessing. I will think of you. Every night, when the moon glides over the mountains, I'll look at it and I'll be right there with you. You, too, look at it. Tt will be our way to be together."

On the way back Rebecca answered Lazarus's questions. "Yes, I knew this meeting would bring you both joy and despair. I knew of Yael's children, but I didn't want to spoil the happiness of your meeting. Now you must forget all this. Stay here. Life here is sweeter than in Castilla. It is not too late to start all over again."

Rebecca was right. What would he do in Spain, where he had nothing if not a brother who had doomed himself? He spent the night thinking about it and then told the El-Kabachs of his intent to travel to Granada. He was contemplating resuming work with their son-in-law, David Medina, if he still wanted him. David was overjoyed.

Ephraim decided to celebrate the event. They had a party for the entire family. Feeling an ache in his heart, Lazarus saw happy children having fun; the three El-Kabach daughters watched over their children while their loving husbands gazed tenderly at them. Melancholy enveloped him. With all the evil he had caused, God had rewarded Joseph with a son; a cool, distant son, raised with a proper Christian education, who might remain a stranger to him; yet, he was a son. Ephraim Medina, named after his grandfather, climbed on Lazarus's knees. They had met at the porcelain factory, and the child had quickly "adopted" the tall man. Little Ruth Medina, with all the innocent gall of her four years, had the gathering laughing when she said, "If Lazarus stays, could I marry him one day?"

After the primitive solidarity of the traveling circus people Lazarus was enjoying the simple but healthy family life of people to whom he meant nothing. To thank them he promised himself to devote himself completely to his new work. Each porcelain tile he would make would be proof of his faithfulness to Yael; thus he would adorn life with his love. This labor perfectly fitted his despair; it required taste as well as precision. Alone with his colors, in the heat of the workshop, he would let life go its course and might end up resigned to its hardships.

The Ben Salfas, Omar's family, received him warmly, delighted to have news from their successful son. If they remained discreet as to why Omar had been banished, they still wanted to thank Lazarus by letting him rent a small house in the Albaicin quarter, under the majectic shade of the Alhambra, a short distance away from the factory.

Lazarus was assimilated easily into this teeming neighborhood. The Ben Salfas were even able to start a rumor that the tall, quiet Jew was a master porcelain maker and that they would be the very first ones to commission him to decorate their house. Lazarus quickly learned the basics of Arabic and settled into his easy but sad life. Each night he watched the moon and communicated with Yael through it. He spoke to her of love; he listened to her, behind her gilded fence, and whispered words of love in her ears. Right then, the world was theirs, but he would have given anything to hold her in his arms.

Many customers came to the factory. Lazarus received them cordially and was soon able to turn David's enterprise into a highly profitable business. Children loved him, and if they happened to stroll by the workshop, Lazarus would stop what he was doing to perch them on his knees and to tell them of his extraordinary travels. Little Ruth prattled in the arms of her "fiancé's"; Ephraim played games of famous Lazarus's terrifying adventures with mustachioed Vaslic on horseback. He had become their best uncle, so amiable, so strong.

Chapter 29

Four months had passed when Rebecca asked to see him. Her eyes were filled with tears.

"Lazarus, I'm just back from the sheik's residence. I saw Yael. Her belly is getting round. She's expecting your child."

"How can she be sure?" he stammered.

"My son, women know these things. She knew it two weeks after your secret rendezvous. That's why she went to her husband's bed so as not to arouse suspicions. It's been four months. It's your child, Lazarus, your child."

"Oh! dear God, a son…"

"It's going to be a girl. Yael doesn't feel dizzy, and she's eating a whole lot of fruit. Everyone knows that a woman expecting a boy devours meat."

"A daughter! Four months! So I'm going to be a father this spring!"

"Yes, Lazarus. Yael is very strong; all will be well. If you could have seen how her face radiated with happiness! Next year, God willing, you'll see her again."

Lazarus had myriad questions to ask. Rebecca answered them patiently. He insisted so much that she had to agree to return to the palace shortly to deliver his messages, one sweeter than the other. But then he remembered Antonio, his messenger at the jail in Toledo, who had paid with his life for helping him, and he changed his mind; he begged Rebecca not to take any risks. It would be better to wait.

She reassured him and promised that all would be well. "And she also told me about the moon. Asked me that you not forget her…"

That evening, more than any other, Lazarus contemplated the star that united him with his beloved. The moon was almost as full as a woman's belly, and it illuminated the white mountains with its pale rays. A new heart was beating inside Lazarus. He began to feel happy to be alive again.

#

Some time later Rebecca described to Yael the reaction of the father-to-be. Wasn't this a dangerous situation? she asked. No, Yael said the sheik was happy to add another heir to his lineage. His two sons welcomed with some puzzlement the idea that they were going to have a little sister, but all the women agreed on this: It would be a girl.

Months went by. In March Rebecca was able to return to the palace a few days after Yael's delivery. Little Yasmina was a quiet baby. If not for her father's dimple in her cheeks, she bore a remarkable resemblance to her mother. Yael was fine; she was overwhelmed with happiness.

Lazarus was moved as he listened to Rebecca, and he tranferred his tender feelings to little Ruth, who, now five, still wanted to marry her hero. When he addressed her he was addressing the other child that he didn't know yet, and the two little girls fused into one in his mind. He was impatiently waiting for the next big sales event in June. Then Yasmina would be ... three months old.

The cool spring mornings has been replaced with the sunny June mornings when Lazarus finally saw his daughter. The same care was taken to disguise him, and the same deception worked without arousing anyone's suspicion. Yael, with circles under her eyes, though radiant, spied her lover's arrival feverishly. She almost rushed to embrace the stooping old woman, but she managed to hold herself back. She greeted Rebecca and exchanged a few words in Hebrew with her before joining the other women's chorus of joyful noises at seeing beautiful, festive materials; she turned this noisy situation to profit by squeezing Lazarus in her arms. A servant carried a small baby. She took it from her gently and revealed its face to her father, who, as an old woman, could cajole the baby tenderly.

"That smile is yours, Lazarus. When I look at her I think I'm seeing you," Yael whispered.

"You have gotten more beautiful. You're gorgeous. Did everything go well, then? Aren't you at risk?"

She told him how afraid she'd gotten when she realized she was pregnant, because she hadn't been with her husband for months. But it had been easy to find her way to his bed and to ask him to father another child before she got too old. "My sons, Lazarus, are proud children but are growing up away from me and the harem, since their father insists they be educated as future kings. I was hoping it would be a girl so I could keep her close to me for a long time. Don't be sad, Lazarus I am torn. The sheik respects me, and my mother's heart cannot make me renounce my sons. But deep down in my heart I am your wife forever, and this child is the fruit of our love." She brought back her youth; she had so much wanted to be his, but she had been sold. Even today, fifteen years later, she still hurt in the very core of her being.

Lazarus felt guilty; nothing would have happened if he hadn't ignored her. But now was the time to forget the painful past and think about the child. They didn't tarry telling each other how their minds thought alike and how their hearts beat as one. "Perhaps one day, Yael, the situation will be such that the three of us will be able to be together and show our love for one another freely. For my child's sake I'll be the most patient man in the world. All I ask is to be able to come see you every year. May God protect us after having put us through so many trials."

Even if Rebecca's ploy seemed failproof, they were still endangering their lives. A slight mishap and Lazarus would be found out and beheaded. When they had found each other again they had, in the heat of passion, cast caution out the window. Death could come to them; they did not fear it. But now there was a little girl with a bright future, and they had to be careful for her sake.

He told her about the blue porcelain he painted while thinking about her. She recollected for him the Hebrew melodies she whispered in her daughter's ears to put her to sleep. He told her about the fabrics he selected for Rebecca to have clothes made for Yasmina. She told him how she waited for the moon to appear above the mountains and how she said the prayers from her past to ask God to watch over them. The afternoon was spent exchanging tender words. Rebecca was on the lookout though no one ever disturbed them. The day ended, and life was tuned to the future. Lazarus held Yael against him one last time and kissed his daughter, and the women with the magical trunks took the road back.

Time was on their side. Seasons went by, and July kept returning quickly. Yasmina turned two. Yasmina turned four. She was becoming a sweet child with an affecting smile. At the harem, if wives could be mercilessly jealous of one another at times, children were kings and grew up enjoying the affection of all the women. Quiet Yasmina had become inseparable from Leila, one of her "half sisters" who was the same age and with whom she spent most of her time. Leila's mother, who was just seventeen, let Yael care for the two little girls.

Lazarus's life was spent according to the cycles of the moon. The people from the neighborhood had come to appreciate him; the small Medina family loved him; the El-Kabachs invited him often if Omar's family hadn't been first to ask. Among them he tried to learn Arabic. The massacres of Toledo began to fade, and Christian power seemed monstruous but distant. In Granada Jewish and Moslem commmunities cohabitated without problems. Even if the news from Spain was good, Lazarus would not be going back. Everything kept him here.

He knew, however, that he could not be satisfied forever with a life without continuity. One day he'd have to do something.

Chapter 30

Around the same time, in Toledo, Joseph resented his ostentatious life more and more. His own loneliness frightened him at times, but he accepted it to make reparation for the evil he had committed. Yes, to be saved he needed to be punished. Lazarus had forgiven him but had left him, forlorn, in the grip of his guilt. What could he have done to redeem himself? Hand his wealth out to the poor, bring his arrogant family to the brink of bankruptcy? He entertained such thoughts from time to time, but wealth had its merits, and, moreover, it was his only weapon

Once in a while he visited Samir, who looked ancient, bent over his perennial white cane, and the two of them would talk for endless hours. He found himself coming by the Jewish cemetery more and more often, as if his father's grave were the repository of all the answers to his questions. But he could not stop there.

Six years had passed since he last saw Lazarus and his grudge against his father began to abate; he was no longer uneasy when he happened to think about the melancholy man who had shown him so little affection. A father himself, he was in a perfect position to understand that a father could grow distant from his child for reasons outside his control. "Everything is quelling, Father. My resentment and my shame. I was baptized, but Christians never consider me one of them. Before it would have chagrined me more than now. Jews are coming back to a better life as it seems a new peaceful period is being ushered in. Maybe one day I will find peace." And he would return home, neither a Christian nor a Jew.

But he paid careful attention to the authorities' changing attitude toward Israel. In 1432 rabbis had been invited to the great synagogue of Valladolid, attended by numerous notables. A new set of regulations and rules had been established to ease Jews back into their rights and to restore their dignity. Juan II signed this decree, known as the "Takkanoth of Valladolid," which put an end to the tremendous cycle of conversions. This important document defined the new directions of Judaism.

Written by the great rabbis and supreme judges Joseph Albo, Joseph Ibn, Schem Tob and especially Abraham Benveniste, it encouraged the faithful to strict obedience to the commandments of the Torah.

It had become possible to be a Jew again. A new breath of life blew over the community. Hope grew in the hearts of newly-made Christians, many of them renewing contacts with their ex-brethren carefully, to be sure, but with genuine faith in their hearts. The new living conditions confused Joseph. He felt even more guilty to have renounced his old religion so easily.

That same year, 1432, his son Joachim turned sixteen. He was still a reserved and aloof young man. A simple look was all it took for him to get what he wanted, if he addressed his mother and grandparents. On the other hand, he asked nothing of his father—not because he feared him, but because he felt no affinity with him. Brilliant and well-read, he was very much sought after at court, where his noble demeanor turned many heads. A luxurious life awaited him, and a noble Spanish beauty would one day become his wife. Because of the education he had received he had completely lost sight of his Jewish blood. A most Christian sun shone for him.

#

The cigarral had expanded with time. There were always many visitors. Painters, musicians, poets and actors were among Joseph's favorite guests. He loved the stories of chivalry or comedy they would tell. Unlearned in the ways to share his enthusiasm, he paid the gifted storytellers handsomely. His wife Isabel, who had not become more intelligent with the passage of time, also enjoyed the adventures of brave knights. She saw her son atop a proud warhorse, attacking hordes of infidels or going across magical forests. People were prone to dream of the Orient in the wintry cold of Castilla. Imagination spilled over familiar borders, and they talked of countries so far away that it took a lifetime to travel there. When in attendance Joachim had a twinkle in his eyes at hearing about those distant lands. His future was bright, but there were times when he'd dream about going on an adventure to the other side of the world and experiencing its dangers.

It was at these times and at these times only that a real family inhabited the cigarral. Everyone listened, and imagination embellished, stories and Toledo, the Tagus, stern Mancha and blistery winters were all forgotten.

Lazarus thought about Joseph sometimes. Joseph thought about Lazarus sometimes. They lived in two different worlds. In Arab lands, the pulse of life beat languidly in the sun. It was fruitless to go after honors; people enjoyed their simple and peaceful existence. Lazarus was often amazed to notice how devoid of violence daily life was. One did not meet contempt in the Arab's eyes. If business was going well, everything was swell; if sales slowed down, it was God's will.

Immersed in the kingdom of money, power and pride, Joseph would never have dreamed of such a life. He often thought about Lazarus. What was he doing? Was he still touring with the circus people Samir had told him about? To give up everything and go on the road… Lazarus was free! Wasn't this the greatest of all riches?

With time Lazarus's opinion of his brother mellowed. What good could it do to live obsessed with the idea of taking revenge? In Granada everyone had a place, with Jehovah for some and Allah for others. Toledo seemed so far away! Their father Eli would never have accepted Joachim, his estranged grandson with an affected manner. Nor Yasmina…in truth, he would have been thoroughly disconcerted by these two children, one raised among Christians, the other one growing up in Islamic culture. Fate had had quite a few surprises in store. Thank God he died a good Jew, nothing had ever shattered his faith.

#

When Santa María died at the age of eighty-three Joseph felt much sadness. With the possible exception of Samir, the priest had been the only one to show him genuine affection.

#

At age twenty-two Joachim-the-proud wed the confidently beautiful Mercedes Delbacia. The young woman's father, a court advisor, organized a sumptuous wedding. Festivities lasted several days, all the

Grandees from neighboring lands were invited, and wine from the Benavistas' wineries flowed abundantly. In the background, Joseph had a difficult time controlling his emotions. In spite of the non-malicious but insurmountable obstacles the da Silvas had set, he was still the father of this child, who had grown into a man and had married one of the most beautiful women in the kingdom. Cooks concocted marvels; jesters entertained; presents piled up in the large room' a painter had been commissioned to paint the couple's portrait.

Nine months later, in 1439, during a beautiful day in May, Manuel Juan Fernando was born out of this union. He was baptized in the huge Toledo cathedral where his parents had been married. In spite of the magnificent service, the couple seemed overwhelmed by the birth. Mercedes, in the full splendor of her eighteen years, and Joachim, with the divine charm, felt they were too young to begin acting as parents.

God, however, had other designs. A month later Mercedes was pregnant again. The young couple confronted each other on the communal bed: "Am I going to end up pregnant each time we accomplish our marital duty?" Mercedes cried out. "Are you so incapable of being careful?"

Pablo Eduardo was born in March. It was an easy birth, but Mercedes was bitter about those eighteen months when she had been nothing but a belly. Pablo and Manuel, however, were strong and good-looking. Joseph, who spied on the relationship between Joachim and his daughter-in-law, felt he had a golden opportunity to express his long-repressed love. He had been prevented from raising his son, but he might be able to share his love with those two lively, screaming babies. He was given one more reason to hope when Isabel's mother, the señora da Silva, passed on; by herself his wife Isabel would not stop him from acting as he pleased. He mourned with a light heart. Manuel already acknowledged him with a smile...

Soon Mercedes deserted the marital bed. She felt she had done her duty. She spent her days in the garden, away from her sons and husband, where she learned how to play the lute under the tutelage of a young music teacher. Joachim would be gone more and more often. He'd ride his bay horse toward mysterious destinations. She was too beautiful and he too handsome. Separately they sought out humbler companions to admire them and love them instead of loving themselves.

Joseph learned timidly the art of grandfathering. His dull spouse's health was deteriorating; he surrounded her with physicians, one more erudite than the other, and slipped discreetly into the kingdom of children.

Fate began to strike a strange balance. Within the same month, Joachim had a fatal fall from his horse and Isabel died after terrible coughing bouts. A scandal was barely averted after Joachim's body was recovered on the small property of don Italo, whose wife had the reputation of being rather loose. After the kick that had killed his master Joachim's horse had galloped back home. Isabel, bedridden for several days, was the one who saw the lone animal. Her mother's heart began to beat furiously, and she sent two servants after the horse. It led them to the corpse. Joachim had broken his neck; his handsome face had frozen in an expression of ire.

When she saw his body, Isabel fainted. Her son had been the shining star in a rather dull life; without him, death could come and take her. When he came back home that evening Joseph got a shock. He wife was stuttering inaudible lamentations, and his son was laid down, white, on his bed. His mind went blank. He felt no sorrow, just a great emptiness.

He felt much empathy for Isabel, however, who died in terrible pains three weeks after her son. She had gone mad and shouted her sorrow between coughing fits, and there was nothing he could do to ease her agony. Then, one day, the house became quiet and empty. Joseph found himself alone with a taciturn daughter-in-law and two energetic children. The mother was buried very close to her son, and new habits took hold at the cigarral.

Mercedes, too, had shown little emotion before the two successive deaths. Now that he was free, Joseph asked her to stay on his property for as long as she would like. He would take care of the children and ask nothing of her. The truth was that a few months earlier he had fallen inavertently under his daughter-in-law's charm. He would sometimes stop what he was doing just to look at her, in the distance, in the garden. To him she represented the inaccessible, true blue blood; he was even resigned to be scorned by her, as if her long neck and dark eyes warranted it. He wanted to talk to her, to tell her the personal tragedies that had made him clumsy but rich, wedged between two religions. But she would never listen to him; she was so far above such mediocre matters.

Doña Mercedes had no animosity toward Joseph. She looked at him as a man in the prime of life, somewhat uncouth, boring, but she appreciated the impunity she enjoyed with him. Everyone at the cigarral knew that the music teacher was her lover; when he opened his home to her, Joseph also granted her the freedom to continue her liaison. He never lectured her on her lack of maternal instincts; quite the contrary. He was glad to assume responsibility for the children's education. This life-style suited them perfectly, and a pleasant routinewas set. Joseph was finally able to experience relative happiness.

Both children grew up surrounded by the love of an amazing grandfather. A little withdrawn, touching at times, he would spend hours talking to them, mixing court stories and fantastic tales of traveling minstrels—and sometimes, though unconsciously, he would interpolate elements from the Talmud. Their mother would make striking apparitions, would kiss them on the forehead and in her low and slow voice ask for news. Joseph hid his nervousness behind a few grimaces to amuse the children before attending to his business.

The vineyard prospered without too much active tending. Samir had died where he had always lived, and at such an old age that Joseph did not know what to have inscribed on the small grave in the middle of his property. On his advice a competent team, knowledgeable in the entire winemaking process, had been created. That gave him the freedom to devote much more time to the children's education.

#

Lazarus saw his daughter each June. Ten years, ten visits. He was forty-eight. By insisting that he reveal nothing about the deception, Rebecca had succeeded in avoiding trouble. Each year the harem received the bent and silent old woman without ever suspecting foul play. Lazarus's only regret was that he had to appear to his daughter as an old hunchbacked woman.

Yasmina had inherited her mother's grace and sweetness. She was a quiet child who sat calmy next to her friend Leila to look at materials and embroideries. Yael, whose face began to show her age, filled with tenderness each time she looked at her child.

"She speaks a little Hebrew, you know, and she knows a lot about our religion. I have also told her the adventures of the hero of the Jews of Toledo, the famous Lazarus Benavista. She knows who you are, though she doesn't know that the man who planted his arrow dead center in the bull's-eye is her own father, but you are a part of her world."

"Aren't you taking too many risks?"

"No. Speaking and storytelling are our main occupations here. I am privileged because I lived on the outside for many years. Almost all the women here were promised to the sheik while they were still babies. The education they received was shaped by that prospect, and few among them have been on the outside. You know, the sheik is nearly sixty, yet last month a new wife arrived, so young and so dainty."

"That's disgusting. Oh, Yael, could he not free you? I only need but one wife! It's so unfair. Yael, I can only think of the time we'll be together forever..."

"Don't scare me, Lazarus. It's not possible ... not now."

"I have studied this fortress. if you knew the thousands of ideas I have to take the two of you out of here—"

"When Yasmina is a woman I will tell her who her father is. Promise me not to try anything before then."

I promise. Ten years have passed, and I have learned to be patient. You see, I was able to wait; I'll go on waiting. But I am going to get ready for your escape. One day, Yael..."

Lazarus lived only for that moment. He had imagined all sorts of schemes: the empty trunks after the sale, the high windows, the moon crescent. At night his disturbed dreams brought about other strange stratagems. He'd try something and would succeed ... God willing.

#

In 1441 Yasmina turned thirteen. She was finally told the truth about her conception. Yael had prepared her so well that she accepted that troubling revelation easily. She even displayed a certain pride when she learned that the "hero of Toledo" was her father. Yael spent a long time telling her about the risks involved and the necessity of keeping the secret if they wanted to stay alive. Yasmina listened to her mother's lecture attentively, absorbing each piece of advice calmly. And when, her face beaming, she stated to her mother, "Then, I am fully Jewish!" Yael embraced her tightly. Away from Toledo, away from Christians, the union of a Monsonego and a Benavista, faithful to their religion, had produced a worthy successor to the people of the Book.

After this revelation mother and daughter saw each other often to talk. The young girl wanted to know everything about the history of her people. Yael regained the ardor of her younger days to share Yasmina's passion. This time the two waited for the month of June to return.

When Lazarus appeared, disguised as an old woman, Yael and Yasmina pointed to a small room in the corner of a hallway where they met him promptly. Yasmina wanted to embrace her father, and more than that, she wanted to see his face and hear his voice. Yael tried to control her tears. Lazarus was very moved. They spent only a few minutes together before returning to the main room. The three of them felt that the time of their deliverance was approaching.

He explained his plan to them. They had to wait for fall, the season when the sheik went hunting. Lazarus would wait for his return and would enter the fortress disguised as a soldier; Rebecca would forewarn Yael as to the exact day.

"I'm already exposing myself to the sun to tan my skin, and Rebecca has told me how to darken my hair. I speak Arabic well, and for the past thirteen years I have considered every possible way to enter this fortress. The harem is located in the left wing in the upper levels. You and Yasmina will have to dress as veiled slaves and place yourselves as close as possible to the wall."

"That will be possible only after sunset, with the third prayer. After that we won't be able to leave our quarters."

"Yes, I know. We'll make it, Yael. We'll succeed because God will not forsake us."

\#

Yael slept uneasily; she spoke in her sleep—in Spanish; fortunately: the other women only understood Arabic. Yasmina, less aware of the danger, came to comfort her mother, who had begun to fear the arrival of fall.

Yet to be free again, after twenty years in Granada, in the sheik's gilded jail, to have the chance to finally live her great love out in the open, overwhelmed her. Her sons had become independent men who rarely visited her. She had resigned herself to that situation and felt she could go on living without ever seeing them again—for her daughter, for Lazarus, for freedom. Would they go back to Toledo? Lazarus had spoken about the money he had that would assure them a rapid escape. But, she wondered, what if everything went sour?

When fall came Lazarus staked out the large entry gate to the domain and watched what went on during the two days of hunting before making up his mind. Everything was ready he had memorized the placing of each of his footsteps, a wagon was waiting close by, Rebecca had informed Yael and had provided her with slave clothing. The sun was beginning to set when Lazarus entered the palace among the sheik's following. He straightaway went for the two women, who were supposed to wait for him in the corridor leading to the kitchens. There they were, their hearts wracked with fear. They obeyed Lazarus's nod; so far so good.

At the same time, however, young Leila was looking for Yasmina in all the rooms of the harem, and she could not find her. She was remembering the strange good-bye Yasmina had bid her the night before. Feeling abandoned by her only friend, she went to her mother to share her concerns. The news was promptly picked up by the other women and quickly spread thoughout the harem; then guards issued a search order. A wife and her daughter had disappeared. The search turned up the runaways on the threshold of the main gate. A guard called out to them. Yasmina ran toward Lazarus while Yael, panic-stricken, froze in place as a guard rushed her. She burst out crying and yelled to Lazarus, "Run, my love. Save yourselves." When he heard Spanish the Moor held her by the shoulder, unsheathed his saber and called his comrades for help. Realizing that all was lost, Yael threw herself on the weapon and was run through. She collapsed while calling the name of the man she had never stopped loving. Yasmina turned to stone.

Lazarus had to act quickly. Without allowing his grief to take over he lifted his daughter in his arms and ran toward the wagon. He dropped her in the back, then seized the reins and commanded his horses to gallop. Yasmina screamed, the horses raced, the palace grew more distant; Lazarus could no longer feel his tears streaming. They drove for hours without stopping or talking, and night slowly fell. They were heading north, leaving a part of themselves in Granada. Yael had only savored a few steps in freedom.

Lazarus drove the horses until they were exhausted. He only wanted to stop in Spain; that was where they would be safer. In addition to his bow and the parchments he had taken blankets, food and clothes. In the back of the wagon Yasmina was crying softly. She, too, had dreamt about happiness, but suddenly she was discovering violence and death.

The horses trotted across the border in the early dawn. When Lazarus caught sight of the first church steeple he came to a halt. He tethered the horses by the bank of a small stream and set up a makeshift camp. Then father and daughter fell asleep in each other's arms.

When they awoke they had to face the nightmare of the day before. It was all too real: Yael was dead, and they were on the lam. Yasmina burst into tears. Death, this stream, these fields, that sky were all new to her. Her father took her in his arms and rocked her silently. He himself was disconsolate and did not know how to comfort her. "Why, why, God of my fathers, do you make those who venerate you suffer? Why did you keep me alive for so long if you're going to end my days now? My God, what do you want? What will satisfy you? What harm have I done that you should be so vengeful toward me? Must I pay all my life for a sin I may have committed but that I do not understand?"

They remained exhausted for a long time, a very long time, until the sun reached its zenith. Then Lazarus decided it was time to do something. He went to the river to wash up and advised Yasmina to do likewise. He took some food out and made her eat. "You want to die," he said to her, his voice choking with tears, "just like I do, before this injustice, before this tragedy. But in your blood flows the Jewish spirit, which weathers all storms and overcomes all calamities. I will teach you the prayer for the dead that we're going to recite in your mother's memory. Then we'll go on the road again to stay alive, Yasmina, for it is God's will."

Thus they prayed by the banks of a river in Spain. In the span of an instant Lazarus relived all the trials of his long life. He would have stopped fighting had he been without his daughter. What would he find in a country that had once been his enemy? Would it be peace or misfortune? What would Yasmina's future be after a life inside a harem? How could he prepare her for existence in a world where liberty had been killed? Shouldn't he choose self-exile, far away, in a land where no one would call him to account, where Yasmina would be happy? But he had to see Toledo one last time. Joseph! What had become of him? What about Samir? Was he still alive? The vineyard, the Jewish quarter, his youth—it all seemed so far away.

#

They made slow progress. Lazarus had brought along a comfortable sum of money, which was meant to facilitate their escape. Yasmina had calmed down; she asked questions and sought in God the response to all her questions. Lazarus tried to reassure her in spite of his own doubts. That first evening they received a warm welcome from a Jewish family in Bailen. Lazarus learned all he needed to know about the new life in Spain, about the period of tranquility that had set in many years ago and which seemed to be lasting. Yasmina smiled weakly when she heard an elder man say to Lazarus, "Lazarus Benavista. That name rings a bell. Aren't you the victor of the tournament of Toledo, in the year fourteen hundred?"

They spent several days traveling the roadways. Landscapes changed, and Yasmina was coming back to life. The child from the harem was no more; she had died the day her mother died, one morning in the Year of Our Lord 1422. An adult Yasmina was beginning to blossom in the shadow of her sturdy father, a Yasmina who was a bit over fourteen and who was discovering her Jewishness, who learned fast and understood everything. Going to Toledo might be a mistake, but who would remember him after thirty years?

And Lazarus had the irresistible urge to go back to his roots.

#

Fog surrounded them as they progressed toward Toledo. Lazarus recounted his youth, the massacres perpetrated against Jews, and how he, too, had been orphaned as his life had barely begun. Late that afternoon they were nearing Madridejo, a small Castilian town where they'd planned to stop. All of a sudden distant screams could be heard. Yasmina cried out, "A wagon, a galloping horse ridden by a child!" Lazarus reacted quickly. He put himself in the path of the runaway vehicle and was able to hoist himself on it and pull back the reins. The animal slowed down before stopping altogether. The child threw himself into Lazarus's arms. A trembling Yasmina caught up with them and sat the little boy of five or six on her knees. Between sobs he told them what had happened: "My two brothers there … and the horse, it just took off. They ran after it, but it was too late. I was so scared—"

Two adolescents ran up to them screaming, "Rafael!"

"He's fine," Lazarus said. "What happened?"

"We got off the wagon for just an second, and the horse bolted—an insect bite, maybe. Wow! You saved our brother. Would you please come to our home? Our father would want to thank you personally!"

They took small, dusty pathways to a beautiful house high on a hill. Lazarus had a shock when he thought he had recognized the cigarral of his youth; he would not have been surprised to see Sarah come out yelling for Joseph. In the span of a minute he forgot how old he was or where he was. Rafael drew him out of his reverie, yelling from the wagon, "It's here, it's our house!" Yes, of course, he was not in Toledo, and he was fifty-two years old. Turning to Yasmina, he said, "You see, our house looked very much like this one. Away from the Jewish quarter, beautiful, large and sturdy."

The child's father, a strong white-haired man, was waiting for them on the threshold. Lazarus realized he was among fellow Jews. Rafael's two brothers recounted their misadventure before Lazarus introduced himself. "My name is Lazarus Benavista, and this is my daughter Yasmina."

Eli Zarka. I do not know how to express my gratitude to you. Rafael is a wonderful child, full of life. Each one of us loves him more than anything, and you saved him. Ask anything you want; My home is your home. Come in and rest. You already know my sons Rafael, Luis and Antonio. My daughter Ines will be along shortly."

Yasmina blushed; she had just found out the name of the pleasant-looking young man she had been staring at. Antonio—the name sounded like a melody. It was the first time that she had observed life outside the harem.

Lazarus explained why he wanted to go to Toledo before leaving the country, for Italy, perhaps. He had just lost his spouse under circumstances he'd rather not retell and wanted nothing more than to start a new life elsewhere. But they were weary and would gladly use the next few days to rest.

Rafael jumped for joy. Lazarus was shown to a comfortable room, and Yasmina was offered a bed in Ines's room. The evening was long and pleasant. Lazarus confessed his emotion to his host; Eli's home resembled the home he had known in his youth and he had the same first name as his father.

When he recalled back the year 1391 Eli Zarka said, with tears in his eyes, "We lived in Valladolid then. I was barely fifteen. I saw my father, mother and brothers die. I was able to escape with my younger sister, and we wandered to the next village, where a family miraculously came to our help. My sister resides in Ocaña now; she is married and a grandmother. As for myself, I married an exceptional woman who has such a tenacious and courageous character that I regained a taste for life. Alas, she passed away four years ago. My daughter Ines has never wanted to get married, so as not to abandon us. Rafael found a second mother in her. She is twenty-five now. My oldest son, Fernando, takes care of my affairs. He's expected to be with us tomorrow. Do you really have to go back on the road? Think about it. My house is large, Yasmina will be comfortable here, and I have work for you."

At the same time the door swung open. "Ah! Ines, my daughter, come on in. We have guests." The story of the wagon was told once more around the table with a flurry of fierce commentaries from Luis and Rafael. Antonio kept quiet. His eyes had crossed Yasmina's. Lazarus caught their gaze and smiled.

He spent an uneasy night. Yasmina was tired; this family seemed so warm. Why not leave her here? He'd proceed to Toledo as he had promised himself, and they'd advise him upon his return: go to Italy or stay here, since the Zarkases had made the offer so generously.

He relayed his decision to Eli when he got up; Eli was delighted.

"Your daughter Yasmina will be fine with us. Ines is already very fond of her."

Yasmina jumped to her father's neck. Antonio lowered his head to hide his joy. Rafael and Luis, the two youngest, clapped. Staid and poised Ines approved with a nod. The following day Lazarus began his journey.

Chapter 31

Toledo! Toledo rose, a proud pink citadel among pale hills. Lazarus remained motionless a long time atop his horse while he contemplated the city of his misfortunes. Over there fields spread out in the open; up there the Alcazar cut an austere figure. He took the path leading to Samir's little house. An hour later he was going across the Benavistas' vineyards. Was the harvest good? Barrels were probably being filled by the hundreds this October. Lazarus would have given anything to inhale the smell in the caves where the wine was pressed.

He could make out the outline of the roof over the small house; he saw a grave. He alit and read the epitaph. Samir had died some six years ago. Lazarus felt an ache in his heart. During all the years he had spent in Granada he had often thought about Samir, and he would have wanted to embrace him one last time. At least he had lived a long and tranquil life, removed from so many tragedies.

He met the new vineyard overseers. He introduced himself under a false name and asked for news of his old friend Joseph. He was told that Joseph spent the majority of his time at the cigarral and that he visited the vineyard once a week, sometimes in the company of his grandsons. He learned of the death of Joachim-the-proud and of his mother Isabel. He heard a few unflattering comments about Joachim's widow, but kinder words about her children. He started toward the cigarral of his youth.

It was the same structure, though perhaps a little smaller than he remembered. The garden where Yael looked for him while he practiced archery... He remembered Sarah and her screams, and Eli, the quiet one. He pictured the way to the Monsonegos' cigarral as well as the longer road that took him to the condesa. Lazarus was over half a century old, and memories from long ago rushed to his mind. Getting off his horse, he asked to see Joseph. The servants thought he was a rich merchant. Lazarus announced himself as a messenger from the Valencia branch and waited.

A beautiful lady was plucking the strings of a lute behind the fountain. Fall was pleasant. She looked in the direction of the stranger, greeted him, and resumed playing her melody. Joseph appeared; he had become rather rotund, and his hair had turned white. Because of his failing eyesight he didn't immediately recognize Lazarus; he invited him in and sat down. Then he looked at him more carefully, and his joy was genuine when he realized who the visitor was. Since he had become a fulfilled grandfather, his personality had changed. He was no longer concerned with appearances; his money helped him live comfortably without having to pay attention to rumors. Lazarus felt this profound change in a brother he remembered as arrogant, vain and petty. He was happy at the change, but showed no emotion.

Joseph insisted he meet his two grandsons. Manuel was almost four, Pablo almost three. The laughing, affectionate kids quickly charmed Lazarus, and the atmosphere relaxed little by little. Lazarus hid the tragedy of Granada from Joseph and said that he had never heard from Yael. Joseph was so happy at being reunited with his brother that he didn't pursue the matter. He wanted to organize a large reception in his brother's honor, but Lazarus refused. He had no intention of staying; he only wanted to see the places of his youth.

"The past is forgotten. Adieu, Joseph."

He went to the Jewish quarter; he was moved more than he had expected. Then he went back to Madridejo. His daughter was waiting. He was now at peace with his past.

#

Lazarus, with Rafael hanging at his neck, related his trip and concluded, "I have definitely turned the page on my past. Only Yasmina matters now." Eli repeated his offer that they stay at his home. Their presence had brightened his home enormously, also, he could tell that Lazarus was experienced. He felt his small business could flourish from that know how. Lazarus accepted. Italy, after all, could wait.

The Zarka family owned a textile business with a small factory in the south of Madridejo. It produced materials with elaborate designs used to make coats for grand occasions. Fernando, the oldest son, managed the enterprise. Lazarus came up with a few ideas to enlarge the workshop and expand business opportunities. He advised Fernando to canvass the neighboring villages and to go even as far as Toledo with samples of the handsome work done by his artisans' "little hands." He preferred staying in the background and attending to the production in Madridejo. He was able to obtain new supplies, threads of rare quality and more efficient tools. In less than a year their profits doubled.

Fernando was a skillful businessman, and orders rushed in. He travelled regularly to southern Castilia to close profitable deals. Lazarus was instrumental in awakening in him a talent that had lain dormant. Yasmina insisted on working alongside her father in the workshop. Ines was thus able to stay home and take on the role of a devoted little mother.

Lazarus also took care of the religious education of Rafael, Luis and Yasmina. When evening fell the children loved to gather around and listen to him.

Their discovery of the biblical world amazed them. "Abstaining from evil and refraining from stealing, lying and hatred is what we must retain. But one must also do good. The Torah contains this wonderful moral precept: 'Love your neighbor as yourself'."

"Even if he is a Christian?" Rafael asked candidly.

"Yes, even if he is Christian or Moslem, because all men are equal before God. But it is toward the weak that we must show goodness and generosity. The written texts are strict on this. We must care for the downtrodden, the widows and the orphans—"

"Like us!" Rafael interrupted once more, happy that the Bible was talking about him.

"Anyone who suffers, Rafael—the poor, the strangers. Don't ever let your heart harden, don't ever close your hand before your indigent brother, God said. These are the precepts of our religion."

"But ... don't Christians also hold these precepts?"

"Yes, the New Testament teaches them to be charitable and to respect their neighbor. But they are forgetful sometimes."

Yasmina never asked any questions but was always attentive. Antonio would join them sometimes and would sit close, very close to her.

"In the beginning our ancestors paid honor to the Almighty by making animal sacrifices or by offering Him flowers and fruit. This was practiced in Jerusalem, at the Temple. Priests, called Cohen or Levi, officiated. Alas, the first temple was destroyed."

"Why?"

"Why? Because it was God's will. This particular temple no longer stands, but anywhere a Jewish community exists, a synagogue is built. But communion with God doesn't necessitate a particular site. Ten men must be present to validate prayers, even in the middle of a desert, for God is everywhere, and he watches and protects us. Just like on the day you were almost killed, Rafael."

"Is He the One Who told you to save me?"

"Yes, somehow. I only had to put into practice one of the principles of the Torah. A human being was in danger; I came to his help. And as a reward, God gathered us here. You see why you have to do good!"

Rafael clapped his hands while Yasmina and Antonio exchanged a tender gaze.

"Our dietary laws seem odd to Christians, yet they are very useful. By forbidding us to eat the flesh of certain animals, our laws protect us from certain diseases."

"Which ones?"

"Well, for example, pork is an unclean animal; its flesh rots rapidly. I have seen Christians eating it and then taking ill. Tt looked as if a demon was eating their guts. God spares us this. With His precepts, he keeps us healthy. There is the Sabbath, the day God makes us rest, which also keeps us healthy! It took the Almighty six days to create the universe, and on the seventh day He rested. We must remain humble in following his example. That holy day must end in joy, prayer, study and relaxation. Friday evening, when the day has ended, we get our homes ready, select the tastiest dishes, dress in our best clothes and light the Sabbath candle."

Rafael's commentaries were disarming. But Lazarus was so apt at finding the proper words to explain each tradition, each precept, that in spite of their age difference the children assimilated the faith of their ancestors easily.

"If our work sometimes prevents us from observing certain holy days, there is one holy day that we must always observe. It's Yom Kippur, the Day of Atonement. On that day we must fast to cleanse ourselves and pray to ask for forgiveness from the Eternal for the sins we committed—even for those we are unaware of having committed, because we may do harm out of carelessness or selfishness. But atoning with half a heart is unacceptable. One must be sincere and convinced. If not, the penance serves no purpose.

"But why did God take my mother? Was it to punish me? Was I sinful?" Rafael asked.

Lazarus, who also wondered why the Almighty had not allowed Yael to live, had no answer. He could only comfort the child. "Of course not, God didn't want to punish you," he said before declaring that it was time for everyone to go to bed. He approached the questions from all angles during his sleepless nights and could find no other response than the one in the Book: "The Lord demands of those he has chosen suffering and compassion; this is why Israel must pay for the sins of others, for it is the Chosen People."

#

In 1443 a royal decree eased Lazarus's bittersweet grief. God had not abandoned them. On all the public plazas of Spain heralds announced that "His Majesty, in an edict published in Areval, took under his care and protection, as his personal property, all the Jews in all the states under his control." Thus all the decisions made against them at the councils of Zamora and Tortosa were null and void. If the 1432 text, the Takkanoth of Valladolid, forbade the persecutions of Jews, the edict of 1443 went much further by restoring them their rights. They would once again be able to open talmudic schools, levy taxes, elect judges, work unimpeded.

This event was marked with festivities in most of the synagogues throughout the country. The double family of the Zarkas-Benavistas was no exeption. All the family members, in their best clothes, rushed to temple. Inside, large makeshift tables had been set up to display trays of pastries. Lazarus choked with emotion as he rediscovered the ritual he had missed for so many years. Yasmina was discovering with wide-open eyes unfamiliar festivities, but she let herself be taken by the general euphoria. The children would remember this day as a new beginning.

That new breath of life stimulated business in the entire region. The Zarka entreprise prospered, and they were able to hire Christians to work in the different shops. Lazarus often thought about his father, Everything was like before.

Chapter 32

1445

Three years had passed since they arrived in the Zarka family. Lazarus had never revealed the secret of Yasmina's birth. His naturally reserved daughter, however, had finally confided in Antonio. Their love wove like a rich fabric. Words had not served to bond them; they were the couple of silences, looks and smiles. Their fathers had no choice but to accept the obvious: These two would be inseparable till death. At seventeen Yasmina was a beautiful dark-haired girl with expressive eyes, although a bit skinny, which gave her an irresistible air of fragility. She took in life through her eyes, was never judgmental, always listened. Antonio literally melted with love for her when she lowered her blushing face. And he, at eighteen, was a young man with a shy smile. His mildness was not a weakness; he forged straight ahead in a tormented life. Yasmina dreamed about running her fingers through his curly hair every night. Without uttering a single word, they had imposed their union as legitimate.

During a meal at which her wedding was to be brought up Yasmina, in her soft voice, asked her father to reveal everything related to her youth. Antonio approved. Lazarus understood that the time had come. Instead of just talking about Granada, however, he related the story of his life, from the tournament to his escape in the Arab kingdom, through his episodes in jail, with the traveling circus, and with the El-Kabachs.

Then Eli understood why the name of his "guest" had been familiar. Of course Lazarus Benavista, deep in the recesses of his memory, was that young man who ... Rafael's eyes sparked at the mention of the tournament, and if Lazarus preferred to appear modest, Eli valorized his deeds by telling all the children the myth of the young hero as it was then being told in the entire region. All the young boys had identified with the famous Lazarus, and all the young girls had dreamt of being courted by him!

Yasmina was moved by the story of her father's arrival in Granada. She asked if he had told the El-Kabachs and the Medinas he would be leaving.

"Only Rebecca knew my plan. I asked her to go see them after the escape, and I begged her, no matter what, to relay only good news to them so that I'll always be a happy memory for them. I do miss them, especially little Ruth, who wanted so much to marry at four."

Rafael wanted to know more about the traveling circus. Lost in his memories, Lazarus evoked starry nights around a campfire, the tricks of the small horse Draga and the strange language spoken by the couple with the snake. A strange fate had made all these adventures possible. In his Soria jail cell where he rotted he would never have imagined running across so many diverse characters. And he still had many more years to live. What did destiny have in store for him at this point? The empire of the Orient, feathered savages, the rugged coasts of Africa?

"Ah! no, you're here now, you are not ever going to leave us!" Rafael said decidedly.

Celebrating a real Jewish wedding as before, in the open, was an immense pleasure.

The synagogue was full that month of June 1446. Yasmina, frail and beautiful in her wedding gown, was living a dream. Lazarus could not keep his eyes from misting as he led her toward the rabbi. Antonio crushed the glass and the music played on, then he took her in his arms before leading her away to make her a woman. Lazarus, who had never known this good fortune, suddenly felt very old. It was as if Yael were disappearing once again. Eli received a similar shock. He held Lazarus by the shoulder and smiled. Such was the lot of fathers!

Soon Fernando announced that he had found his life mate: young Dora Teboul, whose lips were fleshy and whose body was generous. They had been courting for months, and Fernando saw in her a woman who looked fertile and who would give him strong offspring. Young Teboul put her hand in Fernando's.

Then it was Ines's turn. She was seeing Eugenio Laskar, a man of about thirty, a widower, whose heart was bruised. He asked for her hand one cool March day, with such goodness in his eyes that Eli agreed right away. Ines made only one demand: that she stay in her family house, close to Rafael, Luis and her dear father. Eugenio, who had no family, readily agreed. But a family meeting was called: walls were not stretchable; a solution had to be found.

Lazarus volunteered to live in Aranjuez to oversee with Yasmina and Antonio the branch they had opened the year before. Rafael protested. Did his second father want to abandon him? Lazarus smiled. "We'll see each other often. I'll have to leave the two lovers alone once in a while! And you'll join your older brother when he comes to visit us."

They all approved the idea. Yasmina and Antonio were looking forward to living in their own house. Eli was the only one to show some sadness. "Alas! My health won't let me travel to Aranjuez very often."

They left a month later. Fernando's wife already had a very round belly. Good-byes were uttered with some sadness, but a new generation was starting life; hope was smiling.

#

In Aranjuez the Jewish community immediately adopted the new comers. Most of the members worked the land; they were small peasants who led a tranquil and modest life. They never suffered much from discriminatory laws. They were some forty families living peacefully alongside Christians. On Sabbath they gathered in an old structure bought from the overlord that they had transformed into a synagogue.

The store the Zarkas had opened at the edge of the small Jewish quarter was beginning to prosper. Lazarus kept his identity secret; they weren't far from Toledo, and he was still a felon, condemned to life in prison, who was supposed to have died fifteen or twenty years before. He had an uncomfortable house renovated; it turned into a pleasant home, large enough for Yasmina to fill it with as many children as God would grant her. The young couple had the upper floor, and Lazarus settled on the ground floor. The garden, which he designed carefully, quickly became a favorite meeting spot for the men of the neighborhood. They came in the evening to enjoy the pleasant air and engaged in discussions about their children's future, the quality of their work or the interpretation of such and such a passage in the sacred texts.

Women liked to meet, helping one another when there was a need. Sometimes they squabbled. Yasmina, who had been raised in a protected environment, liked the lively and warm atmosphere very much; her large eyes opened wide to take in as much of life as she could. Antonio doted on her with an inextinguishable passion. Working with Lazarus was for him another way of expressing his love for her. He would have learned how to embroider or handle a saber for Yasmina if it would assure their future. Lazarus very much appreciated the young man's enthusiasm; he would protect this couple, who represented everything he had never known, until he was sapped out of all his strength.

That happy union produced a beautiful son in 1447. They named him Simon. He came into the world surrounded with joy and tenderness. He had the most attentive parents and grandfather in the world. The entire Jewish community attended his circumcision in the small synagogue, and all the deeply moved mothers immediately offered advice to Yasmina, as well as clothes and small presents.

Lazarus was a grandfather. He was fifty-seven years old. He had prepared himself for many months for this moment, yet he choked with emotion. Yasmina, the child from the harem, was a mother. "Yael! O Yael. How I wish you were with me to share this happiness!" Lazarus thought.

Two years after Simon, a little girl was born. She did not weigh very much. She was frail like her mother and required much care, but little Myriam began to grow gradually, to everyone's relief. Her brother, standing proudly on his legs, watched with amazament the little newcomer moving in her crib. The two children grew up in playful complicity.

The arrival of those two lively children only increased the deep love of Yasmina and Antonio. Harmony prevailed, and Lazarus was full of tenderness for his grandchildren. Barred from the education of his own daughter, he was able, like his brother Joseph in other circumstances, to transfer his affection onto the mischievious Myriam and the terrible

Simon. The little girl knew how to head off any reprimand with a furtive kiss. And Lazarus, who had erected barricades in Toledo, survived in Soria, seen dear ones die and travelled hundreds of miles, found himself disarmed and happy. Happy finally. Perhaps this was the famous territory he had stil to discover in the autumn of his life. It was neither the Orient nor Africa, just Aranjuez, a daughter who had blossomed, a passionate son-in-law and these two wonderful little rascals.

Yet one day Yasmina got the strange notion to find him a companion. She almost hooked Inna Gouzil, a childless, disconsolate widow. Lazarus refused adamantly. He did not need a wife; he was happy enough to be with Yasmina and his grandchildren. He even excluded himself from outside business decisions, preferring to let his son-in-law take charge. At his age, contemplation was the best exercise he could engage in.

The house in Madridejo was never calm. The small Aranjuez family, Ines, Fernando, Luis, and the children, would travel there once in a while. Like Lazarus, Eli melted before the irresistible Myriam, while Rafael had become Simon's protector. It was a simple life; warmth and family meant something. It was a happy life that made up for all the misfortunes endured by preceding generations. If only it could have lasted forever.

> *You see, little David, they are all there, happy, at peace, even Lazarus, who, at sixty-four, is finally discovering bliss.*

> *Yet clouds are gathering in the distance.*

Chapter 33

When king Juan II died in 1454 Jews grew anxious. They asked a thousand questions: Would his son, Enrique IV, be as benevolent? They had become used to living a life devoid of the demons of fear and humiliation. Would they have to put on the old coat again? History had shown that peaceful periods never lasted very long.

Some refused to let fate decide their future, preferring to pack and go to the other side of the Mediterranean, to Arab land. There there were no winters, no massacres or Christians. Lazarus was not against the idea, but he fully realized the risk he and Yasmina would be taking in Islamic territory: whoever had brought shame upon a sheik in his own domain was relentlessly pursued until death. His travel companions of old, Omar and Ali, would never have dared set foot in a Moslem land because of an untold offense they had commmitted. Enrique IV was not necessarily evil. So why not stay? He accepted the same fatalism that had befallen him thoughout his life.

Trade quickly collapsed. Spain was becoming impoverished. These were times of widespread corruption, of internal struggles at ourt, of misappropriation of tax monies and even of murders among the powerful elite. At the death of Juan II the country desperately needed an iron fist, but Enrique IV seemed to lack character. This worried Lazarus, who had never forgotten meeting the old man from the north, Salomon Sprung, nor his opinion on crimes perpetrated against Jews: "When the populace is hungry and the authorities close their eyes we, sooner or later, are the ones who are made to pay."

He made his family aware of the imminent danger. "Stay alert and stay the course traced by God," he advised.

Chapter 34

In 1459, Manuel, Joseph's first grandson, turned twenty-eight. He was the image of Lazarus at the same age. Pablo was darker, as tall but not as heavy, had a conciliatory nature, and had even succeeded in awakening in his mother, the beautiful Mercedes, a modicum of maternal feeling. More outgoing, Manuel summoned admiration rather than tenderness. Their mother introduced them both proudly as her "big sons."

She had shown a total disinterest in their education, entrusting them instead to their grandfather. She graced their small world with her physical presence only. Joseph had been greatly appreciative; he hadn't noticed how the passage of time had furrowed her beautiful face. He was very fond of her unequaled bearing, her aristocratic gentility. There were times when he felt as if he were cohabitating with a distant, delightful wife, forgetting she was his daughter-in-law. They had almost never spoken about Joachim.

The two brothers got along very well; they grew up in a tranquil and happy milieu. Joseph, however, could still remember the day when a youthful Manuel flashed a smile to him as he jumped atop his horse. Lazarus stood right in front of him. His odd resemblance altered his behavior. The full weight of ever present remorse, in spite of his brother's brief visit some twenty years before, had now shifted to Manuel. "He could be a good Jew, living in harmony with his ancestors. He could lead the life Lazarus never had because of me. He shall be my redemption. Manuel, you are but an accidental Christian. One day you shall reject me, and I will have deserved it," he often thought to himself.

At twenty-eight, Manuel was well-established at Court. Parties that had mostly disappeared during the boys' youth resumed at the cigarral. They divided their time between hunting, the frivolities of parties, and gossiping. Manuel, though, had little affinity with all those wild people whom he very much mistrusted. He had no trust in compliments. Joseph observed him with pride: "He keeps a cool head, unlike that excitable Lazarus. But he does not succumb to the trap of flattery. He remains his own man to the end." Pablo, on the other hand, exuded such charm that he needed no other defense. When he crouched at his mother's feet and begged her to sing and play the lute the two made a charming but hollow tableau.

Both brothers attracted much attention as marriage prospects. Dignified mothers would introduce their daughters to one of the two boys. Neither Manuel nor Pablo, however, was in a hurry to be married' Manuel because he didn't want to commit now that he was getting a full taste of life, Pablo because as he was known to say, "the only woman I love is mother." But Arabella Tortosa, the daughter of the prince of Léon, had set a possessive eye on the charming prince from the court of Toledo, the strong, righteous and proud Manuel. He was the only one not to rush to her side as soon as she made an entrance. How could she resist such wonderful indifference? She became convinced she was madly in love, she quivered if he as much as looked as her. She spent a sleepless night if they exchanged a few words. Her father, Armando Tortosa, friend of Enrique IV, was looking for a trustworthy man; she quickly convinved him, and Manuel was hired in the service of tax collection.

Pablo had no objection to becoming the new overseer at the vineyard. Joseph would have bet the opposite. Pablo went on living at the cigarral while Manuel, because of his new position, was constantly traveling.

His was not an easy task. He had to form a strong team before he could review accounts. He needed to plan the manner in which they would visit the reluctant and delinquent taxpayers.

The prince of Léon was soon satisfied with the services rendered by the efficient, wide-shouldered organizer who knew how to exact his due without violence.

Madly in love, Arabella kept begging her father to make Manuel ask for her hand, but Manuel made a quick exit each time marriage came up. His heart did not beat for the young girl. She was certainly pretty, with blond hair framing her delicate face; she was very wealthy, learned, loyal. But he didn't love her. When he returned to the cigarral and recounted his adventures to his family he would sometimes make fun of blond Arabella. His brother sometimes laughed, calling him insensitive.

Joseph would grow pensive. Hadn't Lazarus similarly disdained a beautiful, powerful, and smitten condesa?

"Whom will you marry, then, Manuel?"

"The woman I love, even if her wealth is but a fraction of ours. A woman who loves me and whom I love. Isn't that the greatest of all riches?"

"Do you think you'll meet her at court?"

"Maybe. But I doubt it. There are so many rules to follow, such protocol to respect, so many interests at play that there may be no room left for love. Still, I have my whole life ahead of me. Poor Arabella. I do hope she falls in love with someone else!"

Mercedes, who rarely intervened, sighed when she heard talk of reciprocal love. When her two surprised sons turned to her, she smiled and nodded. Joseph grew pensive once more. Manuel so resembled Lazarus.

At times he was tempted to tell him about his past, but he got cold feet at the last moment. Manuel was so young; why confuse him with such a horrific confession? That particular evening, however, his grandson encouraged him to go on. Both men went out in the neighboring countryside, and Joseph revealed part of the truth.

"You know, Manuel, I don't know if I ever told you about him, but I once had a brother..."

"No, you have never..."

"Yes, do you remember that hero who won an important archery tournament at age sixteen? You and Pablo used to love that story."

"Yes, you called him Lazarus. But wasn't that a fairy tale?"

"No, this man did exist and he was my brother. His name was Lazarus."

"Yet you have never—"

"He left a long, long time ago for the Orient. I have not seen him since. I was young then, but never mind the past. Manuel, you bear him an uncanny resemblance. You look so much like him that I have often been about to call you Lazarus."

"Why did he leave?"

"Oh! it's a long story. A long time ago Jews had to convert, and we were among them, as you already know. Lazarus refused and had to flee."

#

Manuel listened to these revelations in silence. A mountain of questions rose inside him about this mysterious uncle. Joseph, perhaps regretting having said too much, avoided the subject. Manuel was left perplexed.

Manuel had many other tasks to attend to, but occasionally he caught himself thinking about his grandfather's revelations. Now he remembered: A moved Joseph sometimes watched him silently. Lazarus, one of his youth's heroes, was his uncle. He looked for the resemblance, imagined a young Jew in a different time, aiming at a target and hitting it dead center. A Jew ... and he looked like him.

When Manuel was offered by the chancellor's office the task of auditing the financial reports of the Jewish community of Castilla, he accepted against his better judgment. Taking care of Jewish neighborhoods was not part of his responsibilities, but he was made to understand that his sacrifice would not go unnoticed by the authorities.

In an austere room a huge table was covered with money-filled bags. The bailiff showed Manuel Jacob Aben Nuñez, rabbi, physician and supreme court justice, in charge of collecting the taxes owed by Jews. Jews were the only ones to own gold, while Christians could only settle their debts by giving to the state part of their harvests or cattle. They were not left with much to live on and thus had to borrow from Jews, whom they made the culprits for their misfortune.

This was a truly formidable Church-imposed perfidy to forbid its followers to loan money with interest or risk excommunication. Only the Jews could indulge in such satanic practices, thereby recuperating through usury the money the rich and the nobles did not dare lay claim to, although, in the end, it found its way back into their coffers via the excise of heavy taxes imposed upon the people of Israel.

Manuel peered at the rabbi, searching for a vague resemblance to his grandfather or himself, but he saw none. How silly all this is, he thought. He took the document prepared by Nuñez detailing where the contributions from each of the Jewish quarters had been consigned.

Synagogues in the see of Burgos   30,800 maravedis
Calahorra   30,100

Palencia	54,500
Osma	19,600
Siguenza	15,500
Synagogues in the see of Segovia	19,750 maravedis
Avila	39,950
Salamanca & Ciudad Rodrigo	12,700
Zamora	9,600
Léon & Astorga	37,100
Toledo	64,300
Plasencia	57,300
Lower Extramadura	59,800

The figures looked rather low to him; wasn't it said that these people owned all the gold in the country? Was this man lying to him?

"Rabbi, you brought the sum of four hundred and fifty one-thousand maravedis as payment of the Jewish tax. Where is the difference?" he said angrily.

"This is the total sum that we owe!"

"These figures look ... ridiculous to me. There must have been an error. For Toledo I see sixty-four thousand, three hundred maravedis. Each family pays forty-five maravedis. Therefore, according to your calculations, there would be no more than one thousand, four hundred and twenty-eight Jewish homes!"

Rabbi Nunez was stupefied. He wondered if the young man was mocking him or if he was trying to swindle him out of more money. "It is true," he answered, "that our numbers were far greater, but ... with all due respect, thousands of our brethren have been massacred by Christians, and to avoid a similar fate, tens and even hundreds of thousands of others had themselves baptized. Without these events we would, as you correctly point out, be far more numerous."

The rabbi had placed himself in a difficult situation; the young Christian would never accept such blunt language. He closed his eyes, ready to endure another humiliation. Manuel was dumbfounded. He should call the guards and teach that man a lesson. He hesitated. Hundreds of thousands! Yes, he had skimmed the Book of Tradition where were recorded the names of two hundred thousand people who had joined the Church in the single year 1411 under the pressure of Vincent Ferrer. The scholar Abraham ben Salomon of Torrutiel had undertaken this colossal compilation to salvage from oblivion hundreds of thousands of his brethren.

"Rabbi," he said after a while, "I am willing to forget your outrageous language this time, but you paint quite a bleak picture of conversion. My grandfather willingly entered into the love of Jesus Christ!"

"I do not believe it."

The rabbi said nothing else. Would his verbal insolence bring him trouble? No. He looked at Manuel with kindness. Manuel stood up, troubled, thanked him, and had the bags removed. He left the palace in a state of confusion. He needed to talk to his grandfather.

He arrived home and entered his grandfather's quarters without announcing himself, just as he used to when he was younger.

"What is it, my child?" asked the old man.

"I am upset, Grandfather, and I would like your opinion."

"I'm listening."

"While collecting the taxes from the Jewish communities of Castilla I had a few words with a rabbi. He said things that were completely unacceptable, as much about our family as about the tactics used by the Church. Instead of meting out the punishment he deserved, I said nothing. I listened, and he made me question what I knew."

"What did he say?"

"He said that most Jews were forced to convert or were massacred. Is it true?"

"It is true that there have been massacres. My God, Manuel, you are calling back painful episodes in my life."

"Were you threatened, too?"

"Manuel, some secrets are so heavy to bear that they are impossible to share with anyone. They haunt one's life until madness sets in. Your questions are bringing that inferno back to life for me. Don't ask me anything else."

"Grandfather, I want the truth."

"The truth will hurt you."

"Never mind. What have you suffered, Grandfather?"

"Nothing, Manuel. Sadly enough, nothing … that's why my sin is so horrendous. My brother Lazarus was just a few months old when his mother, along with a great many Jews, was killed in 1391. Our father remarried. This is how I was born. Later, when it had become more and more dangerous to live as a Jew, Lazarus chose to resist. I chose cowardice. I converted outside of any pressure, unlike many others. More than anything else, however, I reported my brother when he was innocent. I lost his wife and took his money. I betrayed an extraordinary man.

"I did not experience suffering, Manuel. I never saw blood. My parents died of old age, peace be upon their souls. I was never threatened. To punish me, God has burdened me with the weight of eternal remorse. Lazarus did not go to the Orient. He was imprisoned for fifteen years, then was declared dead. But I know he is alive."

"Manuel felt devastated. He kept shaking his head, repeating, "Appalling, appalling."

"Yes, it is appalling; yet it is even more appalling to have told you. You can imagine what my life has been since I have had to carry the burden of that secret. I have no excuse. I have paid by enduring the contempt of the 'true' Christians. I, the intruder, was the rich and powerful interloper. I have seen hatred and jealousy in the eyes of those knights. I understood that we, Marranos, would never be accepted."

"Your grandmother, my wife, married me for my money; my son Joachim, your father, hardly knew who I was. My in-laws kept him away from me. What did they think? That I was going to turn him into a monster? In their eyes, even a converted Jew is a monster, barely human! Yet I have raised you and your brother, and you are well-respected at court. I have never spoken about my old faith. As you see today, it was not necessary."

Manuel had a delayed reaction. "What do you mean?"

"I mean to say there is a Jewish soul within you, and this soul manifested itself this morning during your encounter with the rabbi. The milieu in which you evolve does not let you realize it, yet it is so. Your attitude is so much like your uncle's! Don't ever be ashamed to resemble him. He was as righteous and fair as I was weak and cowardly. Your brother is different, he has other roots. I think that Pablo will never understand these feelings of doubt, those emotions that stirred you this morning. That is why I'm confiding in you, not in him. I must also warn you."

"Why?"

"Because the court, as you well know, doesn't forgive any infractions. If you possess the character I think you have, go along with these people for your own protection. Do not oppose them, but always be wary of them. Because whether you like it or not, you are part of the Jewish people. Your behavior and attitude leave no doubt. Sooner or later you'll be reminded of it. Watch, smile, but act with circumspection. I was responsible for Lazarus's demise. I do hope my error can be of help to you."

"Grandfather ..."

Manuel was too overwhelmed to express what he felt. He ran to his room, closed the shutters and, in the afternoon's warmth, let his mind ramble. His own grandfather was a traitor, and a Jewish spirit inhabited him! No, that couldn't be.

When, like a convalescing person, he resumed his life at court, he looked at everything with new eyes. Arabella Tortosa, that possessive goose, her father, a dangerous and powerful man, some of his friends, whose arrogance was boundless ... this was court! Court with its injustices, court concealing behind a flawless organization a degrading, reeking emptiness. Yes, he was truly different. His grandfather's words came back to him relentlessly: "Watch, smile."

He was forced to act curtly to make señorita Tortosa understand that he had no intention of marrying her. During a reception, tired of young Arabella's tireless babbling, he let out a sigh and left the room. She caught up with him, worried, but her concern only angered him more, and he mercilessly told her off. She reacted quickly and publicly. She threatened Manuel with the loss of his position with her father, the prince of Léon. His response rang loudly in many attentive ears: "I do not care about losing this position!" Told what was going on, the prince came running; he found his daughter crying. She cursed Manuel, and Manuel could not disguise his indifference. He never denied saying what he had said, nor did he try to make amends. Antonio Tortosa was forced to officially let this loyal collaborator go.

Manuel had freed himself recklessly from the milieu that was increasingly stifling him. That evening he went back to the cigarral with a light heart. "Grandfather, I no longer work for the prince of Léon!" he said happily. In response to Joseph's carefully worded questions, he said smilingly, "You were right, I am not like these people. Since our conversation I see things in a clearer light. At first I was not looking to make a scene, but Arabella got my goat. I am free! Oh, Grandfather, I have so much in mind, so many plans. I want to travel the world…"

Chapter 35

Months went by. Manuel devoted all of his time to the vineyard, leaving to Pablo the business of attending the court; Arabella was no longer on his mind; he was in good spirits, relaxed and happy. Pablo told him about young Lopez, their neighbor and a newly made noble, and his attempts to win over the disconsolate young woman. She rejected him as harshly as she herself had been rejected. Pablo also brought back all the talk about Manuel. No one had understood his action, especially the prince of Léon, who, quite perturbed, was still looking to replace him.

"Aren't you interested, Pablo?"

"Maybe!"

Pablo also had a hard time understanding his brother's behavior. He was discovering an uncompromising and private Manuel. Manuel's actions seemed to stem from a source only Manuel could perceive. Pablo, on the other hand, knew he was softer, less demanding. Why, then, not take the position Manuel had vacated at the palace? The brothers talked about it at the dinner table; each gave his blessings, and Pablo was hired without a hitch in spite of his brother's scandalous behavior.

Manuel began to study books on Judaism. From a Christian point of view, this was an archaic, violent and absurd religion. The clergy's arguments were convincing, but what about the massacres, the killings and the forced conversions? Were they the acts of the Jews? Deeds were in direct contradiction to the written texts. In the name of Jesus, who preached love, tolerance and piety, why had blood been shed? Manuel was at a loss. How could the Church evangelize using such tactics? "Love your neighbor as yourself"! How could one extol love for his fellow man and prove himself unworthy of that love?

Joseph tried to recall his past in order to come up with answers for his grandson. He had rejected his first religion in an attempt to assimilate, and he had a difficult time putting his past in perspective. Religion of violence? He was able to attest that the only violence he ever witnessed in his youth was the day Lazarus had defended the Jewish quarter to avoid new murders. Not a single blow had been dealt. Archaic religion? Because it originated in the beginning of time? Because, centuries later, its intent had remained unchanged? If the rush to power, the repeated killings and the reign of gold were signs of the new age, then yes, the Jewish religion was archaic. Absurd religion? It was absurd to suffer, to be humiliated, be it inside a church or a synagogue. For God was the same for all. "I am sorry I converted, Manuel. It is too late for me. I am close to death, and I fear the last judgment because of all the sins I have committed. But I would very much like to die as a Jew, because I was born as one."

Little by little Manuel learned, grasped, understood. He began to look at Jews with kinder eyes. Their prayers seemed earnest. Their faith was valid, and the values they championed were his own. He was close to these people. The blood that flowed in his veins took on importance, and a history as ancient as the world reverberated in it. He was more and more tempted to go back to his roots. Joseph knew that death was near, and his recollections of Judaism rushed forward. As he spoke Manuel changed.

A year passed. People gossiped about him. He thought it might be better to make an appearance at court. Young Lopez had borrowed larger and larger sums of money from Manuel, in order to win bitter Arabella over. Yet he could not succeed; the young woman could not get over the rejection of her love and only entertained thoughts of avenging herself. A scorned woman can become a menacing weapon. Manuel met her face to face; with much tact he obtained her "forgiveness," and they became best friends after.

Joseph took ill at the cigarral. To everyone's surprise. Mercedes kept a close watch over him. Her singing was a godsend to the old man's heart. His heavy eyelids he often lifted to admire her. In her forties, she had become even more beautiful. Having been spared life's hardships, she had withdrawn into a comfortable and worry-free existence following very discreet affairs. Now fulfilled, she blossomed near a son who adored her, watched with proud amazement her other progeny and tended to the old man who had made it all possible. At night Pablo and Manuel took turns at their grandfather's bedside.

The dog days of summer settled over La Mancha. Flushed with fever, Joseph gasped for air on his bed. That particular evening Manuel was holding his hand. When the old man whispered, "Come closer," his voice had turned to a rasp. Choking with emotion, Manuel leaned forward.

"I feel I have but a few precious minutes left. Manuel, you are my salvation. May you live a righteous life, and may you not know evil. I'm dying, and I'm afraid to be punished up in the heavens. Carry out my last wish whenever you can, Manuel: Have the kaddish, the prayer for the dead, said over my grave one day, one night, whenever possible. Manuel, hear Israel, the Lord is our God, the Lord is One. Call the others in now. Go."

Grief-stricken, Manuel shouted, "Mother, Pablo, come quickly!" All three rushed to the dying man's bedside. He made out Mercedes's face. "Oh, how beautiful you are," he said. "Your beauty brightened my life. Pablo, Pablo and Manuel, my pride, my sons, I am dying, but I am thankful to you, too. May your fate bring you fulfillment." He grabbed Manuel's hand and squeezed it hard. Then he fell back on his pillow.

He was buried with the sacraments of the Church. Manuel was the only one to know that his soul had migrated on to his own people. He had promised his grandfather he would find someone to recite the prayer for the dead over his grave. How would he do it? He saddled his horse and, pretending to go to Madrid to see a cooper, disappeared for several days. No one would recognize him away from Toledo. He would be at liberty to associate with Jews and learn that prayer; wouldn't that be the greatest homage to pay his grandfather?

Although traveling alone was dangerous, Manuel needed the solitary adventure to cleanse and discover himself. He felt an infinite emptiness. How could his grandfather keep such a secret for so long? How he must have suffered! Manuel felt forlorn; there was no one to confide in and no one to understand him. He was progressing haphazardly toward the morning sun when he suddenly remembered that Horacio del Pereiro, a well-regarded marquess at court, had often invited him to his Aranjuez residence. Both men had grown fond of each other the first time they met: a high-ranked official who didn't care for courtly life, Horacio was rarely seen at court. Endowed with a cynical brand of humor, he had a particular talent for darting caustic comments; Manuel lent an eager ear whenever he knew Horacio was inspired. Yes, he would go see him after looking for the Jewish quarter of Aranjuez, if there was one.

It was still daylight when he entered the city. Everything was quiet; everyone was going home for dinner. Cooking fragrances wafted from every home. Manuel realized he was hungry, but, taken by the purpose of his quest, he began to observe the passersby. Who was a Jew? This man or that one? How does one ask? Perhaps all he had to do was to find the section of town without a church. There, of course ...

He walked down a street and realized he had made the right choice. A six-point star on a building facade indicated the synagogue. He got off his horse and began to walk. A small square, a fountain surrounded by houses, a garden where an old man carefully tended his plants. Manuel felt safe; it all seemed peaceful. He tethered his horse to a bush and stood watching the old man. The old man looked up. They smiled. Neighbors came by. "Hello, Lazarus," they greeted the old man.

When Manuel, who was fumbling for words, heard that name he felt his chest tighten. That could not be. Yet the old man's features were familiar. He tried to visualize him fifty years younger.

"What are you looking for, young man?"

"Well ... I study religions, and I am looking for someone who can teach me the ka—the prayer for the dead. I can—I have money!" Manuel blushed, embarassed at having uttered the last sentence.

"Money! Do you think prayers are for sale? Do I look so pitiful?"

Manuel stammered, angry to have made up such a lame lie. "That's not what I meant. I didn't mean to offend you. I need that prayer."

"And why does a Christian come to the heart of the Jewish quarter to learn a prayer? Because of your studies? Really?"

Moved by a mad hope, Manuel revealed the real reason. "No, I lied to you. It's for ... my grandfather, who just passed away. I promised him. This was his last wish, may God watch over his soul."

"In that case ... come in. Your request is singular. Explain it to me."

Manuel went in. The old man invited him to sit and began asking questions. Manuel offered no answers; he was staring straight into the old man's face.

"Tell me, you look tired. Are you feeling all right? Are you tired from the heat? Where are you from?"

"Toledo. Is your name Lazarus?"

"That's right. What's your name?"

"My name is Manuel. You're Lazarus?"

"How curious you are. My name won't be familiar to you."

"Lazarus Benavista?" The question had been burning his lips.

Lazarus opened his eyes wide. "Yes. Do you know me?"

"I am your brother Joseph's grandson."

Lazarus was struck motionless. The young man had a smart demeanor. He felt as if he were looking at himself tens of years ago. "Don't tell me that your arrival here was unplanned!"

"Absolutely. That's why I—"

"Joseph is dead? When did he die?"

"A week ago."

"And he wanted the kaddish to be said?"

"Yes, and I didn't know how to go about it. Uncle, he's told me everything; he was so full of remorse that I would do anything for God to forgive him. He made me aware of my roots. I want to learn everything about Judaism. God has put me on your path." Then he addressed the heavens: "You see, Grandfather, your family is made whole again."

Lazarus was moved to tears. What a handsome nephew! After two generations in Christianity the lost sheep was coming back home.

#

Manuel spent two days with his uncle. He met Yasmina and Antonio and their two children, aged twelve and fourteen. He returned to Toledo and under the cover of night went to the cemetery to recite the prayer for the peace of his Jewish grandfather's soul. How good he had felt among his family, near that serene old man. It was as if he had found the spiritual father he had been seeking for so long. He had made public his resolution to rejoin his ancestors' religion. Lazarus had advised him, should he pursue his intent, in spite of all the risks it entailed, never to let a single inhabitant of Toledo in on it. He was welcome in Aranjuez anytime. Lazarus's door, the wide gate to the heart, would always be open for him.

Chapter 36

When Simon reached his thirteenth year, the year of his religious majority, Yasmina, Antonio and Lazarus organized a big celebration. This was to be Eli Zarka's last social event; he died two months later.

Rafael had trained as a rabbi; he officiated for his nephew Simon, and his frail voice delighted those in attendance. Rafael's sermon filled many of young Manuel's gaps.

"My dear Simon, you just celebrated your bar mitzvah, and therefore you are responsible for your own actions before God. For the last five years you were taught our religious laws. Yet you have only learned a minuscule portion of what you will learn throughout your life. You now have duties to carry out, and the first one is to remain faithful to our laws. If our people still exists after enduring centuries of suffering and humiliations, it is because it always respected the Torah, the extraordinary legacy left by our ancestors and which you, in turn, will pass on to your heirs. To keep their faith alive our fathers fought, sacrificed their most prized possessions, even their own lives, at times, while reciting: "Hear Israel, the Lord is our God, the Lord is One."

"We are the Chosen People. Let us not draw pride from that. Instead, let it be our guide to help humanity, as we began three thousand years ago by preaching love for our neighbor at a time when so many cities were ripped apart by the basest of barbarism. Do not forget that you live among goys. You shall be judged according to your actions. Woe unto you if you bring shame to your name, because you will have to account for all your deeds during the Final Judgment.

"Even if you are mocked, don't ever turn your back on your heritage. We admire martyrs and saints who are examples of righteousness and goodness for all mankind. Be proud of the glorious role Moses, Deborah, Maimonides and so many of our people have played in the history of civilization. Our ten commandments and most of our biblical texts were shamelessly and straightforwardly copied by other religions. An infinite number of literary and artistic masterpieces were modeled after our poetry and heroes. You must be thankful to the Lord to have been born and raised in the house of Israel. You must ask him to help you remain faithful to it all your life, full of love, fervor and dignity. Amen."

Lazarus looked tenderly on Yasmina and thought how Yael would have liked to live this moment.

Chapter 37

Simon was twenty-one years old in 1468. He had his grandfather's sturdy frame and had discovered a strong aptitude for medicine. His teachers considered him gifted. He learned very quickly and very well; he would become a great doctor. Myriam had developed into a delicate and gracious young woman, and she was full of admiration for her brother. She would always run to him if she got a scratch or if she had been bitten by an insect; to be taken care of by her brother was a great treat to her. Simon, however, was still very much removed from real knowledge.

He was advised to study under the pious and competent Zenouda of Toledo, but Lazarus voiced his opposition to the idea; in his mind, that city was synonymous with danger. He remembered that a great scholar and an old friend of the Zarkas, the honorable Professor Benzimra, was living in Portugal. He would likely be glad to welcome a young and talented mind. When Myriam got wind of her brother's potential departure she ran to his bedroom in tears. Several years without him; what would happen to her? Couldn't she join him? Why did he insist on becoming a physician anyway? Her bad mood hid a profound sadness, and Simon was deeply moved. He, too, would be at a loss away from his lively, cheerful little sister. But a separation now would only bring them closer later.

He comforted her as best he knew how and she finally accepted his departure. As usual, Yasmina let silence express her feelings; her chest tightened when her son left. Fortunately, Antonio was there; time had not dampened their love. A gentle melancholy wind blew over the small Aranjuez family.

Several weeks went by before they received Simon's first letter.

#

Dear Father, Mother and you, Myriam,

I made it fine to Lisbon. Professor Benzimra welcomed me with much kindness. Portugal is a pleasant country. Jews are free. They can study and work freely. Of course, not everything is perfect; Christians do not care for us any more here than they do in Spain. At least we can live peacefully here.

This worry-free existence allows me to concentrate on my studies. The wind often blows; the wide-open sea prevents the stifling heat from settling. Sometimes I watch the sun disappear on the horizon. Where does it fall? That land on the other side of the world exerts a magical attraction on me. I dream more and more often of having all of you here with me. I miss you all very much. We could be happy in Portugal.

I met a man who has impressed me. He is very well versed in medicine, the sciences and economy. We became friends and his family invites me regularly. He is respected in the community by both noblemen and common men. His name is Abravanel. I told him about you, Grandfather, about your past, your deeds and your ordeals. He is convinced that what happened to you is not accidental but that God chose you to fulfill a mission whose meaning we'll understand later. I have a strong hunch that he is right. Distance allows for some remarkable realizations. I have also become aware that I have wonderful parents and the loveliest sister. Write me soon, I am anxious to hear from you. I miss you all very much, but this is only temporary. Soon we'll be together again. Perhaps I will convince you to come to Portugal! Hugs and kisses.

Your devoted son, grandson and brother, who loves you very much.

Beloved son,

We read your letter with immense joy. I want to convey everyone's affection for you.

We noted with great relief that your stay is taking place under the best of circumstances. Don't forget to thank Professor Benzimra for his hospitality.

We miss you very much. Myriam is adorable and very thoughtful. At nineteen, she's is a much courted young lady. She has the attention of two or three suitors from good families, but she shows not the slightest interest in them. "I have time," she keeps saying. In fact, you're the one she misses and she would never agree to marry without your consent. Your mother is sad sometimes, but Lazarus and I are there to comfort her. I am happy that everything is fine with you. I only have one wish: that in spite of this separation your stay be as beneficial to you as possible.

We thought about joining you in Portugal. Your accounts of it make it an attractive place. Your grandfather, however, refuses to consider such a tremendous change. His old age roots him in the soil of Spain even if it brought him more tears than joy. Nevertheless, he has suggested that we leave him to join you, but your mother and your sister refuse to leave him behind. Thus, we await your return home anxiously.

Business is not good. Nothing is simple and we had to get ourselves organized to avoid losses. Your uncle Fernando, who sends his best, does all he can to keep going at work. Fortunately, he has six sons who can support him, which shows that a united family is the greatest of riches. I am worried because the entire country, not just the Zarka family, is stagnant. Four distant cousins left for Africa a week ago. We are all in good health and that's what really matters.

Write us, your letters brighten our days. Myriam wants me to tell you once more that she misses you very much. Kisses from us all. Till soon, Godwilling.

Your loving family.

#

Simon returned home in 1471. His features had changed, he had become a man. He received a hero's welcome. The entire community squeezed into the Zarkas' residence to congratulate him. Although he had not yet begun to practice his art he was already considered one of the most brilliant medical minds of his generation. He was fluent in many languages, had written a commentary on the immortal works of rabbi Moshe ben Maimon, also known as Maimonides, and had translated from Arabic the five books of the great 10th century scholar, Isaaque.

Among his family, a broad shouldered young man smiled. Manuel, reserved as always, had joined them.

Chapter 38

From the time he succeeded his brother Manuel, Pablo felt fulfilled. Collecting taxes for the kingdom gave him a much-envied respectability and attracted a following at court, although he was indifferent to his success. It made his mother smile: Pablo had only one love, his mother. But would he ever marry? Probably not. Manuel had witnessed the peculiar complicity between his brother and mother grow with each passing day. A gaze, a smile, they harmonized perfectly. Life at the cigarral moved along worry-free. The vineyard had been troublesome in the year 1463 only during a period of drought which produced a small quantity of excellent wine. Both brothers had to take a closer look at their financial situation and were happy to realize that they would hardly feel the pinch of a lower production.

Manuel had resumed appearances at the court. He had learned to smile again since his meeting with his uncle Lazarus. The court no longer revolted him. Luxury, hypocrisy and conventions no longer made his blood boil: why be indignant if the world functioned in this fashion? Because he was aware of its weaknesses and because he had entered a world ruled by simplicity and devotion, he was now able to project the persona the courtiers expected of him. He had learned how to deceive; that was the price he had to pay for his peace of mind. Joseph had been right: where Lazarus, at the same age, would have been excited, Manuel knew how to keep his cool.

There was the other life. The one in Aranjuez, the life devoted to study and reflexion, the life of the heart. The fascination he felt for his Jewishness blossomed unrestrained there. He no longer had to pretend and his second family accepted him as one of theirs. He often stayed two to three days in Aranjuez where he conversed for hours with Lazarus, his spiritual father. Then, fulfilled by the discovery of his roots, he went home able to face his mother's innocent gaze and his brother's disarming insignificance.

One day, Pablo had to choose a trustworthy traveling associate to Sevilla, to visit solicitor don Salva, the ex-tax collector. Manuel's ears pricked when he heard about the trip: don Salva, a wealthy, intelligent man, often came through Toledo and Manuel had met him during one such visit. In spite of their difference in age—a good thirty years,.They had developed a mutual appreciation. What a treat it would be to visit with him and, in the process, discover the much-praised Andalusia. He made his intention clear: "Look no further, Pablo, I am your man."

Don Salva's parents had converted during the events of 1411. Would he find with this man he knew to be sensitive and refined, the same doubts and querries?

His arrival in Sevilla, after a long and tiring trip, left him spellbound. The Guadalquivir river, scrawny yet dogged, flowed slowly. Balconies everywhere were adorned with flowers and the whiteness of the walls exploded under the blue sky. The picture of gentleness and hope, the Virgin Mary and Child could be found at every corner. Away from home, Manuel would smile at them: "I am leaving you, the love that you preached is gone from your followers' hearts. My fathers' religion, which survived the night of the ages, paints nothing on walls, does not seek the spotlight but is deep-rooted; centuries have not been able to falsify it."

What a stunning city this was! Andalusian women had a gleeful sparkle in their eyes, and their supple, gracious mien gave the street a festive air. Here heat was not the enemy; it was an accomplice. Manuel got off his horse to stretch and mingle in the hustle and bustle. Accidentally he bumped into a young woman who turned curt on him. Bemused, he took on the role of an impertinent seducer, but the riled young women shrugged him off proudly before turning on her heels. "Beautiful brunette with skin as fine as a cloud, where are you going? Would the dreams you dream at night figure me in?" He felt like following her, but fatigue and prudence prevented it. He asked for the elder Salva's residence.

Ten minutes later he was receiving a warm welcome from the older man. They had so much to tell each other. Manuel told him how wonder struck he had been by the city. Don Salva agreed, but he warned his guest: "The Andalusian is not easy and can prove to be stubborn and uncivilized. The beauty of Andalusian women is a wonderful trade-off, however!"

At dinner don Salva introduced his wife and his youngest daughter, Linda. Manuel smiled broadly; the maiden looked startled. "You know each other?" asked don Salva.

"I awkwardly bumped into your daughter earlier in Seville, lost as I was in contemplation of her beauties—I mean those of the city!"

"Well, since you've beaten me to it, I have nothing else to say! Only that my daughter is a learned person and that I am very proud of her." Looking at Linda, he added: "Manuel comes from Toledo, where he holds a position at court."

"Where I used to work! I went back to my father's vineyard, and my brother is presently collecting taxes. He is the one who asked me to come here."

The young woman remained reserved, but a slight smile was on her lips. An amused Don Salva observed their amiable verbal contest. The charm of Andalusian women! Manuel was very sensitive to it. Ah, Linda's radiance. Linda. She had been given the name of beauty!

Two days later she consented to show him the white city of Seville. She tried to resist the attraction she was feeling for this man; he enjoyed her charm and yearned to declare his love. How would he go about finding the aloofness Arabella had found irresistible? He would be hard-pressed pretending to be cold! He was able to make her laugh and smile, but that wasn't enough. A discussion on a serious topic?

He heard from Linda's mouth her father's words: "Yes, I know, This is a beautiful city, but Andalusians are bull-headed and intolerant. I do not trust them."

"Why this distrust?"

"In the heart of a city, one social blunder can make you suspect."

"I know that only too well, having taken that risk in Toledo. But what social blunder could you risk making?"

"None!" she stammered. "I have not made any social blunder, no. What are you trying to say by that? What about you? What risk did you take in Toledo?"

"None! I ... no, no risk, I don't see what ... Well..."

Manuel slowed down; an idea had just crossed his mind. He turned to the young woman. "Perhaps we share the same secret!" he said.

That unsettled her. She blushed and shook her head. "I don't understand. Let's go back."

He followed her, joyful. That cautious demeanor was almost a confession. Linda's behavior, bearing and education did not match that of a Christian. "Statues of the Virgin Mary spy on us at each street corner. I have never seen so many churches!" he said feigning surprise.

"One has to be careful in this city! No, I mean ..."

"You mean to say that the Christian spirit is very powerful here! That it is omnipresent, just as in Toledo?"

Linda did not answer.

"In Toledo," Manuel went on, "the love of Christ does exist, but so does a certain level of violence. If, for example, some nonconformists do not follow the precepts of Christianity, they can suffer dire consequences."

"Well, here these nonconformists would keep a low profile, enabling the Church to deny their existence. As long as the populace at large believes ..."

Back home and away from indiscreet ears, Manuel took her hands in his. "I once learned that my ancestors were Jewish. I wanted to know more about them and ended up discovering a religion that has touched me in the depths of my soul. Linda, I know you know what I am saying..."

She lowered her head, but when she looked up at Manuel she was smiling.

They were married a short time later in the church of San Salvador of Seville. A few days afterwards Rabbi Moshe Karrel united them secretly in accordance with Mosaic law. Each had traveled his own path toward the other. In her quest for Judaism Linda had held the same fascination, the same obstinacy as Manuel. By mingling their faiths they made them real.

Manuel was discovering a world where Jews and Marranos, prayed together fearing being found out. He could now understand Linda's apprehension when he had first arrived, for if the city held out its attractions, one could still feel the pent-up violence. If there were to be renewed attacks against the Jews of Spain, they would originate right here. He confided in his beloved spouse: "To feel so much animosity around us is unbearable. In Toledo things are less tense. Close to the capital, at Aranjuez, Lazarus and his family would be delighted to hear about our marriage. Close to them, we'll be able to grow together."

They went to Toledo. The large and beautiful cigarral occupied by the heedless Pablo and his feckless mother would permit them to build a comfortable hideaway. Their first visit was to Lazarus; he was more than eighty years old, with a long white beard and unsteady walk. He blessed them.

Chapter 38

Simon became a physician famous throughout the region. Availing himself the teachings of his mentor Benzimra, he performed miracles—at least, that's what the sick dubbed their healing. His dearest wish, after three years in Portugal, was to remain with his family, especially Myriam, but his success was such that he was called upon throughout the country. Under such conditions, would he be able to find a wife and become a father?

After a year he dedicated himself to the cure of serious illnesses. He would be called on by a messenger; depending on the patient's health, he either started immediately on his way or postponed his visit to the following day. He was present the day Myriam introduced Abraham Sananes to the family. He gave her his assent with a single look and she clapped her hands with joy.

Abraham was twenty-five years old; his deep shyness hid an immense generosity. He had been able to make Myriam laugh while her dear brother was in Portugal. Decent, though a little awkward, he worked hard to be able to provide her with material comfort. He was madly in love with this incredible elf. Myriam had lost none of her youth's liveliness as she grew older.

Simon, Fernando and his wife and their nine children, Luis, who was back from Italy, and Ines, with her husband and daughter as well as Manuel and Linda, attended the wedding. Abraham, overcome with happiness, was beside himself. His little princess was dazzling in her embroidered dress; for as long as one could remember, Aranjuez had not witnessed such a happy celebration. Lazarus thanked God to have lived long enough to have seen that day. Myriam the imp ... her grandmother had been passionate, bold, whole, her mother was gentle and curious about everything, and this third generation carrying the same blood relished life as passionately as the former and as innocently as the latter. Myriam would be happy; God had created her for that purpose.

A short time later Simon met Rachel at the honorable Falco's residence; he was a great friend of Uncle Rafael and a famous medical doctor in Toledo. She had dazzled him not with her keen beauty but through judicious pieces of advice dealing with medicine. She had not been impressed by either of them. Such a strength of character allied to a great intelligence attracted Simon. He often spoke about this woman to his grandfather and parents: "She is so feminine and so strong at the same time. She is ..." Antonio proffered the answer everyone expected: "Marry her! You love her. Marry her!"

Simon settled in Toledo in spite of Lazarus's fears and married the beautiful Rachel with the aquline nose. He found in her a true confidante and an assistant. How right his father had been! The simplest pieces of advice often turned out to be the best ones: "You love her. Marry her."

In the distance, dear little David, the thunder rumbled.
Yet the skies were still blue.
But when the sun went down, the horizon turned red.

Chapter 39

1474. The country was teetering on the brink of collapse. Life was expensive, and the gears of the economy were in total disarray. Because of repeated plundering and confiscations, businesses, controlled for the most part by Hebrews, had become moribund. Industry and commerce tottered, and the authorities no longer controlled anything. Anarchy ruled.

Spain was decadent. She no longer thought about reclaiming territories occupied by the Moors in the small kingdom of Granada. Noblemen were wasting their time warring among themselves instead of uniting to drive the enemy away. King Enrique IV had neither the competence nor the personality of his father Juan II. He was not respected at court, and everyone wished for his death.

On the other hand, his half-sister, the Infanta Isabella, won everyone's heart. Her charisma and piety were such that most of the grandees of Spain had recognized her authority.

One day a group of officers requested an audience with her.

"Princess, the situation is catastrophic. The king no longer rules, and people are ready to revolt. A word from you and we'll place you on the throne."

"I'm thankful for the trust you have placed in me, but it is not yet time for reform. King Enrique IV is of my blood, and it is not for me to judge or blame him, much less overthrow him. Still, I am touched by your proposition and will accept the crown only when God has given it to me."

"If this is your wish, it is also ours. Know, madam, that all the nobles will stand behind you. There is, however, one important topic we would like to discuss and which will help strengthen our loyalty to you."

"I'm listening."

"There are in our country converted Jews who still practice their old religion in secret. We cannot stand idly by while they insult our Church. In 1441 the Pope, in a brief to the Bishop of Osma, ordered the creation of a special court of law to deal with this type of infraction, yet the king has refused to enact this decision."

"I am aware of the problem. Torquemada, my confessor, has told me about it many times. He is ready to sacrifice his life so that justice be served."

"The establishment of the inquisition is a prerequisite for the protection of our creed in Spain. Your agreement with our position is the principal reason for our support."

"Sirs, do know that I share your point of view. Rest assured, in due time I will take the steps necessary to punish such infractions."

Isabella did not have to wait long. On the twelfth of December of the same year, 1474 God called the king to His kingdom. She forced destiny by appropriating the crown of Castilla, which legally was to go to Jeanne la Beltraneja, daughter of her brother Enrique IV and the true heiress to the throne.

Shocked by Isabella's behavior, King Alfonso V of Portugal came to the aid of his young niece Jeanne to restore her rights. He raised an army to bring the usurper down. But he was old, and the flame of his youth was flickering. In spite of valiant efforts, he was unable to thwart Isabella's intentions, and in 1476 she asserted her full authority over Castilla. The queen's appeal was huge. She was very popular and knew how to arouse crowds, be they Jewish or Christian. Her succession to the throne was even celebrated in every synagogue with prayers and festivities.

"Friends and brothers," they began, King Enrique is dead, and we must pray for his soul. But we can only rejoice, because the good doña Isabella is sitting on the throne. An era of peace and prosperity is about to begin in Spain. This righteous and noble woman will restore our dignity. Yet our joy must be tempered, for many converts to Christianity among us are in turmoil. But keep hope alive. Isabella, in all her wisdom, will know how to solve this situation."

Manuel did not share this optimism. The queen's entourage was too fiercely anti-Jewish to accept even a semblance of compromise. Pablo could have told him much more had he still frequented court. Five months earlier, however, he had accepted the post of ambassador to

Florence. Leave! He talked about it to his mother and brother, and to everyone's surprise, Mercedes professed how extremely pleased she would be to accompany her son. Italy, her painters and her dolce vita had always fascinated her. Manuel and Pablo were unaware that the faithful and discreet lover of their mother had just died and that at fifty she was ready to start life all over again. The long sea crossing did not scare her, after an entire life spent quietly in the heart of Spain. The cigarral felt a bit empty to Manuel. Mercedes had never been excessively demonstrative, but her presence was imprinted on all the walls, and her absence became painful. Manuel also missed his brother's gentleness.

Manuel and Linda found themselves freer in their movements. They let go some of the servants, opting instead for a quiet and private home, even if it was huge. They could, at night, in the privacy of their garden, talk about the Isabella Manuel was so afraid of. He believed she would go to any extreme to secure her power, and among the claims, be they from the people or the nobles, the ancestral hatred for the Jews would occupy a privileged place.

Yet since the decrees of 1445 Judaism was recovering slowly from the blows of mass conversions. It took more than fifty years before new generations rejuvenated it. Little by little the converts themselves had begun to return to their old religion. Tensions, however, were now rising.

"I do not trust Isabella," Manuel would repeat. "Too many among her entourage are plotting our destruction, and sooner or later she'll surrender to their influence. They have no conception of the beauty of Judaism, and their fear becomes contempt with some, violence with others. One day Isabella will turn that fear into a powerful weapon to solve her problems. Linda, I am quite concerned."

He shared his feelings with Lazarus, who fully agreed with his assessment. Lazarus tried to alert Yasmina and Antonio, but they could only listen distractedly, isolated as they were by their love for each other. In their world there was no place for Isabella.

Lazarus then turned to his grandchildren. Simon had just become the father of little Judith and looked to the bright future ahead. He then talked to Abraham, who shrugged him off. He was too busy with his family to begin worrying about a hypothetical future. Even Myriam complained there was nothing to justify such pessimism; Lazarus was too old to come to terms with the new Spain.

In fact, Isabella's first years in power seemed to prove Lazarus and Manuel wrong. Inquisition was not on the agenda. In a country on the brink of anarchy, there were many other priorities. Isabella enacted rigorous administrative and financial reforms. She brought back the "Santas Hermandades," those groups dedicated to the preservation of law and order; they reestablished order in an implacable fashion. Thieves, arsonists and murderers who for decades had openly committed the worst of offenses without fearing arrest were now prosecuted to the full extent of the law. Panic set in among robbers; they had to find new outlets. Not even the grandees were spared; scheming and dealing and illegitimate favors came to an abrupt end at court. Nobles were put on notice.

Isabella had a unique goal: the reconquest and unity of the country. Everything functioned better. The nobility acted carefully, roads were safe, peasants harvested unbothered, Jews were no longer worried. This lull reassured Manuel. Simon might be right; Spain was becoming more humane, more tolerant.

Yet he practiced Judaism, and that was still against the law.

> *David, dear little David, you have known that terrible storm. The tempest did not spare you. You are navigating toward a land of hope, Simon is reunited with his family in Heaven, and the history you are reading is going to get bloody once more. After the sword, fire. The Inquisition is going to cast its huge shadow of suffering and death over writhing human beings. The mere mention of the word will evoke fear in mankind for centuries to come.*

Chapter 40

Don Salva died in 1477. His daughter Linda went to Seville with Manuel to pray over his grave. They stayed only a month in Andalusia. Diego de Susan, a rich Marrano neighbor who had befriended Manuel, promised to take care of the house and make sure it would be well maintained. Then the couple returned to Toledo.

That is when, as she was beginning to lose hope, Linda became pregnant. After the first euphoric moments she quickly succumbed to helplessness. That birth would engender quite a few problems: how to raise the child? As a Christian? That would be a betrayal. As a Jew. This would not be possible in Toledo. Go abroad, then? Manuel didn't have the strength anymore.

Five years after she got married Myriam was still without child, and this protracted sterility produced in her a deep sense of loss. When she learned of Linda's pregnancy and the questions the parents were raising she volunteered to raise the baby. Manuel approved of the idea. Linda, whose belly was getting rounder, had some reservations. Her own child! Not to be able to see him every day, not to be able to hold him in her arms with each new day! But she looked at the problem from all angles, and this seemed the best solution. Holding back tears, she agreed, meeting the luminous gaze of Myriam, for whom this baby was a divine gift.

They agreed that Linda was to show herself as little as possible in Toledo. Two months before she was due to deliver she would settle in Aranjuez, where she would give birth and breastfeed the newborn. To answer the unavoidable questions relating to his wife's long absence, Manuel would explain that she was visiting her gravely ill mother-in-law in Italy. Manuel knew that the lie itself was not important so long as it was said convincingly and casually.

Thus, in February, 1478, Linda gave birth to a beautiful boy who was named David …

David, do you remember the broad-shouldered man who used to hold you in his arms when you were just a little boy? Do you remember the lady with the deep voice who showed you so much love every time she would see you?

He was your father; his name was Manuel. She was your mother; her name was Linda. They wanted you to be the proud descendant of their ancestry. Alone aboard your boat, stay strong, resist, and you shall survive, for the Eternal watches over you.

Chapter 41

Isabella had envisioned a powerful and healthy Spain. To realize that ambition she first had to settle a thorny problem: the kingdom of Granada. Enrique IV had been able to live with that shameful blot on the map, but Isabella could no longer endure it. Especially since, some ten years ago, Moulay Aben Hacen had refused to pay his annual levy, which helped maintain the semblance of a peaceful state of affairs both kingdoms enjoyed. Before undertaking a reconquest, which would certainly be difficult, the queen opted to send the pious and valiant knight don Juan de Vera to negotiate with Moulay Aben Hacen. If the latter repaid his debt, an arrangement would be worked out. If he refused, war would be inevitable.

And after war would come victory. But at what price? Protected on the north, east and west by rugged mountains, buffered by the Mediterranean Sea in the south, the kingdom of Granada could resist for a long time. It was true that Muslims had lost their appetite for war and had only rudimentary weapons; unlike Christians, they did not pursue the perfection of weaponry. Fertile plains and two harbors, Malaga and Almeria, opening to Turkey and Africa, made it a rich kingdom. A small, prosperous and tolerant people who enjoyed the pleasures of living— this was a powerful moral weapon that ought not to be taken lightly.

Don Juan de Vera suggested that Manuel accompany him on that journey. Manuel did not mind the company of this exemplary nobleman; his strong sense of duty made him different from the majority of the courtiers. Granada! Manuel welcomed the offer. In the service of the queen he was protecting his own interests. Life in Toledo was becoming unbearable. Linda was due back at the cigarral shortly, but without his son the atmosphere would most likely be morose. Having Myriam raise David could only be a short-term solution. Sooner or later a permanent solution had to be found … going abroad, maybe.

When he arrived in Aranjuez he muted his dark thoughts. His son babbled, surrounded by his mothers: Yasmina, Myriam and Linda, who looked on him with equal affection. He took the little guy from them to kiss, then approached Lazarus, who, as was his habit, was sitting near the window. The old man was staring at the sky.

"Uncle, what are you thinking about?"

"At my age one thinks about what one has done, about those who have departed, about those that are left behind. One prays God to protect them ... yes, one prays to God, that's the only thing we have left. We are too old to work. The only comfort we are able to provide at this point is on the moral plane. This, my son, is what one thinks about when one is eighty-eight years old."

Manuel was moved; he kissed his uncle's hand and told him about his trip to Granada. Many images rushed back to the old man, who, in turn, related his remembrances: little Ruth, Rebecca Cherki, who had helped him so much, the El-Kabachs, who had most likely died long ago, and sheik El-Moktar, who had an heir, perhaps one of Yael's sons. He asked Manuel to inquire about all these people. "What a strange twist of fate," he concluded. "Yael will have had three children, two raised according to Islamic faith and the third one raised as a Jew."

Leaving Lazarus to wax nostalgic and Linda with her baby David, Manuel left, fortified by the mission his great-uncle had entrusted to him. What a strange destiny, that old man had outlived everyone.

Preceded by a small escort, Manuel and don Juan de Vera entered Granada through the renowned gate of Helia. A crowd gathered around them. Valiant knights often arrived in their city in search of glory and fortune, challenging Moor champions to one-on-one tournaments. Were these two of that mien? Manuel read curiosity and arrogance in the eyes of the Arabs.

"I bring a message from Queen Isabella of Castilla to Prince Moulay Aben Hacen," said Juan de Vera to the guards coming toward him.

Seated under a magnificent canopy and surrounded by notables from the kingdom of Granada, the prince welcomed them in the Alhambra's Hall of the Ambassadors. Manuel had heard about this paradisical palace but gasped in awe at the splendid rooms and gardens they went through. Could such beauty be earthly? As for Juan de Vera, nothing could distract him from his mission.

"I come in the name of our beloved queen to claim the two thousand gold pistoles that make up the sum of the annual tax paid by the kings of Granada to the kings of Leon and Castilla. Until 1465 this arrangement was honored. At that time you succeeded your ancestors and have since refused to pay your debt. The king and queen won't allow this situation to go on any longer."

The prince smiled, glanced at his advisors as if to share the humor of that speech, and in a slow voice said, "Go and tell your queen that the kings of Granada who paid their debt to Christians died long ago. Tell her that in Granada only scimitars and lancespears are being forged against our enemies."

These were the words that were going to launch the ultimate phase of the Reconquista.

Juan de Vera wanted to return to Toledo at once, but Manuel had another mission to carry out. The two friends took leave of each other. Juan retained the escort; Manuel would travel on his own. Striding up and down the streets of the city where Lazarus had grown older brought about mixed emotions. Where would he ask about the El-Kabachs, the Medinas, and Yael's two sons? He found the Jewish quarter with great difficulty; in Spain everything was well marked. No Jew could have lived among Christians. Here the separation was not so obvious. "Around there," he was told, "most of the merchants are Jewish." See if you can get your information." He sensed no mistrust when he asked questions along the way. Finally he was shown, on the western edge of town, the large earthernware factory managed by a certain Ephraim Medina.

A stout man in his fifties welcomed him. "Lazarus Benavista! Oh, my God, he's still alive? He was like a second father to me; they still talk about him in the Alhambra neighborhood where he once lived. Arabs and Jews, everyone loved him. What has become of him? You're his nephew? I am so glad to meet you! Ruth is going to be so surprised! We talk about him often. I'm going to let her know!"

Overwhelmed by such warmth, Manuel relaxed. A thought passed through his mind. Why not settle in Granada? "No, impossible," he thought. Suddenly he remembered the main purpose of his visit: the failed negotiations with the prince. Soon this part of the country would be bloodied and burning. As it was, he had to warn these lovely people who were so intent on celebrating his visit.

That evening he saw little Ruth, who wasn't five anymore. Brother and sister talked about Lazarus with much emotion. When he had suddenly vanished from Granada no one had understood. Later a friend of their grandparents, Rebecca Cherki, had told them that he had found his wife and daughter and had left with them. Before she died old Rebecca recounted the true story of Yael, who was buried one night in a pauper's grave as punishment for her treason and how some mysterious arms had placed her body in a grave on the outskirts of the city. For the Jewish community this took on the proportions of a myth; the story was recounted as a tale linking two pure souls, and one could often see a small bouquet of flowers on the grass-covered grave. Moved, Manuel asked to be taken to the cemetery to pray.

Then he asked about Yasmira's brothers, Anouar and Mourad. One had died in a riding accident. The younger Mourad, had broken with his father and married a young woman who lived near Malaga. Sheik El-Moktar lived many more years. He was described as a melancholy man. Some eight years ago he had died.

"This Mourad and myself had a common parent. Isn't that a strange fate?" Manuel confessed to his anonymous interlocutor.

"You can meet him if you wish."

Manuel accepted the offer. The two men met the following day. They were so moved that they spent a long time looking at each other silently.

Manuel was first to break the silence: "We have, I believe, the same great-grandfather, Isaac Monsenego."

"Not exactly," Mourad answered. "Isaac was my great-grandfather, and he must have been your great-great-grandfaher. You see, I am very familiar with our family tree."

The men got along famously; they shared the same generous spirit and had the same sense of values, even though they had been brought up in different religions. They talked for a long time, delighted to compare their life experiences.

"I am very touched by your words, yet they make me uneasy, knowing that our peoples are going to wage a war that will take us to the brink of perdition. Adieu, cousin, and may God bless you."

"Insh'Allah, may it be God's will," the sheik answered. Thus they took leave of each other.

#

A few days later Manuel was back in Toledo. In briefing Juan de Vera he learned of Isabella's latest decision to get ready and wait for the opportune time to attack. Manuel was pleased that he had warned the people back in Granada. Then, he went to Aranjuez to tell Lazarus and Yasmina the results of his inquiry.

When he recounted the story of Yael's grave Yasmina collapsed tearfully. Lazarus took her in his arms as he used to. God! How he longed to join Yael; he had lived a long time. What else did the Eternal expect from him to grant him such a long life?

> *The state was getting ready to go to war. In the meantime, the rumor was spreading; too many new Christians were again observing their old Jewish rites impunity. The most disturbing rumbles being heard now:*
>
> *Inquisition,*
>
> *INQUISITION,*
>
> *INQUISITION…*

Chapter 42

SEVILLE 1480

It was an evening of festivities. Jews were celebrating Passover while soldiers patrolled the outskirts of the Jewish quarter. Everything was calm; Christian Seville would celebrate Christ's resurrection the following week. That evening two guards, sniffing an odor of smoke, went up the small Isaac-Shaprut street and came upon an eerily quiet disturbance: a good ten men were busy extinguishing a fire and glancing in panic at the entrance gate to the Jewish quarter. When they saw the newcomers their behavior turned strange.

"What's going on here?" asked one of the guards.

"We were celebrating Passover. One of the candelabras toppled to the ground. Fire spread quickly, but we have it under control now. There is no danger anymore."

"Are you sure? We'll check."

"No, no, everything's fine, there is no danger, really!"

The man looked scared; his companions were staring at the ground. Their unusual behavior aroused the guards' suspicion. They moved toward the group of men, staring them in the face one by one. One of them tried to step back and disappear into the street, but a guard caught up with him and recognized him. "You're Simon de Rosas, aren't you? What are you doing among these Jews?"

"He's a convert, he was celebrating with them! He follows the Jewish rites! Go get help!" said the other guard.

The authorities were quickly informed. They sent search teams throughout the entire Jewish quarter and soon flushed out many converts, who were caught praying alongside their old correligionists. It turned into a general outcry in all of Spain, and this seemingly minor incident would serve as a spark.

The king and queen drafted an official request to Pope Sixtus IV to resume the Inquisition in Spain in order to fight the perverse behavior of the heretics. A papal bull brought them the satisfaction they had sought, and in Seville Miguel de Morillo and Juan de Martín were chosen as the first inquisitors of the Iberian peninsula.

Horror and dismay fell upon the Marranos. In less than a month's time the movement swelled considerably. Danger lurked at every street corner. The number of converts who had returned to Judaism was enormous, and only a handful of them remained secretive. They ran the risk of being turned in at any time.

Diego de Susan, the Salvas' neighbor in Seville, sat on the city council. He volunteered to meet with Torquemada to nullify the enactment of the court of shame and instead solve this problem without bloodshed. Torquemada refused. He made a similar plea to the queen; she, too, refused. There was no room for heretics in the powerful and pure Spain she was building; a baptized Christian who repudiated the word of Christ was a danger to the faith. Thus, for the country and to boot the Moors out of Granada, the kingdom had to be cleansed of all its destabilizing elements first. Miguel de Morillo and Juan de Martín were about to move to Seville. The results would be a telltale sign.

The "affair of the Jewish Passover" had aroused the people. This time they were not going after the Jews, but that was immaterial. There was an ongoing investigation, betrayal was in the air, people spread rumors, minds awakened before the task of helping the purification effort of the Inquisition… Thus, for a few observers, Diego de Susan's insistence seemed suspicious. At the city council he did not tarry, speaking against the abominable tribunal of the Inquisition. They began to keep tabs on him.

He called on several friends who practiced Judaism to attempt to find a solution. A pious few recounted how careful new "Christians" had to be to get together. For what purpose? The indiscreet ear of a pious Christian knight, who happened to be very much in love with Diego's daughter, picked up fragments of their conversation: "two emissaries," "prevent this tribunal to function," "use of violence." He related his fears to the public authorities. The heretic Diego de Susan, along with a few accomplices, planned to kill Miguel de Morillo and Juan de Martin. Diego and his fellow plotters were quickly apprehended.

#

Locked up inside a damp and pitch-dark grotto, Diego had lost all notion of time when one morning he was led to a large room lit by huge torches. His accusers were seated behind a long table.

"Diego de Susan, you are accused of having plotted against the regime by planning to assassinate Miguel de Morillo and Juan de Martín, two representatives of the Holy See in Seville. You are present here to confess your crimes and to atone."

He attempted to justify his behavior but was interrupted; he was to answer the charges only. Before this tribunal he was no longer a human being. He was like a trapped mouse about to be cut up because they wanted to pry a confession out of him. A person who had been apprehended did not stand a chance of a fair trial or a gentle, quick death. Hell would descend to earth. Diego was about to learn it.

First he endured the poulie torture. He was hung from the ceiling by a rope, to come crashing down; the rope, however, kept him suspended a few inches from the ground. With each fall, he ran the risk of dismemberment in an unbelievably violent crash. Diego was hardly aware of the screams he let out. They kept this up until he succumbed to answering every one of their questions.

"José del Castillo, Eduardo Uva, Pedro Sunis are therefore guilty. You must provide us with the names of your other accomplices."

Diego could only feel pain and could not think of any names. They repeated the question. They forced him to gulp gallons and gallons of water. He was gasping for air. Then his torturers lay him down on a hollow bench topped with a heavy slab; it was not uncommon for bodies to burst under such pressure. A strange inertia invaded him intermittently, robbing him of the inquisitor's questions. Exhausted, he lost consciousness. He was led back to his cell. He had been condemned to burn at the stake.

On January 6, 1481, Diego and the richest Marranos of Seville were the first to feed the spectacle of fire. They burned on the public square in front of a crowd of more than fifty thousand. Torture, however, had already broken them. They had become nothing more than ghostly shadows letting out last cries before flames devoured them.

#

The Inquisition organized itself swiftly by setting strict rules for seizure and arrest. Informing was a right, a duty. Anyone wearing his best clothes who did not profit from making fire on a Saturday, or who refrained from eating pork, was suspect.

Children were encouraged to turn in their parents, with the guarantee that the informer would remain nameless.

A mere altercation could take on enormous proportions. Life was becoming impossible in Andalusia. Because of jealousy or a debt men were denounced to executioners, sometimes by their very enemies. In Seville the number of convicts grew to such proportions that the Holy See moved from the San Pablo Convent to the Triana Castle. Hugely successful, the Inquisition spread to most of the important Castilian cities under Torquemada's direction.

Rabbis were required to denounce those who still followed the Mosaic law. In exchange for relative security in their Jewish quarters they had to become a part of the cleansing effort. At risk for losing their lives, and in spite fo the pressure put on them, not one complied with this evil command.

The Inquisition cast her gigantic shadow over all of Spain. For the first time in decades Jews did not have to live in fear. By an ironic twist of fate, those who had held on to their ancient religion were almost rewarded for their conviction; it was the others, the Marranos, the authorities were after.

Manuel cursed the destiny that put him in an important position in Toledan society. Had he been born poor, he could have vanished in Aranjuez and disappeared amid the small Jewish population. Life was about to become unbearable. They had to leave. They had to go far away, perhaps to Italy, to Florence, where many Marranos had already found refuge. Linda, whose features were marked by worry, readily agreed. No need to sell anything; they only had to gather enough money for the journey and to begin a new life. Most importantly, they should proceed cautiously and act discreetly, since no one suspected anything thus far.

They took the utmost care planning their trip to Aranjuez. David wasn't at all certain who his mother was anymore. Mama Myriam cared for him every day, while Mama Linda showed up for short visits only, and the old man, Lazarus, would tell him stories in his broken voice. The child felt a bit lost being passed from arms to arms. Myriam agreed stoically to give him up. She had not lost the hope that she would become a mother one day, but the pressure was such that she took ill. As she needed to recover, it was decided that David would spend a few weeks with Simon and Rachel in Toledo. His small cousin Judith would be his companion.

Linda and Manuel were losing heart. It would be even more difficult for them to see their son. They agreed that Simon should bring him to them. Because he was a physician, it would be perfectly plausible that Linda required his services and even more so that he be accompanied by his daughter or nephew to enjoy the delightful gardens of her home.

Rachel was the first one to guess that Myriam was not sick but pregnant. Simon confirmed her diagnosis; it wasn't unusual for a menstruating woman to dismiss the possiblity of a pregnancy. Aranjuez celebrated; ten years after their wedding God had finally heard the couple's prayers. Abraham fell to his knees when he heard the news. Manuel realized that it would now be easier to take David back; Myriam, sweet Myriam, would have been brokenhearted had she remained childless. There was still hope.

#

In Granada, following the official visit of the knight don Juan de Vera, the sheik had decided to teach a lesson to the arrogant queen, that woman who reigned over a kingdom as garish as it was vacuous. Spaniards had forgotten how to fight, and a small army would drive that point home. In December, 1481, the Moors encountered little resistance as they took the fortress of Zahalca by surprise. This act of war fanned the flames.

Spanish princes set their differences aside. A large show of force was organized; nobleman or peasant, everyone rallied under the royal banner to liberate the country. In 1482 Ponce de Leon, prince of Cadiz, captured Alhambra. Then important strategic cities like Coil, Cortona, Ronda, Cambil, Alhabar and Valea also fell. Manuel was in no position to refuse to participate in the war effort; everyone was aware of his most Christian righteousness and complete devotion to the crown. He fought alongside those whose fanaticism had murdered his friend Diego.

Anyone could have vouched for his courage. In the midst of battle, in the gallop of horses going at full stride and in the cries of the knights he found a level of energy that soothed his anxiety. When fear had to be repressed the best remedy was to let himself succumb to noise and fury. Devotion! It was also a moral guarantee to deflect the suspicion of heresy while the Inquisition wracked havoc. With sadness he thought about his friend Mourad, who was risking his life in the opposite camp. At least he was defending a cause he could agree with. Torn between faith and military duties, Manuel was not as fortunate.

Chapter 43

In Toledo Simon picked up as much information about Italy as he could to share with Manuel. Life was good for Jews there. Travelers and exiles were always welcomed warmly and taken in for as long as needed, to rest up or adapt to a new society, if that was what they came to seek. Manuel realized he could settle there and began to plan accordingly. Quietly, via an Italian-Jewish banker in whom he confided. His intentions, he had a bill of exchange drafted in his name.

Linda put her father's property in Seville on the market, although in these troubled times few people could afford such sumptuous residences; the state automatically commandeered heretics' homes without compensation and would often give them to those who helped the Inquisitors. It took Linda close to a year to find a buyer. The buyer got for it a song. Manuel reviewed their finances; there was not have enough to begin a new life. But time was running out; he had to act. There was a solution: Lopez, his neighbor, owed him an important sum of money. Before claiming his debt Manuel proceeded to the second phase of his plan. Forging his brother's handwriting, he sent himself a letter from Italy in which Pablo invited him and his spouse to Florence to visit and care for their ailing mother. No one would have suspected Manuel of wanting to leave the country; however, the letter gave him the confidence he might need to lie and deceive. There wouldn't be a problem for David, because Simon would entrust the child to him just before the boat set sail. Manuel went to see Lopez.

Lopez! His grandfather had been one of Santa María's henchmen and had been involved in the arrest of Lazarus. To thank him, Joseph, whose grand gesture had been dictated from above, had rented Avi Monsenego's cigarral to him for a symbolic sum after Avi moved to the Jewish quarter. His son, Juan Lopez, had moved into the house after declaring that this home was not worthy of him. Joseph had said nothing, ashamed as he was to have accommodated these devious people so close to his own home, like an eternal reminder of his guilt. Juan's son

Alberto, who was as little liked as his father, had drawn attention to himself because of his assiduous courtship of Arabella, but she humiliated him by marrying the prince of Salamanca. Lopez stayed a bachelor; no noblewoman wanted him, and his own pride made him despise the town's bourgeoises. He had borrowed a considerable sum of money from Manuel while courting Arabella. Alberto had relations with loose women whom he introduced to rich roués. This activity provided him with enough to get drunk in the company of like-minded rascals and afforded him a comfortable life-style in the cigarral his father had stolen. That man whom Manuel had never liked and feared like cholera was the one he was paying a visit to on a beautiful morning.

Lopez was still asleep in his city clothes. He was awakened and grunted, but upon learning the identity of his visitor he got up quickly. Manuel almost took fright when he saw his disheveled and wine-stinking neighbor come toward him with the usual sly smile on his face.

"I came," Manuel explained, "to talk to you about the money you owe me. Let me say, first of all, that I did not keep an accurate record."

"Well... neither did I."

"I think we should be able to agree on a figure. For the past fifteen years I have loaned you large sums of money. Moreover, this house still belongs to my family, even if both our fathers have forgotten it. Let's keep on forgetting it. But I would like to be reimbursed the money. I know you can pay me back."

"Well ... why the sudden rush? They say that you've sold your wife's property, so why this urgent need for money?"

Manuel saw red. He had to justify his actions! He lost his cool. "You owe me a fortune, and I am here to come to an amicable solution. You dare take this tone? Don't you think you ought to be more civil?"

Lopez blushed. "I was only inquiring about you! I do hope that you are not in trouble, that's why I was asking those questions!"

"You are too kind. No, I am not in trouble; however, I need to go to Florence to see Pablo and my mother, who is dying."

"Oh! Then why aren't they coming?"

Manuel tightened his fists and screamed, "Because she's very ill, I told you! Listen, Lopez, you have four weeks to pay me back the money

I've lent you. All of it. According to my calculations, it comes to about fifteen thousand maravedis. Out of friendship I ask nothing for this house, which is family property. You can go back to sleep. A word to the wise should suffice!"

On his way back home Manuel wondered if he hadn't gone too far. That man was dishonest; wouldn't he look to start trouble? But he reassured himself; nothing bad could happen to him. He was, after all, well considered at court following the Andalusian expedition. He benefited from the Grandees' friendship. It would come down to his word against that of a ruffian!

Lopez was distraught. Manuel had been so curt with him, and he asked for the impossible: fifteen thousand maradevis within the next four weeks! He might as well have been asked to grow oranges on a bed of stones! What arrogance! This offspring of Jews thought himself the equal of a prince and had even dared accuse him of having stolen the house his grandfather had obtained by the sweat of his brow; what impudence! What vanity! Lopez kept replaying the scene in his mind. Manuel was powerful and respected and could easily have him evicted; Lopez would never be able to produce the property deed.

Was he about to lose everything? Without this residence he would not be able to continue his corrupt dealings; this was where he invited a few rich bachelors or some neglected husbands for wine and music before offering them young and beautiful and illiterate but dedicated peasant maidens. Everything was working out so well and so discreetly. To be chased from the cigarral would be to lose the "business." He had to act quickly.

The next day at the Alcazar he ran into the knight don Perez of Avila, who had entree with the Inquisition. Ah! if only he had the same contacts, he would be ready to sell a few souls to bask a moment in glory! His face suddenly lit up. He only had to accuse Manuel of observing Jewish rituals to be freed of his debt. Why not plant a compromising object on Manuel's property?

The next day, before leaving to meet the royal armies in the south of the country, Manuel warned Linda and Simon: "Lopez is a dangerous man. We have to remain cautious. I will be back in about a month, at which time, God willing, we shall sail for Italy."

Lopez soon devised a perfect plan. With a few accomplices he went to loot the house of heretics who had just been arrested. He made off with whatever the guards had not carted off. He stole a seven-branch candelabrum, some small oil lamps used for Sabbath, and a few other objects whose use he was unfamiliar with, and slipped all these objects into a large canvas bag. When night came he sneaked into Manuel's garden and buried the candelabrum and the oil lamps in full moonlight. "Tomorrow I shall denounce this son of Jews," he said to himself. "The cigarral is mine. Debts be gone!"

He went to the Alcazar early the following morning. Crossing paths with the knight Perez of Avila, he said unhappily, "My dear friend Manuel, whom I thought to be so noble, has told me some unbelievable things; I am dumbfounded."

"Manuel? He's such a brave man. He has fought valiantly for his country!"

"That's what I thought, but after a few drinks he kept saying that he went to war in the service of the assassins who killed his Marrano friends in Seville."

"What? Those heretics that God has forsaken?"

"Yes. He is said to be hiding religious objects in his garden, because he secretly follows the Jewish rites. I can't believe it. Yet he suddenly looked so demented!"

Although unbelieving, the knight was shocked by the accusation. He rode with four royal guards to Manuel's house. Lopez went to a tavern, shaking with apprehension. He was about to spend the longest day of his life.

Linda stood frozen when she saw the guards. She was supposed to be ill to explain Simon's presence; she had no trouble convincing them. By the greatest coincidence, Simon was not accompanied by David. The two of them felt the pangs of anguish. Avila entered the room. He had the house searched and, looking at Linda, said: "You are accused of practicing the Jewish religion. Who is this man?"

"My name is Simon Zarka; I am a physician."

"Simon Zarka! Your name is well known beyond Castilla! What are you doing in this house?"

"I am attending this lady, who suffers from a blood deficiency."

"Are you also attending to her heretical practices?"

"No, my lord. We, the Jews, have been instructed to denounce Christians who practice Judaism. If this were the case, be assured that I would have done so right away. This lady, however, is gravely ill, in a very Christian way. As for her husband, who as we speak happens to be fighting in the queen's service, I don't believe that anyone would suspect him of such ignominious acts!"

Simon's aplomb and reputation impressed don Perez of Avila. Linda was too frightened to talk; she was ashen. Don Perez hesitated before asking Linda to recite the Pater Noster. She obliged him in a low and broken voice, dredging from her memory the words from childhood. Guards burst in in the middle of her prayer. They were brandishing the candelabrum and the oil lamps they had dug up in the garden at the spot indicated by Lopez. Don Avila frowned and had Linda arrested in spite of her screams. Simon was shaking his head and kept repeating, "I don't understand."

On the contrary, he understood very well. Lopez was probably responsible for this frame-up. Manuel had talked about him ominously. He called don Perez back to tell him, semi-confidently: "There is, on the other hand, a man who I was told spends a lot of time with his fellow worshipers. He lives not far from here. His name is Alberto Lopez. Question him. He'll be able to tell you a lot more about his accomplices!"

Simon was hoping that by accusing him Lopez he would succeed in getting the latter to recant and confess his lie. If the tribunals of the Inquisition ever rendered true justice, then Linda and Manuel might be spared. Alas! He hadn't yet realized how mercilessly the nightmare crushed everyone who had to face Christian justice, even those of Lopez's ilk. As he watched Linda being led away a small hope remained alive in his devastated heart. He galloped to Aranjuez, where he related the events that had just taken place. Everyone was dismayed. David was asleep. He was only five.

Manuel was apprehended. What he had feared most since Isabella ascended the throne had happened; the world was crumbling. He was kept in solitary confinement and wasn't told anything, although he didn't doubt that Lopez had been swift to devise a counterplan. What had happened to Linda, Simon and David? Had they escaped? Who could tell him? He would die without ever knowing his wife's and son's fate. He begged don Perez of Avila to tell him; this man who had respected him until now could fulfill his ultimate request. Avila looked ill at ease; he answered curtly, violating the rules of the Inquisition, which demanded complete noncommunication from judges. "Your wife and your accomplice have been detained. Don't ask any more questions."

Manuel almost lost consciousness. Linda … and who could this accomplice be? Simon? David, he knew, was safe. But Linda, lively and loving Linda, had been ensnared in the Christians' cruel trap, too? He would have liked to be struck by lightning.

For her he braved torture. In spite of torture he refused to perjure himself; he wasn't guilty, he wanted to be part of a religion which fascinated him and appeared more wholesome to him. He was born a Christian; he would die a Jew. That very first prayer he had learned for his grandfather he was now humming to himself; he wasn't dead yet, but life was growing distant. "Linda, would a single glance reveal all of my love for you, how my passion never weakened in the midst of the storm?"

He was shocked back into reality by an unexpected question: "Do you admit that a certain Alberto Lopez, who denies all charges against him, was your accomplice?" So Lopez had been arrested; he was the accomplice don Perez had mentioned. This time, Manuel said, "Yes, yes, Lopez works against faith." At least the executioners had gotten that confession out of him. Manuel was condenmed to die at the stake. He never knew how the sentence was reached.

Linda died the same way. As for Lopez, he brought about his own perdition, because a search turned up the unfamiliar ritual objects he had not buried in Manuel's garden. He, too, was condemned to die at the stake.

Chapter 44

A FEW MONTHS LATER

An imposing amphitheater had been erected on the Zocodover square of Toledo for the sovereigns to preside over. To the right were the most important guests, the different councils of Spain and the inquisitors, led by Torquemada. To the left were narrow, sturdy cages to hold heretics. It had been an eventful night. Many peasants and villagers had slept in the open in order to secure the best viewing spots.

The grandstand filled up quickly, and at exactly eight o'clock the king and queen appeared on the balcony and were cheered by the crowd.

At the same time the procession left the church. Coal-heavers armed with pikes, praying Dominican monks, high dignitaries of the Inquisition, wearing coats decked with white and black crosses, and halberdiers dressed in black and white proceeded feverishly. It did not take them long to reach Zocodover square. There the mob shuffled impatiently as they awaited the arrival of the heretics.

The night before, prison guards had gathered all the heretics in the jail's main hall. They were kept standing up all through the night while Dominican priests exhorted them to repent.

A terror-stricken Manuel caught sight of his wife. He could neither come closer nor speak to her, but he managed a weak smile that seemed to say "I am with you, you know." He was stunned to see his brother among the prisoners. He looked at him with sadness and wondered how he could have been apprehended in Italy. Had the lie he made up about his mother's health backfired at Pablo?

The priests had been relentless and prodded them until the early morning hours. They were forced to slip on the san-benito, a narrow, yellow wool scapular embroidered with a red cross reaching the knees. Manuel understood the significance of this symbol: They would die at the stake. He felt weak for a few seconds but quickly regained his composure. He was determined not to let his executioners see his fright. With a look at Linda he let her know that they'd be reunited in heaven.

They each received a paper miter on their head and a woodwaxen wreath around the neck. A green wax torch was placed in each one's hand, and they were marched out of the jail. The show was finally underway.

At the head of the procession were the paper effigies of those who had died in their cells or had fled Spain. One could recognize Pablo's face in one of the figurines; in fact, it was meant to be Joseph Benavista's, but his grandson's facial features were used to represent him. His remains had been unearthed and placed in an urn to be thrown into the fire. Then came those who had been convicted of minor heresy; they would be flogged on the main square and would spend the remainder of their lives in distress. There were around thirty of them.

The "obdurate" ones came last, surrounded by a flock of priests. One of them managed to lower his gag and yell, "Shame on you, Isabella, woe to you, people of Spain! God will never forgive your crimes against the Jewish people." He was not able to go on; the prison guards were mercilessly lashing him with their whips.

The condemned arrived on Zocodover square. They were placed between dignitaries of the Inquisition and religious people praying fervently. Torquemada, wearing a miter, walked toward the king, followed by officers of the Inquisition. He was brandishing a cross and a book of the Gospels. Raising his royal sword to the sky, the king stood up and swore on the official book of oaths, engraved with gold letters, to defend the Catholic faith no matter what. Mass began.

Heralds read the sentences. When his name was called out Manuel was dragged to one of the cages set on the amphitheater. He felt neither shame nor remorse but regretted only one thing: not to have seen his son one last time.

The ceremony lasted a few hours, and Torquemada gave absolution to those few who agreed to repent. Then the king left and the condemned were led out of town, into the vast prairie where stakes had been set up. The crowd followed, except for a few sensitive villagers who went back home.

First the effigies of those absent were thrown to the flames, then the remains of heretics who died in jail or those dead for a long time, such as Joseph and Joachim. Next the executioners turned their attention to the living. To shorten their suffering, they strangled two men and three women who had repented at the very last moment. They tied the incorruptible ones to pillories.

After he had confessed his crimes and given names Pablo, in a surge of pride, recanted. He who had been weak and fickle had transformed into the equal of the most courageous in a few weeks' time. He accepted his Calvary as Jesus had accepted his. He climbed the stake with peace of mind, surrounded by three Dominicans who had understood nothing and who kept hoping for a last-minute confession.

Manuel, tied to the next pillory, was able to speak with him briefly. "This is it, brother," he said. "Now is the moment of truth, but one has to continue believing, because contrary to what our executioners are telling us, we shall soon be reunited near the Almighty. As it is written in the Old as well as the New Testament: 'Thou shalt not kill, and thou shalt respect thy neighbor.' Today's Church, however, seems to have forgotten it. If you really feel Christian, there is nothing to fear, since the kingom of the heavens will be yours. As for me, I rejoined Judaism and found peace. I do not consider myself a heretic because there is only one God for all. May He bless you and may He let us meet in a better world."

The spectacle of death began with Pablo. He vainly attempted to undo his ties, screaming with pain under the gaze of an angry and jeering mob, but he quickly quieted. The coal-heavers were loath to use green wood because when it burned it produced a thick smoke that caused too quick a death by suffocation. But that particular day there had been so many condemned that the fires had to be stoked with freshly chopped wood. In some ways, Linda got lucky; she suffocated almost instantly and died even before flames reached her, to the crowd's great disappointment.

Manuel would have liked to comfort her, but she was too far away and had already left the world. The heat became unbearable, he began to suffer cruelly, but he wanted to remain dignified, show that he knew how to die. He tightened all the muscles in his body, and with a superhuman effort, recited the prayer for the dead in Hebrew. Then he addressed the crowd. "May God forgive you," he said, then his body slackened. He had joined his ancestors in eternity.

#

In less than ten years 114,000 people were condemned to the stake or to prison. Isabella and Ferdinand wanted a united, powerful and sound Spain, Spain born of fire and blood, where suspicion, fear and denunciation were daily staples, where stakes cut their gruesome shadows. A Spain united, powerful and sound.

Chapter 45

Aranjuez was struck with consternation; everyone was dismayed. Lazarus caught himself sobbing. "Why this hatred, why this curse? Has Manuel ever done any harm in his life? Oh, God, he had come back to you!" he kept repeating

Myriam had a difficult pregnancy. She would not be able to take care of David anymore. They lived in a world filled with anxiety and cruelty; bearing an innocent child became a very serious responsibility. Simon had a hard time remaining focused; he had nightmares every night. Being powerless at helping loved ones is the worst curse, he thought. He prayed all day long that Heaven would welcome Manuel and Linda after the earthly horror they had just endured.

He began to doubt, wondering why the Almighty let humble and innocent people suffer, why He allowed men to act like beasts. A bizarre whim of a vengeful destiny had touched Joseph's family through three generations. Lazarus had forgiven, but the malediction had spread to David, David the orphan, the new blood on whom all the hopes of a renewed alliance with the Eternal rested.

"This child is mine," Simon told his grandfather, "I will reveal everything to him when he becomes an adult."

Simon was not allowed to muse long. He needed to resume his activities so as not to arouse suspicion. Myriam's health worried him. Would she carry her pregnancy to term? A frightful heat crept between the sheets, relentlessly reminding the living of the martyrdom suffered by those who died at the stakes.

Lazarus required close supervision; his advanced age made him vulnerable He had become sullen. Only Antonio and Yasmina stayed united, almost oblivious to the drama that had played out. Simon divided his time between Toledo and Aranjuez; he cared for the powerful and the common people while the Inquisition raged on.

Jews, testimony to human error, that useless and deicidal brood, proved the existence of evil. They had killed Christ, and for that they would be cursed and forever exiled.

In 1487 they were five years away from the final solution.

Chapter 46

The war against the Saracens was intensifying. Peasants turned warrior, leaving their wives and children to bring in the harvest. Jews had joined the king and queen's camp and assured the continued administration of the country. They made the economic survival of the country possible by supplying weapons, provisions and uniforms. Abravanel and Abraham Seneor, two important figureheads of contemporary Judaism, took the role of intermediaries between their people and the Christians, proffering instructions and advice to maintain solidarity.

After he conquered Loja, Illorca, Noclin and Velez Malaga, Ferdinand seized Malaga. It was the second largest city of the Moorish empire, although protected by the Alcazaba and the Gibralfaro, two forts reputed to be impregnable. It proved a total defeat. The many Jews who had sought refuge in these lands welcomed the victors with great apprehension. How would they fare?

Their spiritual brothers who accompanied Ferdinand attempted to reassure them. They had nothing to fear. Renewal was upon Spain; God had enlightened the good sovereigns, who had only words of praise for the help brought by Israel. Yet rabbis remained reserved. What fate awaited the Marranos who, in order to escape the Inquisition, fled to Moorish kingdoms? The answers were still ambiguous and vague, and much was expected of Isabella's compassion.

As they were trying to make sense of the new turn of events the king captured Baeza on December 4, 1489, Almeria on the 23rd and Cadiz on the 29th. Granada was in sight, they only had to lay siege to it.

"The sovereigns," the authorities told Abravanel, "are willing to forget the support your community lent new Christians if you bear the total cost of the siege of Granada. Make yourself worthy of his trust and you will not regret it."

Rabbis, merchants and respected community leaders all agreed. "These sacrifices are nothing if they are the price to pay for freedom and security," they said. Gunsmiths worked day and night for no compensation. Toledo, Valladolid and many other cities throbbed with the blows of hammers. Helmets, lances, swords, axes, armors, coats of mail and musketoons were making their way toward the Moorish capital. The best artisans built a gigantic tent city at the gates of Granada, reserving the most spacious and beautiful ones for the lords. The most skillful tailors, the majority of whom were Jewish, came to the battlefield to make, for next to nothing, sumptuous clothes. It was eminently necessary for the Spanish elite, which had followed its king, to renounce its taste for elegance. Jews provided goats, cows, sheep, hens and game. They got their supplies from Arab farmers to whom freedom was promised in exchange for their active cooperation.

To head off a possible Saracen attack they set up, a short distance away from the tent city, a field hospital where numerous priests worked alongside Jewish physicians. Simon's competence and reputation made him a natural choice for difficult cases. Even away from his wife and children he did not feel isolated. He was with many of his spiritual brothers and would often converse with them. Yet he could not share their optimism, which he found excessive. He would often recall the words his grandfather had said to him right before he came to Andalusia: "My son, beware of empty promises. The sovereigns are driven by a blind faith, and I am suspicious of the sincerity of their feelings. Hatred and scorn cannot be made to vanish in so little time; only self-interest incites them to alter their attitude." In spite of his unsteady gait and broken voice, Lazarus, at one hundred, was clear-minded, and facts rarely contradicted his judgment.

Simon was at this juncture in his thoughts when he was told that a member of the king's family, Lord Alfonsi, was critically wounded. "His horse reared, and as he fell the prince's thigh was run through by his sword. He is bleeding a lot," they said as they pointed to the stretcher.

Simon directed those who had carried the wounded each to get a hold of a limb. He then swiftly removed the sword from the thigh and had the extremities of the wound compressed. Finally he heated up the culprit blade until it glowed red before applying it to the edges of the wound to cauterize it. Although he had passed out, the prince flinched, but the hemorrhage was over.

He was far from saved, however. He was laid down carefully in his tent while Simon prepared and administered his secret remedies against fevers and contractions. The prince spent some difficult days before he came to. His life was no longer threatened.

The entire army at Granada learned of the doctor's prowess. The king, who had come to visit his troops, hailed the recovery. As to Alfonsi, he insisted on thanking Simon personally. "Sir, you have saved my life. I am indebted to you. Even if your religion was and always will be an obstacle between us, I shall never forget what you have done for me." And Simon was congratulated from tent to tent. Simon was grateful, yet he was ill at ease. "Am I the man who saved don Alfonsi's life or the Jew who saved the Christian prince of the Christian army of very Christian Spain? All men are equal before suffering, they are all afraid of death, but once they recover their health they rediscover intolerance. Perhaps the very same man I saved will be the one who will strike at me later. Mine is a strange and beautiful profession."

He was given a few days' leave in Toledo. He was about to reintegrate into his own world, see his beloved little Judith, who changed from week to week. Did she have suitors? He did not know. This war demanded so much of him that he was no longer able to focus on what really mattered. He stepped across the threshold of his home with much relief. There he found a helpless Rachel, who tearfully told him that Antonio and Yasmina were dead. Coming around a curve, their cart had jumped a cliff. They were a little over sixty and had never been away from each other for more than a day. For the last three days, since she found out about the accident, Rachel hadn't stopped crying. She was crying for Simon because he had just lost his parents, for Lazarus, who had such a powerful tenderness for his daughter, for Yasmina and her eloquent silences, for Antonio and for his, love which had transcended time.

Simon stayed a few days in Aranjuez. He needed to hold his sister in his arms and to hear his grandfather. "Are they up there, Grandfather? Do you think they see us?"

"Yes, they are near the Almighty, and they protect you, my children. Soon I shall be with them because that is where I belong."

Simon headed back south, filled with nostalgia. War no longer interested him; he had nothing to do with the reconquest. This was not his struggle. He knew he stood against a people, the Moors, who were not his enemies and to whom he felt close. Jews had suffered too much not to be affected by the adversity of these men and women whose physical and spiritual being was being debased.

At his grandfather's request he visited, near Malaga, with Mourad el-Moktar, his uncle, Yael's child, the son of a Jewess. He found his uncle in the throes of a deep distress, at the mercy of his Christian victors. Simon explained the difficult role his correligionists had to play, forced to lend their support to Isabella and Ferdinand to stay alive. He recalled, his voice choking with emotion, his mother's death, Manuel's memory. Tears streamed from the Arab's eyes. "Yasmina, my God! The sister I knew so little. It's all so far away, so unreal. And Manuel. I have good memories of him, we understood each other well."

"I know," Simon answered. "He told me everything about your encounter. My grandfather would have liked to have met you. How strange life can be! Our customs and manners are so similar, yet we traveled different paths. What an ironic twist of fate! To think that together we might have been strong, almost invulnerable… Christians made the most of our differences; that is why they won. Don't take this badly, but you, the Arabs, are partly responsible. You never trusted us. You are so entrenched in your moral superiority and the belief that the truth is yours, and here is the result: this logical, implacable defeat. I am speaking thus with you because the Jewish fiber in you still exists somewhat; unfortunately, your descendants will come to forget it."

"Yes, you're right, Simon, we are quite close to one another. We have the same God, whom you call Elohim and I, Allah. Will we be intelligent enough to one day clean the slate of all our differences, to join together and recall the time we used to be brothers and allies?"

"May Heaven let our children remember. May God protect you, Mourad."

"May He protect you, too."

And they parted ways forever.

Simon found the outskirts of Granada as he had left them. The siege was underway, passive, without any heroic act except for a few forays, inconsequential skirmishes which did not benefit either side.

In the hard-pressed city refugees and cripples appeared in great numbers. Some lamented, others prayed, yet others repudiated the Koran. Despair of men who could no longer have faith in anything, distress of old men seeking refuge in the reading of sacred texts, terrifying wailings from the wounded awaiting death.

Elsewhere the country, which had become Spanish again, was beginning to organize. Isabella had promised freedom of worship, but was this believable? Many Muslims set sail for Africa. The Church took over mosques; the shadow of the cross extended over every home. People were rebuilding, involved in petty disputes over newly conquered lands. Ten years of Catholic war, discord spreading within the Emir's family, a dreadful siege—all this contributed to bring proud Granada to her knees. On January 2, 1492, Muley Boabdil handed over the keys of the Alhambra to Ferdinand and Isabella. The flags of Castilla and Aragon flew over the city. Moslem Spain was finished.

Bells pealed in every city of the peninsula. With spontaneous or elaborate festivities, from north to south and from east to west, everyone celebrated the repossession of the country from Moslems after seven hundred and seventy-seven years of occupation. Isabella and Ferdinand of Aragon were the monarchs of honor regained. Now Spain was cleansed.

Almost.

Chapter 47

The Alhambra! Who had not heard of the astounding beauty of this palace, sung by troubadours, described by storytellers, painted by artists? Ferdinand made his entrance into the palace the symbol of his victory. The whiteness of the snow made the summits of the Sierra Nevada sparkle. The royal procession entered through the monumental gate after it had climbed the hill. Luxurious alleys planted with a thousand flowers, fountains rippling with pure water, tranquil basins reflecting the charms of life, they all led to the "red one," the Arabic name for the sumptuous palace.

After Ferdinand had taken possession of the premises the queen joined him and together they visited each room with renewed rapture. There, precious tiles; here, niches sculpted with an intoxicating precision; farther on a golden room with an intricately carved ceiling. They discovered the octagonal Room of the Whispers, where one only had to whisper a few words against a wall for his accomplice, positioned on the other side of the room, to hear them perfectly. The Arabic architectural magic so delighted Ferdinand and Isabella that they forbade a single stone of the building be touched. Destroy all evidence of Moslem Spain, but keep this work of art intact!

Ferdinand organized a debate in the magnificent Hall of the Ambassadors, the room where he had received the keys to the city. He had summoned the highest dignitaries of the kingdom to discuss the future of Spain.

"Must we, can we really respect freedom of worship for the Moslems we have just conquered? This would be an insult to our country, to her kings!"

"Perhaps so, but we have signed an agreement with Boabdil, and if we do not abide by it we may have to contend with the rest of the Moslem world."

"What about the Jews, then? No Jewish empire is likely to call us to account. We can no longer tolerate them. Spain can remain great only with Catholicism. Let's drive them out.

"Their wealth is an insult!"

"Their temples stand as a persistent challenge to our holy Church!"

"We should rid the country of heretics. Now is the time to take care of them!"

"I agree with everything that's being said," Ferdinand answered. Do not forget, however, the promise Isabella made and, more importantly, that Jews control a large segment of our economy. Can we really do without them?"

"Make them convert, or else we shall replace them!"

A voice rose among those assembled. "Why such harshness? Must we forget their dedication and the help they lent us in our struggle against the Moors?"

Torquemada cut short the spoiler. "They only acted out of financial self-interest. We understand your concern, Prince Alfonsi. You owe your life to one of them. The heroic deeds of a few, however, do not give absolution to all the others. They must choose between exile and conversion."

#

At the same time Simon was enjoying his victory, proud to have carried out his duty. The monarchs could only have praise for the way Jews behaved during the Reconquista. He had one immediate need: to return to Toledo, see his family, and pray over his parents' grave. It was Judith who had felt his absence the most; she was at an age where the advice and the presence of a father were all-important. A happy teen in her marrying years, she was patiently awaiting a sign from destiny. But everything was about to change. He would talk and listen to her, and he would find her a husband. He felt less guilty with David, younger and more impressionable. Rachel! He would finally see her. And his grandfather, the pillar of the Benavistas, still alive by the grace of God … Yes, he needed to see his family, to fall back into his old habits. He had to forget this nasty war, the despairing people down there in the south. He had given too much of himself; now he needed to think about himself, to be comforted by Rachel, to live selfishly.

He was getting ready to leave when he was told of Lord Alfonsi's unexpected visit. He was surprised that such an important person wanted to meet with him. A proud smile lit up his face. He thought he knew the reason for this call: a reward? words of thanks?

"Sir," the prince began gravely, "I have turned protocol on its ear to come see you. A tragedy is brewing which will affect your community. The Grandees of the kingdom, who gathered this morning at the king's council, have agreed to expel the Jews from Spain. My efforts to intervene were in vain. I am dismayed by this decree, but I lack the authority to change it. I am beholden to you and will never be able to repay my debt. The information I have brought you will be made public in a few days. Make the best of whatever time you have left to make your arguments prevail. War was too costly; the country is left bloodless. Even if you have already given much, offer still more. Ferdinand may be swayed by this argument. May God protect you!"

Simon was devastated. He told Abravanel and Seneor what was afoot. They railed at the authorities, unable to make sense of this new turn of events. They were furious but needed to come up with an alternate plan. Overcoming their indignation, they requested a meeting with Ferdinand.

"Sir, worrisome rumors as to our future are circulating. Should we give them any credit?"

"These rumors are true indeed," the king answered solemnly. "Your presence on our land has become intolerable. It is a disgrace to our Lord Jesus Christ."

"I do not understand," said a surprised Seneor. "We have always been your faithful servants."

"Times have changed. The new Spain can only be Christian."

"What ungratefulness, sire, what an injustice!" the rabbi shot back. We are as much a part of this land as it is a part of us. We have lived here for many centuries; no one has the right to expel us."

Seneor was devastated; the decision seemed irrevocable. He spoke loudly before opening his heart; the king had to go back on his decision no matter what. For an instant Abravanel thought he could detect an emotional response on Ferdinand's face. That was the moment to advance the most decisive argument.

"Sire," he said, interrupting Seneor, "you honored me by consulting me on the affairs of the kingdom. However, as you are well aware, the state's coffers have been emptied. War was costly, and rebuilding the country will require enormous sums of money. Our community has made important sacrifices to lend you help. Yet, on behalf of my community I hereby pledge that we shall continue our help. We shall work day and night if necessary to provide you with anything you might need. As proof of our goodwill I offer you, right now, thirty thousand gold ducats."

The king, impressed, said he had to think about it. Abravanel breathed freely; all was not lost. Unfortunately, Torquemada, hiding behind a door, had been listening to the entire conversation. He burst into the room in a fury and held out a crucifix toward Ferdinand. "Judah sold Our Lord for thirty ducats. You would do it for thirty thousand. Look, here he is!"

Ferdinand was startled. He looked at the crucifix for a long time before kneeling and asking for forgiveness. After he regained his composure he dismissed the two Jews.

Christian Spain had just won one of its most brilliant victories.

Helpless, Abravanel and Seneor joined Simon, who had not attended the meeting. Simon lost his temper. "All our sacrifices were for naught. The monarchs are not trustworthy. After they have destroyed our souls they are bent on our physical destruction. What reprehensible deeds have we ever commited to deserve this new trial? Is God putting us through a new exodus from Egypt?"

"Enough with the jeremiads," Seneor answered. "This is no time for giving speeches. We have to think about all those who won't have the strength to leave. They will convert or die on the spot; their despair will be total. Since God made me rich and influential, I shall stay to assist our people in these difficult times as best I can."

"You are right," Simon asserted. "Many will not be able to leave Spain by the set date and will seek to escape later. They will need assistance, and I can lend them my help. Thus I shall convert and be ready to help them. But when my work is done I will leave this accursed country, because I want to live as a Jew."

"I admire you, Simon," Abravanel went on. "As for me, I count too many enemies to be able to stay behind. We only have four months to get ready; that's not much time. There are small but long-established Jewish communities in Barbary, in Oran, Fez, Djerba and elsewhere. They have freedom of worship. We can join them as others among us already have."

"Won't a mass exodus of our people scare the Saracens?" Simon asked. "Our language, our culture and customs are so different. Won't they seek to reignite a holy war? We helped Christians defeat them; won't they make us pay for it?"

"There are risks," Abravanel conceded, "but the sacred texts of the Koran command its followers to respect the people of the Book. Moreover, Moslems are hospitable and do not turn away those who need shelter.

"May the Almighty hear you, Abravanel," Seneor answered. "However, only our brothers who live in the south choose to go to these lands. They have built some very good relations with Arab states, and going there won't be painful for them. On the other hand, those of us who live in the middle of the country or in the north will prefer to go to the Turkish empire, Navarra, Portugal, Sicily or Italy."

"How do we organize the departures?" asked a worried Abravanel. "There are so many obstacles to overcome. Are roads safe? Won't we be robbed on the way? It is true that since Isabella ascended the throne the situation has gotten much better."

"There are close to four hundred Jewish communities scattered throughout Spain," Seneor went on. "Some consist of just a few families; others are more important. We will need to pray that nothing happens to them. They will have to gather in some large cities, which will serve as points of departure for large convoys toward Portugal, Navarra and important harbors. We cannot trust any soldier or mercenary to escort them. We'll have to depend on ourselves. Rabbis will be our spokespersons. They shall comfort the unfortunate and make all the necessary decisions. The bravest and youngest among us will make up our army. We'll need to think about provisions and carts for the sick and the wounded."

"Portugal and Navarra won't be much of a problem. I am, however, worried about those who will choose to go to Africa," said Abravanel. "Which harbors shall we gather them at? Will we find ships? More importantly, will we be able to trust the captains and their crews?"

"We have many difficulties to solve!" Simon said conclusively. "God has to be with us. I believe that now is the time to take leave of each other and to inform community leaders. Good-bye, my friends. May the Almighty grant us his protection."

Simon left for Toledo with a broken heart. The world was collapsing. For a moment he wished to be dead, leaving a world full of hatred, but his own people desperately needed him. With Rachel and his two children he went to Aranjuez, where he revealed the news.

"Conversion or exile. Four hundred Spanish Jewish communities are wandering on the roads of Spain. This is Isabella and Ferdinand's reward. Their decree will soon be made public; we need to think about our departure. Life is pleasant in Portugal; that is where we should go. What do you say, Abraham?"

"We shall never leave."

"Conversion or exile! Do you wish to convert?" said Myriam in tears.

"They have no right to chase us out."

"Alas! Abraham, one doesn't question Isabella's dictates, the commandments of all of Christendom. No, the king will never change his mind. People would not understand. I can already hear them celebrating the news of our imminent departure."

"We shall not leave. This land is our land. I was born here," Abraham said stubbornly. He could not bring himself to accept the inevitable.

Simon left him to think and went through Aranjuez to urge his fellow Jews to attend a meeting. His serious air convinced them. That same evening he told the terrible news to the entire community gathered in the synagogue. He answered questions he had asked himself a few days before, expressed some of his ideas, suggested they organize. The small Jewish population of Aranjuez, however, reacted much like Abraham.

Be exiled? That was preposterous. Unfair, therefore preposterous. They'd stay, the king would go back on his decision, life would go on in Spain as it had for some twenty, thirty generations before them.

When a few days went by without the news being made public they began to think that perhaps they'd prevailed. Simon shrugged and went back to Toledo. Everyone knew he was mistaken.

Chapter 48

At the end of April, 1492, on every public square and before huge crowds, heralds read the decree of the expulsion of the Jews.

Don Ferdinand and doña Isabella, by the grace of God king and queen of Castilla, Leon, Aragon, Sicily, Granada, Toledo, Valencia, Majorca, Sevilla, Sardinia, Corsica, Murcia, Jaen, the Algarves, Algeciras, Gibraltar, the Canary Islands, count and countess of Barcelona, lords of Biscay and Molina, dukes of Athens, count of Roussillon and Cerdagne, marquess of Oristan.

To prince don Juan, our dearest and dearly beloved son, and to the infantes, prelates, dukes, marquesses, counts, representatives of all social classes, peers, rich men, commanders, governors of our kingdoms and fiefdoms, counselors, judges, mayors, men of arms, officers, jurors and good men of all cities, villages and localities in our kingdoms and fiefdoms, to the synagogues and to the Jews who frequent them, to all Jews and private citizens be they men or women, regardless of age, to everyone else from whatever social class, law or dignity, importance or status, to all those who, in one way or another, this chart affects or will affect, may you be blessed with health, grace and salvation!

Know that we were informed that there exist and that there had existed in our kingdoms wicked Christians who were practicing Judaism. We decreed at the Cortes meeting last year in Toledo the creation of Jewish quarters in every city, village or any other locality where Jews would continue living in their sinful ways. Moreover, we ordered that the Inquisition establish a foothold in all our kingdoms and fiefdoms. As you are all aware, the Inquisition has, in its twelve years of existence, captured many culprits, as we were told by inquisitors and other religious persons who, because of their relations, discussions and communications with Jews, were deceived by them.

"Jews use many means and schemes to turn believers away from our holy Catholic faith, taking them back to their dangerous beliefs, instructing them in the customs of the law, inviting them to attend meetings where they are explained Jewish holy days they are expected to honor. They want to circumcise them and their children, offering them prayer books, telling them which fast to respect, teaching them to transcribe copies of the law, letting them know about Passover ahead of time, explaining to them how to celebrate and plan for it. They give them and they bring to them unleavened bread and the meat of animals slaughtered according to their own rites, they warn them against all the things that are forbidden to eat or against their commandments. They convince them of the superiority of Mosaic law, making sure they know there is no other law, no other truth than theirs. All this was verified through a multitude of declarations and confessions, coming from Jews and from those whom they had tricked; all this undermines, harms and debases our holy Catholic faith.

As we became aware of these events in all parts of the country, and because we know that the real remedy to these ills is to forbid Jews to communicate with Christians, we expelled them from Andalucia, where they seemed to have caused the most harm, in the mistaken belief that this would be a sufficient measure to prevent Jews in other cities, villages and others localities in our kingdoms and fiefdoms from committing the same offenses. But it was brought to our attention that neither this nor the pardons granted to certain Jews guilty of crimes against our holy Catholic faith sufficed to deter them from offending the Catholic religion. Because with each passing day the aforementioned Jews perpetuate this state of affairs, and so that there no longer be opportunities to offend our holy mother Church, we must rally to fend off the main offender, namely by the expulsion of Jews from our kingdoms.

Because when a serious and odious crime is committed by whatever body, it makes sense to dissolve that body and punish its members; likewise those who pervert the good and honest way of life of our cities and villages should be driven out.

Consequently, we, following the counsel of and in full agreement with prelates, grandees and knights of our kingdoms and other persons present at our council meeting, have, after full deliberation, decided to order the expulsion of all the Jews in all our kingdoms, and may they never return. This is why, with the present edict, we hereby give notice to every Jew, man or woman, regardless of age or place of residence, living in the aforementioned kingdoms and fiefdoms, whether they are natives of these localities or not, that after the end of the month of July of the current year they leave with their sons and daughters, male and female servants and Jewish family members, the young as well as the old, regardless of their age. They will not be allowed to return to our territories either purposefully, or in transit, or under any other circumstance. If they ever set foot back in whatever fashion or are discovered living within our borders, they risk losing their lives and having all their possessions confiscated by our chamber of taxation.

Furthermore, we hereby order and warn who ever, be it a single individual or a group of individuals from the aforementioned kingdoms, regardless of class, condition or dignity, agrees to give shelter or is giving shelter or welcomes or defends either publicly or privately a Jew or a Jewess after the end of the month of July or beyond, forever, whether it be on his lands, in his home or in any locality belonging to the aforementioned kingdoms and fiefdoms, that said individual or group risking loss of his possessions, vassals, fortresses and any and all other inheritance. Further, he shall lose our support vis-à-vis the chamber of taxation. Moreover, to allow the Jewish men and women, during the time granted to them through the end of the month of July, to make arrangements, we hereby extend our royal protection to them and their possessions so that, during that period, they be able to attend to their work without fear, sell, trade or divest themselves of all their goods, furniture and property and dispose of them freely. We hereby grant them the permission and the opportunity to take with them, outside the borders of our kingoms and fiefdoms, their possessions and treasures, by sea or land, with the exception of gold, silver and any other stamped currency, as well as any other object forbidden by the laws of our kingdoms, and also excepting spices whose exportation is prohibited.

Furthermore, we hereby give notice to all councils, courts of law, administrators and knights, as well as to the good citizens of said kingdoms and fiefdoms and to all our subjects, to enact, respect and legislate these directives to the letter and lend help and assistance if need be. Anyone acting contrarily will have all his possessions confiscated by our chamber of taxation. In order that our orders be known to all and that no one can ever claim ignorance of them, we ask that the present letter be publicly read on all city squares, markets and all other public places in cities and villages by the town's crier in the presence of the public scribe.

And furthermore, we hereby order that anyone asked to participate in this effort carry out his duties or risk being arraigned before us, in front of our tribunal, within fifteen days and dealt the punishment mentioned above. Every public scrivener asked to testify in a case involving a contravention to our orders will communicate using his private seal, so that we may know how our orders are carried out.

Executed in the city of Granada, on the thirty-first day of the month of March in the year one thousand four hundred and ninety-two of Our Lord Jesus Christ.

For the king, the queen, Juan of Coloma, secretary to the king and queen, our lords, done at their request.

#

The news was received with victory shouts in every city. Spain was about to become the proud and united country the queen had described when she ascended the throne. After the Inquisition, this expulsion came as a crowning achievement for Isabella. They were rich! By dividing the exiles' possessions, Christians would regain their wealth, whispered the populace as they applauded the heralds.

Then mobs entered Jewish quarters not to destroy them but to yell their joy. They railed at the dismayed residents and knocked on doors, boiling with impatience to take possession of these homes. In an expression of goodwill the queen had forbidden attacks against Jews. One could only wonder why these people looked so depressed; they were allowed to live!

Simon left with Rachel and his two children for Aranjuez. This time they could no longer deny the obvious. In Toledo the Jewish population had decided to rally around the rabbis and organize convoys. The last one would leave three weeks before the fateful deadline of July 31. Meanwhile, they had no choice but to sell their possessions to sniggering

Christians, who were letting prices drop with great jubilation. Yet always the same remark: "We are letting you live, so why the long faces?" They had to buy, very expensively now, provisions, horses, wagons, blankets, barrels, goats, hens... the banging of hammers resonated in the Jewish quarters; carts were reinforced. They worried about cold nights, about potential rains, about the hot summer sun. They wanted to cart off everything—pieces of furniture, memories—unwilling to realize that a single horse would never be able to pull an entire house.

Simon used Toledo as an example for the people of Aranjuez. In the smaller villages, however, it was more difficult to sell than in the larger ones. Some Jewish quarters were still not quite convinced. If they had ever considered moving elsewhere, perhaps in a distant future, the thought of selling their homes for a song to their own tormentors left them with a sour taste in the mouth. Thus they moved backwards toward the fateful date.

Simon talked at length with Rachel before making his decision. Finally, as he had told Abravanel, he would stay and undergo a temporary conversion. He would assist his people in need, would close his grandfather's eyes before leaving the country.

Myriam collapsed when she found out her brother's decision. "Be separated? How can you even conceive it? If we do not stay together, we become weaker. Oh, Simon, I was so unhappy during the three years you spent in Portugal. What about David, what about our grandfather? Father and Mother are buried here! How can we abandon them?"

Lazarus stood up with great difficulty before taking her by the shoulders. "It's very hard, Myriam, but I cannot, I cannot leave with you. I must die here. Simon and Rachel are not staying here just for me, they are staying for those who would have converted. My dear granddaughter, when I am reunited with my family up in heaven Simon will join you, and you shall be together once more. This is an accursed country, and you must escape it. It is perhaps the road toward a new promised land. God looks after us, don't you ever forget it, even if the path to be taken is sometimes difficult to understand. You, Abraham and your daughters are a small part of Israel. My heart is and always will be with you."

Myriam collapsed tearfully in his arms.

Abraham, resigned, shrugged. "My sister doesn't want to leave with us. She is a little crazy since the death of her husband. What a tragedy, what a terrible tragedy! Oh, Simon, we can't sell the store, the horse has seen better years, it's not feasible, how are we ever going to be ready? Myriam, when I think about the happiness that was ours ... my dearest little daughters ..."

And time ticked away. Weeks went by at a prodigious pace. Abraham counted the days wandering through the house. Simon gathered them all in Toledo. Thus Lazarus, a few decades later, was back in the city of his youth. Simon's home was huge and resembled the cigarral on the banks of the Tagus. At his request Lazarus settled in the large main room. He could see the park through the window and the outline of cruel Toledo in the distance. For another week every relative of the old man could still partake of his wisdom and love.

He told them of the faith that parted waters, of children who passed on to future generations the words of an old man who had lived a whole century. He spoke about all those he was going to meet up in the heavens: the mother he had never known but who had always been there for him, his father, Yael, Yasmina and Antonio, Manuel and Linda; and also all those who had crossed his path: the faithful Samir, the condesa, his brother, who betrayed him and paid for his sins, Zorra, the Moslem woman who helped him at a critical time, the circus people from all four corners of the earth, the El-Kabachs from Granada, Rebecca Cherki, old Eli Zarka..." At my age death is not sad. From above I shall watch you, and when you remember me, I will be happy."

Then came the day to part. Judith was sad; she would no longer see her cousins, her friends, nor the boy she was so fond of and who was leaving for Africa. Myriam fell apart and sought refuge in her grandfather's arms just as she used to do as a little girl. Lazarus also had a difficult time repressing his tears. He blessed his granddaughter one more time, and then it was time to leave. Myriam turned around on the wagon and waved her hand and heard her grandfather's broken voice: "Farewell, my dear."

Simon escorted them to Aranjuez. There he realized that Abraham had paid scant attention to what was the most important: the strength of the cart, the endurance of the horse. As to the provisions, there wasn't too much. A convoy two thousand persons strong was leaving from Ciudad Real for Portugal in two days. If they wanted to join them, they had just enough time. Simon gave them a small amount of gold—not to take across the border, which was forbidden, but to buy their way out of ambushes along the way. He also gave them, although he was very attached to it, his young and energetic horse. He took the other tired beast to ride back; that one would not have lasted long. Then he pushed up his sleeves and tried to strengthen the cart while advising Abraham against taking too many useless things.

At dawn they prayed over Antonio's and Yasmina's graves, and then the horse-drawn wagon pulled away. Abraham had fallen behind and had lost many precious hours; he was the last one to leave Aranjuez. If he would not be able to join the large convoy out of Ciudad Real, they would have to manage on their own, and things could get much harder. In spite of Isabella's prohibitions, there would certainly be highway robbers poised to take advantage of events.

His heart breaking, Simon stood alone at the entrance to the village and waited a long time after the wagon had vanished. A terrifying silence had fallen upon the Jewish quarter. He went back to the empty house and climbed to what, as a child, had been his room. There he surrendered to his misery.

Chapter 49

Abraham had only two days to join the convoy out of Ciudad Real. He mentally thanked Simon for that energetic horse, which would allow them to get, he hoped, to the rendezvous point on time. Myriam could not stop crying, while the children, their heads resting against their mother, were silent.

They had not gone more than fifty miles when the rear wheel got stuck in a rut, throwing everyone to the ground. Miraculously, it had not broken, it had only jumped the joint on the axle tree. "The Almighty has not given us up yet," Abraham proclaimed.

"The children are all right. Everything else is nothing important," Myriam answered.

Everything was fixed before nightfall. They spotted a small grove, which they used as a shelter until the next day. They left early, hoping to reach Ciudad Real by evening. Abraham was somber. He kept close watch on the wheel he had repaired with great difficulty and which, by some miracle, was still attached. "I am worried," he said after a while. "We're not going fast enough. I am afraid we might get there too late to catch up with the last convoy." Myriam said nothing, praying for a miracle. Unfortunately, they advanced at a snail's pace, and Ciudad Real came into view only on the third day after of their departure."

Abraham left the cart in front of the Puerta de Leon. "Wait for me here. I am going to find out. The wagon is too weak to go into the city." He crossed the bridge and walked up to the small Jewish quarter. He was one of the last Jews to travel this path. The silence was oppressive. He did not see a soul. He looked gloomily at the empty houses, abandoned forever. He saw an old man with a long white beard meditating before a portico, gazing into space.

"Who are you?" the old man asked.

"My name is Abraham Sananes. I come from Aranjuez. I am looking for the last convoy going to Portugal."

"It left yesterday."

"That's what I feared. I just arrived. My God! It is too late."

"Don't worry. It can't be very far. You see it, it's over there, on the road that goes to the west. I watched it until my eyes burned. For hours I witnessed wagons and people on foot. The women were crying, the men praying. Some spent three days at the cemetery to give a final tribute to their dead. It seemed as if the convoy would go on forever. Those in front were already far away when the last carts disappeared behind the hill. They proceeded slowly, a whole people, our people. Don't be fearful. There must be other people lost on the way. Regroup, and by riding faster you shall catch up with the convoy."

"What about you, aren't you going?"

"I am too old. In a few days I shall become a Christian against my will. Over there are two other neighbors who chose to stay. We are alone. All the streets are empty. Without us Spain will fall. We were her glue, and she didn't realize it. Our rabbi, who organized the convoy, tore down an entire wall of his home so he could take one of the stones with him. A stone from Salomon's temple, which his family had venerated for centuries."

Another old man joined them. "Take our faith far away, you who are leaving. Pray for us. Thinking about you will help us live through whatever little time we have left. And you, brother, listen to the story of Joseph Ibn. Oh! I realize you are in a hurry, but you must hear it out. That poor man left a week ago. He was ailing, without any private means, without a family. He staggered forward on the road. He came upon a representative of the Church. The latter offered to help him if he agreed to convert. At first Joseph refused, but the man was stubborn and followed in his own chariot. Two days later, exhausted, he agreed to be baptized. He reached Ciudad Real in a state of utmost confusion and hanged himself a few hours later. Drunk with rage, the priest lifted the body down before throwing the corpse to the ground and exhorting his followers to trample it. We witnessed this scene. What a disgrace!"

"Priests go to such extremes to torment us? It's terrible!"

"They might be reluctant to go after large convoys, but if they come across a solitary family in need or a man alone, they do all they can to convert them. Think about this story, my son, and tell it."

"Why don't they let us go and retain our dignity? If we do not catch up with the convoy, I wonder what might become of us."

"You seem worried."

"My family is waiting for me at the Puerta de León, and our cart is in a sorry state. I need a new one. I can pay."

"Keep your money. We have here a wagon left behind by a man burned by the Inquisition. I am happy to let you have it."

"Yes, it behind the synagogue," the other old man said. "Come, take it."

Abraham looked at the two old men and was unable to repress his emotions. "You remind me of Lazarus Benavista, my wife's grandfather. Like you, he stayed in Toledo because he is too old to travel. You comforted me as he would have. I don't know how to thank you."

"Lazarus Benavista! He's still alive?"

"Yes, he is one hundred years old."

"Lazarus Benavista is alive! Thank you, Abraham, for bringing us this news. Go get the cart and get back to your family."

Without losing any time Abraham set Myriam and the two little girls in the new, larger and more comfortable wagon and rode away from Ciudad Real.

They met several families along the way. Abraham felt relieved; they would no longer travel alone. He was hopeful again. They shared their thoughts about leaving, spoke with emotion about those they left behind, about old men who refused to leave and who, although baptized, would continue to live as before, in spite of the Inquisition. "Our past is dying and will disappear into the vortex of time. Our descendants, wherever they might be, will never know of the struggles and the suffering these men sustained." Abraham recalled the memory of Joseph Ibn. One of his traveling companions told the story of the "Sefers" he had taken along, and which his family had passed on from one generation to the next. They were old, worn-out parchments, almost illegible, dating from the seventh century. According to elders, they had been instrumental in preventing a massacre.

At that time the Grand Rabbi da Costa, his ancestor, stood before a maddened mob ready to exterminate Jews. Brandishing the sacred rolls, he began to shout in Hebrew, imploring his God. It was then that a miracle happened. The sun, reflecting off the metallic support holding the Ten Commandments, blinded the gang leader's horse. The animal became scared, reared, and unsaddled his master, who fell heavily. The ruffians tried to put him back on his feet, but he was dead. Shocked and frightened, they fled. Centuries later the story of the miraculous scrolls was still being told.

Few people knew this tale or the numerous and equally miraculous tales which had marked the history of Israel in Spain for centuries. There had been so many massacres that no one had felt up to writing the chronicle of these remarkable events. Abraham and Myriam then spoke about Lazarus and of his deeds and his fascinating life. From legend to tale the small group covered a great distance while unrolling the memory of an exiled people.

They had to think about food. Abraham decided he would buy a goat at the next village. Its milk would be good for his daughters; as for the rest, some bread and some dried meat would quiet growling stomachs. They reached Don Miguel a little after noon. A group of peasants stopped digging to watch them go by. Abraham climbed down.

"We would like to buy a goat."

"A goat? What for? Do you want to convert it?"

"No, we need a goat for its meat, for the milk!"

"We need! 'We need!" Hey, do you hear that?" yelled one of the peasants to his companions. "How arrogant Jews are! It's a good thing Queen Isabella is getting rid of them!"

Abraham clenched his teeth but went on. "We can pay!"

"You can! Why, did you think we were gonna give it to you? Well, in these parts, a goat costs five hundred maravedis."

"That's an incredible sum of money!"

"It's that or nothing."

"I have two hundred maravedis. No, three hundred."

"Three hundred! Deal."

Abraham took the coins out of his purse and handed him the money. The man put the money in his pocket before leaving and returning a few minutes later with a goat.

"But it's a dead goat!" a bewildered Abraham observed.

"Yes, we never agreed on whether it had to be dead or alive! A live goat will cost you a thousand maravedis!"

The peasants laughed uproariously.

Abraham turned pale and tightened his fists. Rage and frustration surged through his body. Would he strike? Jacob Moha, his traveling companion, pulled him back. "Don't do anything stupid. Your kids need you!"

"Yeah, don't be stupid, coward!" the mocking chorus of peasants piped in. Some villagers had joined their group and seemed to enjoy themselves very much.

"We have to go," whispered Jacob. "The situation is getting out of hand."

"What about the goat? You paid for it, it's yours. Say a few of your prayers. Maybe you'll get milk!"

Abraham picked up the dead animal, and they left amid the jeers of the villagers.

#

Abraham reflected. How could they ever come to accept conversion if they had as models people incapable of expressing even a modicum of pity? What would they find in Portugal? Abraham's brother had preferred not to wait for the answer; he chose to go to Africa. Moslems were violent and direct, but they respected Moses as much as Jesus or the Prophet Mohammed. Living alongside them might turn out to be hard, but they would no longer be humiliated.

Overwhelmed by a profound distress, Abraham cried out, "Let's not go there, Myriam. Instead let's go to Africa or Turkey or to the end of the world. We are not animals, we are human beings being trod on, even though we have never harmed anyone. Was I rude or arrogant? Why did they have to humiliate us so? Oh, Myriam! I feel like killing, like destroying myself..."

Myriam was discovering in her husband a violence she did not know. In Aranjuez Lazarus had been the rock, and Abraham's personality had been eclipsed. As for important decisions, it was generally Simon who made them. But now he had to take charge, be a leader! She tried to calm him down with her sweet voice. "They say that in Portugal the authorities are tolerant. Spaniards are arrogant and proud, granted, but that doesn't mean that all Christians are the same!"

"Myriam, my love, we have become accustomed to accepting so much because it was the best thing to do, and also because we were brought up to live in fear. You might be right about Portugal. We'll find out once we get there. But I cannot accept what we just endured."

"What do you plan to do?"

"Something. Make myself be respected. How would you look at me if I give in over and over again? I'm going back to Don Miguel."

"You're mad! What do you intend to do? Take on the the whole village?"

"No, I just want to take a goat and all the food I find. I'll go at night."

"That's thievery!"

"Didn't I pay for the goat? Who robbed whom?"

"But you might get killed! How will we manage without you?"

"You do not need a coward. I suffered all my life, and I do not want to be afraid of my shadow any longer. I will never again heed the whims of Christians. Your grandfather and your brother have shown me the way. They stayed at the risk of losing their lives. I do not feel right about it, and I need to resemble them. I have lost all my scruples, you know. I now consider myself a stranger in this land, impervious to her laws. I shall defend my life fiercely, but don't worry, I shall not die. Remember what your grandfather used to say of his encounter with Salomon Sprung: Jews do not have to bow down. Our people must not give in to despair; it has to stand tall. That's what I am doing. Nothing and no one will stop me."

Myriam, startled by her husband's determination, felt neither sorrow nor pain; he had passed his sudden strength on to her. Instead she felt an admiring trust in him and kissed him for a long time before letting him go.

He spoke to Jacob, his traveling companion. "If I am not back tomorrow morning, pray for me and, with your brothers, take my wife and my children to Portugal. We are far away enough from Don Miguel so that you should not fear reprisals if anything happens to me."

"Since you are so sure of your purpose, follow your conscience," Jacob answered. "I promise to look after your family. May God protect you."

He hugged his two daughters. Myriam whispered in his ear, "I love you." He smiled back at her, armed himself with a thick staff and left.

#

Night fell late, this time of year. The air he breathed was invigorating, he was surefooted, unafraid. When the last purple hints of sunset disappeared on the horizon he was within a couple miles of the village. He waited. The children's screams died down, then he could hear the adults. Domestic noises, doors, pots, shutters, animal bells clanged. Then nature was taken over by crickets. Night had taken possession of the earth.

Barns cut thick, dark silhouettes under the pale moonlight. A little farther on the white houses glistened. Abraham made a mental note of a few landmarks before moving quietly toward two barns standing next to each other. He jumped with each insect rattle, each time he stepped on straw; he was breathing heavily. He was in front of the first door, with its flimsy lock. He needed to lift the heavy latch and hoped to God it would not grate; open up the swing door, let his eyes get used to the darkness, look back one last time before going in. After a few seconds he was able to tell what was stored: an impressive quantity of food the peasants had stocked in anticipation of the winter months. Dried fruits, onions, dried meat. Abraham filled his sack. But no matter how hard he listened, there was no animal nearby. A goat, just a little goat. He had bought it. If he wanted to erase the offense, he had to find another one. He left the barn very cautiously.

The outline of the other building revealed an animal shed. He stole inside and let his nose inform him. The strong smell was unmistakable, there were animals sleeping in here. "Sleep, good animals, and you, too, good people, sleep your good Christian sleep," he told himself, with fear gripping his guts. He went inside the shed, his thick staff in one hand,

and smiled. "Myriam, my wife, I almost won. My children, look at all these animals. There is even an old snoring cow over there." He spotted five goats among the sows and donkeys. He untied the one closest to him, stroking it gently to awaken it. It worked; the animal did not bleat. It staggered up and followed him. Blood was pulsing in his temples. He walked toward the door of the animal shed, seconds felt like hours. Then to the deserted path leading to the road that would take him to his family. His lungs filled with the air of night.

A punch on the back sent him reeling to the ground. Breathless, he lifted his head and distinguished the huge outline of a bearded man.

"Well, ruffian, you rob from honest people! Do you know how we deal with your kind?" He grabbed him roughly by the arm, stood him up, then let out an angry scream. "I know who you are, you're the Jew with the goat! You're as good as dead. I'm taking you to the village."

In the darkness Abraham's hand groped for the staff he had dropped. He leapt to his feet and struck the man violently. He collapsed, his neck broken.

Abraham caught his breath. He took a long time to assess what had just occurred. He had killed a man! He fell to his knees and recited the prayer for the dead in Hebrew. Then, almost in tears, he took the goat by the cord and fled to a thicket. There was no witness. Who would suspect a Jew? Thou shalt not kill. Thou shalt not steal. Would God forgive him?

He went forward, wild-eyed. He made tens of excuses in his mind: milk for his children, a proud attitude instead of cowardice, a life traded for another. But the blood on his hands burned his skin; the dead man's face pressed against his. Walk, go forward, feel the clawing of the bushes, stumble on a root but get up again, still pulling a sleepy goat at the other end of the rope. Abraham quickened his pace, praying for daylight to break, for the blue sky to wash away the nightmare. He was a murderer.

Several hours later, his forehead burning, he caught sight of something through half-opened eyes. At the end of the path, on the other side of the hill, was the last car of their small convoy. He was arriving with dawn. He let everyone sleep, sat on a rock after he tethered the goat to a tree, and took his head in his hands. Nothing would ever be the same.

A child began a gentle whimper near one of the wagons. Then, little by little, the convoy came to life. Abraham joined his wife and daughters. Myriam ran to hug him, Lea let out a joyful scream and Luisa clapped her hands. "Papa is here, he has the goat, he is alive!"

He fell asleep quickly, leaving to his wife the responsibilty of driving the cart. He woke up later that afternoon with a horrendous headache and a rabid hunger. He ate voraciously while answering questions but said nothing about the dead man—not out of shame but because he wanted to remain cautious. If the story accidentally reached the ears of the Inquisition, they would all be accomplices in the involuntary manslaughter. He proceeded to ask a multitude of questions: Was the goat still there? Were they heading the right way, had they run across other people on the way? Hearing reassuring answers and seeing the happy expression on his friends' faces, he realized they were out of danger. The accidental death of the previous night was beginning to blur; soon it would vanish completely from his mind. If it was God's will.

As they had done since they had left, they set up their night camp toward the end of the day in an isolated location, a little past Medellín. The next day they washed up in the pond that lay at their feet and renewed their water supplies. It was the first time they had relaxed since they had left. The children had met one another, and their crystalline laughter could be heard. Myriam observed her husband; her love for him was getting stronger. Abraham had had a brush with death and no longer feared Portugal or the unknown. As long as he had his wife and daughters close to him he would be able to overcome anything.

That afternoon they saw four chariots in front of them. Obviously it was not the large convoy out of Ciudad Real, but one probably made up of a few lost families. The men were on foot, desperate, dead tired. The women and children, lying down inside the carts, seemed to await death. Suddenly Abraham realized that the three characters in the last wagons were priests. They were brandishing Bibles and bread.

"What's going on?" he asked briskly while jumping off his cart.

"We are exhausted, we haven't eaten in two days. These priests stay on our heels. They want to trade our conversion for a meal."

Abraham shook his head. The old men in Ciudad Real had spoken the truth; the roads to exile were littered with inhumane deeds. He ran toward Myriam and told her what was going on. Luisa quickly helped him gather some food, and the two of them ran toward the unfortunate group. "Here, eat. Your problems are over."

He then addressed the priests. "You are monsters! You want to destroy our souls when you already dispossessed us of everything else! The country is yours, as well as all our past wealth. Let those who want to leave this land, their land, be in peace!"

"Your conduct is an aberration. You would rather die of hunger than accept the love of Jesus."

"Jesus spoke of tolerance, of mutual help! Not of blackmail!"

"The Jews killed him!"

"Jesus forgave them! Where does forgiveness fit in your vile attitude?"

A shout interrupted them. A woman in the first wagon was holding her baby in her arms; the baby was motionless. He was dead. The priests approached the devastated woman. "Convert. He took your most precious possession to bring you back to Him."

Abraham was startled. He leapt toward them. "Quiet! how dare you carry on this odious blackmail! Leave now, leave!"

The priests backed down but did not turn away. Abraham clenched his fists and repeated, "I killed once, I shall not kill again. Murder will never be the solution ..." There was so much pent-up violence in him that he was frightened. How could these execrable vultures let a child die? Were they so obsessed with their mission than they forgot their famous mercy? The Bible they brandished spoke of love and sharing. Nothing else mattered for them except the methodical destruction of the Jewish people. That dead child meant one less "murderer of Jesus." Around him no one, not a single soul, protested. Oh, Jewish people, bowing under your yoke ... lift up your heads, refuse this abomination!

They rolled the small body in a cloth before putting it in his parents' cart. The three wagons joined Abraham and Jacob's convoy.

It had been a trying day; no one said a word. Everyone was thinking about the baby. They comforted the harrowed couple, but on the heels of the surge of optimism of the morning their illusions were now shattered. Abraham tried to hearten his companions. "Portugal is getting closer," he said. "Our exodus is soon to end, even if we are unable to catch up with the large convoy before crossing the border. Take heart, brothers."

Abraham did not recognize himself. "Lazarus would have acted very much like this," he thought, "and now it is my turn to make decisions." As he walked he went over his life's deeds, wondering what logic underlay this plan, incomprehensible to any simple, mortal man. He could not understand how his people had let themselves be crushed by Christians, when they were so many and had been the country's first inhabitants. Israel let herself be chased from her land without a protest, in spite of her renowned scholars, her important contribution to the development of science and her noble philosophical principles.

From the dawn of the Middle Ages, the Church had preached contempt for this people and had succeeded beyond her wildest expectations. Jews were born to suffer. If, by chance, one of them refused to surrender to his fate, Christiendom was there to remind him that he was nothing but a descendant of the "damned race" that had killed Jesus.

Abraham prayed for the coming of the Messiah on earth to make mankind better.

Exhausted, mostly disheartened, they stopped as night fell without concerning themselves with shelter. An evening of soul searching and great sadness was about to unfold.

"Over there, in the distance, there's a fire," shouted Jacob Moha suddenly as he peered into the horizon. Abraham had a start. Problems? Highway robbers? Would the small, passive troupe defend itself in case of an attack? Abraham and Jacob left, armed with sticks.

An hour later, just as the children were falling asleep, they returned in the company of four men. "It's the convoy from Ciudad Real! We caught up with it! The fire over there, it's theirs. Everything is fine."

"We came to help you," the four men said. "Climb back on your wagons. In a half hour you'll be safe among the rest of us."

They did not have to repeat it. Everyone loaded their mules up and joined the encampment. They were received warmly, and they resettled around a campfire. They all fell asleep quickly except the disconsolate couple, who kept a vigil over their son's dead body.

#

Early the next morning Abraham got up and stretched his legs while the rest of the camp still slept. There were wagons as far as the eye could see, lined one behind the other on the shoulder of the road. There were easily three hundred, a few of which were loaded with food. A little farther down three carts were used as the infirmary. Wails were coming out of one of them. Abraham came closer and looked inside.

"What do you want?" a woman asked him.

"Nothing. I just joined the convoy."

"Oh! She refuses to drink. Come on, sweetheart, drink up!" She was holding up the head of a young woman whose belly was rather round.

"Is it serious?"

"Normally this would be a happy event. But under the present circumstances it is difficult to give birth. She is weak and very distraught. Like many of us, she left behind members of her family in Spain, especially older people. Her husband went mad. Poor thing …"

"She'll get over it. There is life inside her. So many others only have dead ones."

"We've had seven deaths since we left. Old people and children."

"It's horrendous. What do you do with the bodies?"

"We inter them before moving on. It's so difficult for the families. There are even priests showing up at gravesites to encourage the grieving parents to convert. One couple did not want to leave their dead child behind. They watched the convoy leave, found they were alone, baptized, and with nothing more than the knoll where their son rested. Late arrivers told us the next day that the man and woman had hanged themselves from a tree."

"I saw priests let a child die of hunger. They wanted to buy the baby's family conversion with some bread. I hope they'll let parents bury their children peacefully."

"They don't dare attack our convoy. We don't threaten them; we simply prevent them from attending funerals."

He offered some comforting words to the expectant mother and resumed his exploration. The encampment was stirring back to life slowly. He recognized, coming from the bank of the river, a neighbor from Aranjuez, the carpenter Joseph Pinto. They fell into each other's arms; at home, on a good day, they would have exchanged only a cursory greeting. Joseph told him about their departure and how worried they had been when they did not see them, him and Myriam. "Yes, our entire community is here—Ephraim Delara, Daniel, old Sarah—come!"

Abraham followed him and shook hands, happy at seeing familiar faces. Then he asked to see a rabbi. He wanted to confess his crime at Don Miguel. Rabbi Toben listened to his confession, understood his turmoil and found the right words to comfort him.

Abraham rejoined Myriam and his daughters. The camp was getting ready to push forward. The sun was shining. The deadline given in the royal decree had been extended two days. It ran out the second of August, 1492. The convoy crossed the frontier on the eve of that day.

#

Abraham and his family had joined the people of Aranjuez in the middle of the convoy. The little girls found girlfriends, and time was spent in idle talk. As they crossed the border Ephraim Delara's son applauded. "We are saved! We are saved!"

"Perhaps," Abraham answered, nodding his head, "but we are far from an end to our troubles. What are we going to do here?"

"We must not lose heart," the teenager replied. "Commerce and industry, the ports and cities of Spain are doomed to fail. In a few years they'll beg us to return! What a victory that'd be!"

"No," said Abraham. "Our departure is final. Christians follow a demented logic that leaves no room for us in their society, knowing all the while that by expelling us they deprive the country in the most dynamic group of her population. They'll have no use for converts; the latter will lose, with their religion, the desire to undertake new business ventures that is a characteristic trait of our people. Spain might celebrate a few easy but passing successes, but then misery and decadence shall descend on her. She will be incapable of building or creating. She will find herself isolated, the bane of all nations. She shall pay until the day she realizes her errors, the day our descendants will be allowed back in this country."

The chariots weren't moving forward anymore. Jacob saluted Abraham and said he was going to the head of the column to see what was afoot. He returned ten minutes later. "I witnessed the conclusion of a discussion of epic proportions. Some wanted to rest here for a few days, while others wanted to push directly to Lisbon. Rabbis had the last word. We stop here. The weather is pleasant; we have enough food and plenty of time. The ninth of Ab in the Hebrew calendar, the second of August in the Christian calendar, will be a historical day. If all the convoys that left for Arab territories, Navarra, Italy and Portugal make it within the time ordered, there shall not be a single Jew left in Spain. Let's pray for those who stayed behind, and let's rest up before we begin a new life."

Chapter 50

During the week preceding the ultimatum the roads of Spain were crisscrossed by large convoys, small groups and individuals. Those of Old Castilla and Asturias entered Portugal from the north; few had chosen Navarra, hemmed in by two strongly Catholic countries; Catalans and people living along the coast had sailed for Italy or Arab lands. A few adventurous ones had pushed all the way to Salonica or Turkey. Abraham's sister, Sarah Zucoth, lived in the surrounding countryside of Aranjuez. Her husband had died, killed by brigands, a few months before, and since then she had become indifferent to everything except her two sons, aged five and ten. When Isabella's edict was made public she remained impervious to the panic taking hold of all the Jews of Spain. What point was there in fleeing; what use was there in being alive? Two weeks before the final deadline, while everyone around her was busy getting ready to leave, she kept nodding, her eyes aimlessly peering at the distance. Her neighbors were aware of her incurable melancholy. They did not press her; they let her be.

When, three days before the expulsion date, she found herself alone with her two sonss, forsaken in that small part of the village that used to be so lively, it finally dawned on her. Her children, the living memory of their father, should never have to convert. She clapped her hands together, took her two sons and led them to her husband's grave. In a voice made hoarse with emotion she told them. "There, my little ones, pray one last time for your father; he gave you life and his love, but the Almighty called him to His side. Wherever you might end up, whatever you may do, don't ever forget him. We are going to leave you, Joseph Farewell, my love. Know that you shall always be with me. Watch over us."

She returned to the house and brought out the old cart, along with the goat and the mare. In one hour she had gathered all she would need; without wasting a second, without panicking, she left.

The road was easy. She was one of the last ones to travel that route, going at a good pace and without fear of highway robbers. She expected to cross into Navarra in two days, following in tracks left by her spiritual brethren. The day ended uneventfully. They set up camp in a sheltered area. The goat had given milk, the tree its shade.

Just before day broke she awake without making any noise and went to survey the surrounding area in search of a water hole in which to wash up. She came around two small brushwoods but did not notice on the ground the sharpened extremity of a tree limb that cut a gash in her foot. She screamed and, as she bent down, lost her footing and fell a good ten feet down to the foot of a slope. Her leg broke. She attempted to stand up, but that was impossible; the pain was too great. She called out to her children; they were sleeping soundly. Then she began to cry, wondering why God was punishing her. She crawled, but the slope was too steep, the pain too unbearable, and she lost consciousness.

It was just about eight o'clock when José, the smaller one, woke up. "Mama, where are you?" he yelled.

He startled his brother. "Why are you screaming?"

"Mama is not here."

Marcelo rubbed his eyes and looked round. They were all alone. He tried to comfort his brother. "Mama is probably picking flowers, or else she's ... Or else ..."

"Mama! Mama! I'm hungry. Where are you?" José yelled.

Very worried, they called out a long time before giving in to their hunger and deciding to milk the goat. Sated, they resumed the search. José was crying, and Marcelo marshaled the experience of his ten years to think of a solution, but their anguish was growing. "Mama, I want Mama," José was sobbing.

That was when Sarah came to. She called out to them. Guided by her voice, they ran through scraggy bushes and found her farther down, her face shriveling with pain. "I got hurt when I fell, but it's nothing serious," she said reassuringly. "Help me go around this brushwood to get back to our wagon."

But José and Marcelo were not strong enough to support her, and she made it around practically by herself. The rugged terrain was ripping her belly. Feeling about to faint again, she drew a weak smile. "Let's stop, children. Being here or at the cart, it's all the same. Bring me some milk. I'm not going anywhere." They obeyed, then they lay down next to her, hoping for a charitable soul to come by and offer them help.

A man, a clothes bag on his shoulder, came by an hour later.

"What's going on?"

"I am hurt, I can't move."

"I'll help you," the man said. "Where do you hurt?"

"I'm afraid I broke my leg. We are Jews. We are going to Navarra," Sarah said, as if apologizing.

"I'm heading there also. Let's see the leg!"

She showed him the swollen ankle that was hobbling her with pain. The man made a face and asked for a piece of cloth to use as a bandage. He made Sarah speak to distract her and, when she least expected it, pulled on her foot. She howled and almost fainted again, but he had set the fracture.

"I'm sorry, but that was necessary. Your troubles are now over. Children, what did you find?"

He took the sheet tendered by Marcelo and ripped it to make bandages. His makeshift splint made the pain bearable. The man helped her onto the wagon.

"We left at the very last moment! I did not want to convert. It is the same with you?"

"I ... I am not Jewish."

Sarah's mouth gaped, her eyes open wide.

The man smiled. "It is against the law?"

"No, no," she stammered, but it's the first time that ... that I meet a good Christian."

"Yes, it is true that many have forgotten the precepts of charity taught in our books. But I am only a traveling entertainer, and I often run into feelings of contempt from believers. For us, the homeless, mutual help is important, and we are not concerned with religion or place of origin. A few years ago a man saved my life. I did not speak his language, yet he fed me and carried me for miles across a forest and put me out of harm's way before leaving. I will lead you into Navarra."

Sarah was moved. She trusted him. His name was Alfredo. He drove the small carriage slowly, careful to avoid the potholes and bumps of the road so as not to rattle the wounded ankle. The children listened with great delight to his adventures. He told them about the dawns, the marvelous landscapes of the north, the many strangers he had run into. They crossed the border at nightfall, their heads filled with images.

The man, who knew this part of the country, took them to the main road of Spain, used by many exiles during the previous weeks. He left the three fugitives in their trust and bid them farewell. Sarah felt tears welling up in her eyes. He noticed.

"It's as I told you: It's the law of the roads. You meet people and you never see them again. But I will remember the three of you."

"How can I repay you?"

"By remembering me, by remembering that not all Christians are as evil as those who dispossessed you."

He left without waiting for a reply, but Sarah caught his hand just in time to whisper, "May God bless you."

#

Twenty thousand people sought refuge in Navarra and settled there permanently. Many converted. A few courageous ones continued east in the direction of Constantinople; others stopped in Carpentras, a city under the protection of papal authorities.

> *Here, little David, is the story of the exodus. The malevolent*
> *Christian maelstrom had done its work well. There was nothing left*
> *except for the dust of the roads and the deafening silence. A list had*
> *been made of all those who were to be baptized before the fateful date.*
> *On the ninth of Ab of the Jewish calendar, the second of August,*
> *1492, there was not a single Jew left in Spain.*
>
> *Except one.*

Chapter 51

NINTH OF AB

At a hundred and two, Lazarus was the last witness of an era forever gone. In other circumstances, in other places, a whole people would be showing him respect. Mothers would ask him to bless their children; hordes of young people hungry for advice would gather at his feet. In Isabella the Catholic's inflexible Spain; he was nothing. The entire cultural heritage he stood for had been swept away; no one would remember him.

He spent long hours leaning his elbows on his perennial staff, seated under the shade of a large oak in the garden, waiting for a death that seemed to elude him. His gait was tentative, but he still had that same fire in his eyes. His long white beard and his abundant hair hid many wrinkles. His hearing was impaired, but he remained very clear-minded.

What beautiful memories he held in the recesses of his mind! The passing hour of his youth's glory; Yael, who died as she was about to be his. Yasmina, the shy daughter who would not close his eyes; Myriam, his favorite child, whom he would never see again. Pity!

He was tired. He meditated for hours. He had come to understand that the power and honors so many men fought for were bait to snare the unbelievers. Real strength did not exist on earth.

He had spent a long time wondering why his people had not reacted before the persecutions. He had finally figured out the answer: The placid strength of Judaism, shaped by millenia-old traditions, had turned on him. The refusal to resort to violence, the respect for others, solidarity, the will to settle every matter via discussion rather than through the use of force, the founding principles of the Jewish religion were felt by Christians as weaknesses and acts of cowardice. The Church, thus, had built a war machine that had no difficulty crushing the Mosaic law, too passive and too contemplative to offer any resistance.

On the twenty-ninth of July Simon, his wife and their two children returned home as Catholics after they brought their books, prayer shawls and ritual objects to a bonfire. Because of his advanced age Lazarus had been granted permission to be baptized at home. Yet his conversion still had not taken place. The authorities, overwhelmed by the large numbers of Jews to baptize, had forgotten about him.

On the ninth of Ab, 1492, he had yet to be visited by priests. That evening he decided to stay outdoors longer than usual. He was sad. This accursed day marked the end of Judaism in Spain.

As he was lost in his thoughts he felt a sharp pain in his chest. "I don't have much longer to live," he thought to himself. He laughed at the trick he was about to play on Christians: He would be the last Jew to die in Spain.

Judith arrived just then. "Grandfather, it's getting late. We have to go in now."

"I know it, child, but I am living my last hours as a free man, and I need to look at the sky and the stars. Go get your brother. I need to talk to you."

She was his sunshine. She was always dancing and singing. She had the carelessness of youth. She always spoke to him very softly, brought him treats, asked about his health, helped him walk.

She returned with David.

"Sit near me and listen," the old man said in the same breath. "On the first day of the third month following their exit from Egypt the children of Israel camped at the foot of Mount Sinai. The Eternal then spoke to Moses: 'Come to the mountain. I will give you the precepts and the doctrine I have set for my people.' When Moses was knowledgeable enough God gave him the two tablets on which were inscribed the ten commandments you are familiar with but that I want to remind you of because as of tomorrow you shall not be allowed to recall them. 'I am the Eternal, your God, who brought you forth from Egypt, where you were a slave. Thou shalt have no other God but Me, and thou shalt not venerate any idol. Thou shalt not use the name of the Eternal your God to tell a lie. Sanctify the day of the Sabbath, when thou shalt not do any work. Honor your father and your mother. Thou shalt not kill. Thou shalt not commit adultery. Thou shalt not steal. Thou shalt not bear false witness against THY neighbor. Thou shalt not covet thy neighbor's house or wife, manservant or woman servant, nor his steer or ass or anything else that belongs to him."

"Later, much later, Solomon sat on the throne of Israel. One night the Eternal appeared in a dream and said, 'Ask me what you want.': Solomon answered, 'You made me Your servant, a king, yet I am young and inexperienced. Give me a sensible heart to rule over Your people with fairness and to know how to tell evil from good.' God agreed to that request and answered, 'Because you asked me neither for long life nor riches, nor your enemies' death, but wisdom to give justice, I grant you your wish, and moreover, I give you riches and glory'."

"That," Lazarus went on, listened to with much emotion, "that's because they respected the Almighty's commandments. Many among us were blessed with wisdom, intelligence and wealth. That is also the reason our people have been, is and will be persecuted by Christians and many other peoples."

"I wasn't always the meditative and quiet old man you know. A very long time ago I wanted to fight against evil by stirring up our people against those who oppressed us. Unfortunately, I wasn't successful. Christians, through my brother, threw me in jail. They tried to break me but could not, because God never forsook me. When in my misery I began to doubt, I would recall the words of our sages, advising us to be patient and to wait for the coming of the Messiah. That would bring me comfort and the strength to endure more persecutions."

"You must, my dearest children, no matter what happens, never deny your origins nor renounce our values. Even if we are temporarily forced to submit to the law of the strongest, remember that the Almighty is there, and that He watches over you. Today marks the end of our history in this country. It's a day of mourning." He grimaced. His chest was hurting him more and more. "Soon I shall no longer be on this earth, and this was the message I wanted to leave you. Kiss me now, and may God bless you."

He took Simon aside. "My time has come, my son. Take me to what was my fathers' land, the Benavistas' vineyard. You said that the small house was empty, I would like to die there and show you the place where, many years ago, I buried parchments and the bow with which I won the famous tournament of 1406."

Rachel held him in her arms a long time. He kissed Judith and David and left with his grandson.

Simon drove slowly. He was following the itinerary his grandfather had marked. Lazarus opened his eyes wide for this last voyage into his past. The Jewish quarter, empty and quiet, would never again bathe in blood, but never again would it be enlivened by the children's laughter or the women's voices. The Alcantara bridge, the almost-dried-up Tagus winding around the city... Farther, on the arid soil of La Mancha, the verdant cigarrals lazed in the sun. Lazarus felt a great surge of emotion as he passed the cigarral of his youth. The road leading to the condesa's residence was the same, he noted. In the private gardens of the beautiful María he saw a young woman playing the sitar and thought he was seeing his old lover. In the span of exchanging glances he had turned nineteen again. He had just caught sight of doña María's granddaughter.

Then the vineyard with its ripening grapes came into view. "Land of my fathers, dry and rich, hardy vines, grapes bursting with life, how I have missed you! How often have I dreamed of seeing you again." They were coming near the small house Lazarus closed his eyes, a peaceful smile on his lips. He was breathing with much difficulty but insisted on taking off his own shoes to walk barefoot on the soil of his youth. He took a few steps while holding his grandsons arm to show him, to the left of the small house, the place where he had buried his treasures.

Simon made him sit down before digging. A few minutes later he was holding the precious objects. Lazarus took the bow and bent it. He closed his eyes, exhausted but happy to have relived feelings of so long ago. A coughing fit interrupted his remembrances; each gesture he made depleted the small amount of energy he had left. He gasped, "Simon!" Simon turned around and, seeing his grandfather with his mouth agape, rushed to him.

"Simon, thank you for having brought me here. I am grateful. May God bless you. Farewell, my son." Simon kissed him and held his hand until he gave up his last breath. The sun's intense heat on this thirty-first of July beat down on the entire country.

Lazarus was the last Jew to be buried in Spain.

Simon remembered the sentence uttered by Abravanel while he was a student in Portugal: "God chose your grandfather to carry out a mission whose purpose will be made clear to us later, much later." Today he knew his grandfather was a chosen one, a righteous man, the last one in Spain. He was born when the large-scale massacres were going on, and the Lord summoned him to Him the day His people had been banished.

Simon retired to the house, covered his head, and asked God to forgive him for not respecting religious laws requiring the presence of ten faithful men to honor the memory of the dead before he began reciting the kaddish, the ultimate prayer said over the departed.

"MAY THE NAME OF THE LORD BE EXALTED AND SANCTIFIED THROUGHOUT THE WORLD WHICH HE HAS CREATED ACCORDING TO HIS WILL. MAY HE ESTABLISH HIS KINGDOM AND CAUSE HIS REDEMPTION TO SPRING FORTH. MAY HE HASTEN THE ADVENT OF THE MESSIAH FOR THE WHOLE HOUSE OF ISRAEL."

"MAY HIS GREAT NAME BE BLESSED AND GLORIFIED FOR EVER AND EVER. MAY HIS HALLOWED NAME BE PRAISED, GLORIFIED, MAGNIFIED, HONORED AND MOST EXCELLENTLY ADORED; BLESSED IS HE FAR EXCEEDING ALL BLESSINGS, HYMNS, PRAISES, AND BENEDICTIONS THAT ARE REPEATED THROUGHOUT THE WORLD."

"MAY THE FULLNESS OF PEACE FROM HEAVEN, WITH LIFE, PLENTY, SALVATION, CONSOLATION, FREEDOM, HEALTH, REDEMPTION, PARDON, EXPIATION, ENLARGEMENT, AND DELIVERANCE BE GRANTED, TO US AND TO ALL HIS PEOPLE ISRAEL."

"MAY HE WHO MAKES PEACE IN THE HIGH HEAVENS BESTOW PEACE ON US AND ALL ISRAEL. AMEN."

Chapter 52

Simon read and reread the parchments with much emotion. With his most trusted writing implement he picked up the thread, recounting the recent nightmarish years up to the accursed ninth of Ab Then, he thought about his sister. Where was she? He decided he'd better be patient and, as they had agreed, wait for news from her before focusing on his escape. With Lazarus now dead he no longer wanted to remain in this soulless country.

At this particular juncture, however, he was left to his own devices. He could not distance himself from the Church, which was now even more vigilant than ever. The Inquisition would deal with him mercilessly if he were to commit the slightest blunder.

"We are going to leave," he announced to Rachel and his children. "When? I can't tell you, but I swear to you on Lazarus's and my parents' memory that we shall be Jews again. In the meantime we must exercise the utmost caution. Do not ever let anyone find you out. I want you to lie, to be two-faced, because our safety is at stake. Judith, you are as pretty as a button, and you shall be courted. Smile always, and do not rebuff any of your suitors. David, they'll teach you the Gospels. Don't resist their efforts. Agree with everything, and never mention Judaism. Let's apply ourselves in this endeavor knowing, all along that our sacrifices the next few months will be the price we have to pay to salvage our faith."

Judith had inherited her mother's fine intelligence. She shone. As her father had predicted, she met thoughtful young men, new converts or Christian-born, that she kept at distance with exemplary courteousness. Rachel became her faithful accomplice and turned into a very hospitable housewife. As for David, he still held in his eyes that trace of anxiety that had lodged there in the early years of his life. Silence was his trump card; he rarely spoke and had no trouble taking Simon's advice.

Although David enjoyed pampering his happy and playful sister and found solace near Rachel, he had a boundless admiration for his father.

Simon had said they had to be careful and pretend to be Christians, and so he weighed each word in his mind before he would begin to speak. Simon had said that they could not forget Israel, and so David, each night before going to bed, would recite passages from the Bible. Everything was well near his father. Since he was back from the long war against the Saracens, David was no longer afraid.

Simon finally had the time to take care of his children and to listen to them. He wanted the conditions to make their departure perfect. If news from Myriam was late in getting to him, then he might go straight to Portugal and find her. In the meantime ...

In the meantime, at court, the great physician Simon Benavista was immersing himself in the Gospels. A true scholar, he didn't cut any corners and read and reread the New Testament, not to imbue himself with it, but in order to undestand the basis of Christian hatred and contempt for Jews. He understood that evil did not lurk in the writings but resided in the interpretations proffered by men throughout the ages.

His behavior satisfied the religious court watchers, who enjoyed meeting him at the palace's library. Simon was even approached by students, the scions of noble families, who sought to benefit from his vast erudition. Once more he realized that Christian intolerance did not just foster obstinate fanatics among its young people. They were curious about everything and open to new ideas. It was among those who held a certain position of power that evil lurked: the power of a priest who wanted to keep his hold on his parish, the power of a rich merchant who feared for his gold, the power of a nobleman who sensed his dominance over his subjects starting to dissipate. These were the Christians who could at the drop of a hat whip up the hatred for the Jew for their own profit. Simon felt almost amused; now that Israel had left Spain, who would they turn against?

His worries grew when a royal emissary informed him he had been chosen to help his old religious brothers to find their place in Christiendom: "The king is well aware of your interest in your new religion. You are an example to all those who, praised be the Lord, have converted. We have set up many schools in the environs of Toledo where the Gospels are taught. But ours is a difficult task; every single one of these lambs needs the guidance of someone competent, of someone they can trust. Our beloved kings believe you have the qualifications to take on that role. You will be assisting your people to their new existence by showing them the right way. Should some of them resist your efforts, you are responsible to bring them back into the fold. If you must, you will denounce them to the Inquisition."

Simon had no choice. He had to accept this role in spite of the uneasiness he felt following the meeting. Inquisitors! That Church never could get her fill of blood and pain; she still needed to destroy innocent souls! He felt strongly that he might be in a position to save many new Christians from the fate that awaited them if he could offer them reassurances and tell them what he understood to be the spirit of the Church. But never, oh God, would he turn anyone in. Once again Rachel knew how to comfort him by stressing the positive aspect of his mission. And wasn't it precisely why he had stayed? To help his people before escaping this country? He decided to put a good face on his misfortune.

When he ran into the ex-rabbi Abraham Seneor, who since his conversion had changed his name to Coronel, he became agitated again.

"I am happy to see you," Coronel said. "It has been ages since we last saw each other. I am getting used to my new life better than I imagined. I am relaxed and no longer distressed. I find the Gospels fascinating. We were short-sighted not to go beyond our books! But let's talk about you. How are you?"

Simon could only utter small talk. Shocked by the sudden change, he became almost mistrustful of this man who had been his friend. Was the man's jollity genuine, or was he pulling the strings of an insidious Inquisition trap? Simon couldn't bring himself to believe in so radical a treason and when they took leave of each other he felt terribly distressed. Vanity, race against the wind…

He realized his own vanity when he began to fulfill the terms of his mission. He visited a new Castilian village every day, hoping to meet helpless men and women to whom he might offer moral support. He quickly realized that his mission was bound to fail. Streets and marketplaces, always so crowded during hard times, were now deserted. Many shops had closed. Gone were the merchants who enticed you with their novelty items. Here and there some cloth merchants waited idly for a potential customer to show their scanty display; there were no children to be heard anywhere.

Although they were numerous, the converts didn't dare leave their homes, which effectively reinforced the feelings of forlorness and despair one could sense when walking through the empty quarters. They went forward like golems, avoiding their neighbors' gaze. Only a few of the old, very old men dared to look at the stranger who roamed their streets; they had nothing more to lose as they waited to die a proud death in their isolation. Simon greeted them; smiled at them, but was not able to initiate a conversation. Christians, satisfied with the expulsion of the Jews, purred near fountains on the front porches of their homes, unaware that everything had gone down a notch. A pleasant torpor had taken hold of the cities. It was an exalted torpor, drunk with its own power, the calm forerunner of the decadence to follow. The country's vitality was gone. Isabella could go on financing the extravagant voyages of seafarers who played with eggs, but without Jews and Arabs Spain would be nothing more than vanity, a race against the wind.

No one had any need for Simon, and he went back home disappointed the first few evenings.

Rachel had a hard time believing there could be so much fear and indifference. "No one came to you, no one spoke to you?"

"No one."

Why had he stayed? For Lazarus, primarily, but also for all those who were fleeing from him. A letter from Myriam, sent from Portugal, deepened his depression. Things were fine, she wrote, and they had just set foot on the land of their exile. It had taken almost two months for the letter to reach him. He missed his sister. He got up every morning to trample the same desert, from Maqueda to Ocaña or from Mora to Madrid. After a few weeks he returned terribly discouraged.

"This time they spoke to me. Oh, God, what a disgrace!"

"What did they say, Simon?"

"Some converts asked me why I was coming around to torment them. They pleaded with me to let them be."

"But did you tell them you were there to help?"

"They have no trust left in them. They mistrust everything and everyone. They know that the rewards for their conversions are scorn and mistrust."

"They're right, I'm afraid."

"I'd rather know that their guard's up. Down south people are saying that the Inquisition is already back at work. They show such distress, and I can't even help them. They know their sons and the sons of their sons will assimilate and that our faith will not survive—that they are a generation lost to Christian madness. Rachel, I'm ready to leave. Everything is ruined. It's almost October, and Myriam, Abraham and everyone else left us two months ago. Let us get ready."

"Oh! Simon, I waited every day for you to say this. The children, too, are impatient. Will we go to Portugal?"

"No. I received some very bad news from Portugal. Some terrible news."

Chapter 53

Myriam and Abraham's long convoy, which had crossed the border two months earlier, stopped for a few days in the countryside before heading for Lisbon. The exiled were beside themselves with joy. Some went hunting; others picked berries or fished in nearby ponds. Abraham strolled through the camp, going from one group to another; paid a visit to the young pregnant girl with Myriam; made himself available with the nurse; chopped wood. Everyone had a role to play, everyone knew how to make himself useful. Hope sprang anew even though their thoughts often turned to those who had remained in Spain.

Some inventoried what they had been able to salvage. A man in the prime of his life boasted about the good trick he had played on the Spaniards: He had devised an excellent hiding place in which he'd placed his most precious possessions. "This is gold the queen won't have!" he said in a loud burst of laughter. The others stared him down sternly; they hadn't dared take that risk, mindful of the royal decree against the flight of precious metals. If caught, one could be sold as a slave to Turks or thrown in jail. Everyone remembered poor Abraham Juikot, who, on the eve of crossing the border, had hidden a few silver coins under some blankets. Although the infraction was not serious, guards arrested him and led him away. He was not heard of again.

The most stricken among them had gathered. They spoke little, evoked the past and prayed to God. Near them were the cartloads of the sick and the wounded whose condition had worsened during the trip. It broke one's heart to hear their wails; they were comforted with stories about their new land, and of a newfound peace. The young people had become acquainted with one another and formed a separate group. They talked about their ideals, the dignity for which they'd fight, if necessary. They had their whole lives ahead of them. Abraham ran across a teary-eyed sixteen-year-old boy. "Well, what are you doing here with the adults? Why don't you join those in your age group? They're singing and laughing. You belong with them."

I don't feel like it. I am too sad. My parents died a year ago today, and I think about them a lot. I will never be able to meditate over their graves."

Abraham grabbed his arm and led him to the group of adolescents. Then he went in search of a rabbi who might know how to comfort the boy.

#

The convoy stayed in the clearing near the river for three days before taking to the road again. Most of the immigrants had never been to Portugal. How would they be received? They had been told that the Portuguese were peaceful and that no harm would come to them. But the travails they had endured had made them suspicious.

They were about to start when eight carts carrying about forty people broke ranks with the others. Their spokesperson addressed rabbi Toben. "We are not going to go with you; we can only think about those we left behind in Spain. If we must change our religion, then so be it; at any rate, deep in our hearts we will always be Jews. If we are doomed to die, it may as well be on our own land."

"Go in peace, and may God bless you," the rabbi answered. He had seen too many guilt-ridden exiles not to understand their plight. "I swear that for the rest of my life not a day will go by that I won't pray for your souls."

Myriam took the opportunity to entrust the group with a letter to her brother to inform him that everything was going all right. The small group pulled away from the larger convoy headed for Lisbon.

Soon a village came into view. Women held their children close, pleading with them not to make any noise; men went forward with their heads low, hoping not to be noticed. But the reception they got was far from hostile. The silent travelers were stared at; children started waving their arms and running behind carts. The exiled relaxed. They greeted the onlookers with a smile. What they had been told turned out to be true: This people was neither scornful nor violent. The convoy hurried its pace progressively while young girls sang. They longed to reach their destination.

#

A few days later, as they reached the environs of Lisbon, some fifteen correligionists came toward them. "You must be the tenth convoy to get here. Others reached Braga, Porto, Coimbra, Leiria, even Faro. We are scattered all over the country. We are here to help you. The authorities have agreed that you should settle on the west side of town. Because there are so many of us, the Jewish quarter cannot accommodate all of us. Our Portuguese brothers are to be commmended, and their wives and daughters are very dedicated. They have provided much comfort to our sick and to our children."

The first few days went by without a hitch. The weather was pleasant and their provisions adequate. Carts were used as infirmaries or as dormitories for the children and the aged. The others made their own makeshift housing; here it was a couple planks put across two trees; there, just some moss; elsewhere, a blanket stretched by stakes. Most of them would have liked to be working, even if for a pittance, but there was no work to be gotten.

Portugal was too small to absorb that many people; king Joao II allowed the immigrants on his territory for only eight months. Moreover, he set an entry fee of eight cruzados per person. Surprise followed by consternation descended upon the outcasts, who had hoped to remain indefinitely in this country. Most of them paid scant mind to the deadline, certain that their distress would stir the king's compassion and that he would rescind his order.

Joao II's first act was a rather reassuring one: He addressed in most compassionate terms the commanders of ships that were going to transport Jews. "I hereby entrust you with men and women who have endured a great deal of suffering. I ask that you treat them kindly and that you take them to the country of their choice. As the good Christians that you are and in accordance with the promise you made to me, the fare to be charged for the trip will be reasonable. You are the last hope of these forsaken people."

Encouraged by such words, two thousand five hundred people embarked on some ten ships leaving for Africa.

Abraham, Myriam and their two daughters were among them. Since it was difficult, if not outright impossible, to stay in Portugal, they might as well continue their wandering before it was too late, before they lost the drive or the strength to go one more step. Myriam cried, "What about Simon? And David? We shall never see them again!"

"If we stay here, we will relive the nightmare, I'm afraid. Let's go to Africa. I want to offer you a new land and peace. I entrusted someone going to Toledo with a message for Simon so he'll know where we are going."

It turned out to be a good idea. Aboard a small merchant boat Myriam thanked God to have endowed Abraham with so much common sense. It was an uneventful crossing to Larache, a small Moroccan harbor that some ten families exiled from Spain a fortnight ago were now calling home. The locals, their eyes the blue of the ocean, paid scant attention to the newcomers.

Mutual aid among the Jewish families was immediate. They shared information and their possessions; each child, each woman found an occupation while the men began to raise a roof. Abraham wrote Simon a third letter; it traveled around the Mediterranean basin before getting lost in Barcelona one year later.

Abraham had made the right choice. Later, when they heard about the fate a great number of their people had met, they spent many evenings praying for the souls of all those victims they could have joined. For if those who reacted immediately arrived at their destination safe and sound, the others lived through a nightmare. Ship captains were quick to realize the potential for huge profits to be made from their cargo of lost human beings. They suspected they were carrying gold or other negotiable goods and set about to take advantage of a desperate situation. The respect extolled by Joao II went up in smoke.

Thus, aboard the frigate *God's Will* two days after they'd set sail, Manuel de Santos, the only master on board after God, let Rabbi Eli ben Zaffran, acting as the spokesperson for the two hundred and fifty wretched souls he was ferrying, know of the decision he had come to. "If you want to continue your journey, you must pay a supplement."

"But we settled everything before leaving! How do you expect—?"

"I'm taking too many risks with you. You smell bad, your children, are sick and how do I know you don't carry the plague."

"You have no right. You promised."

"I don't have the right! Well, we shall see, you son of a bitch!"

He summoned two sailors who seized the rabbi and threw him overboard. The sea was calm and there was no wind, and everyone heard the cries of the man for a long time. Then silence fell.

Then the captain spoke to the outlaws who had congregated in the front of the ship. "That, you scum, is my answer to your rabbi. Now pay up and I'll take you to your destination."

A slight human form broke away from the lines.

"I can't give anything else. I have nothing left."

"Is that so? You have nothing left," Santos snickered. "Tell me, you have a family, don't you?"

"Yes."

"Show them to me."

He shakingly pointed his wife and daughter.

The captain then spoke to his men. "They are yours, do with them as you please."

Six mad men rushed the two Jewesses while another two beat the husband, who had tried to intervene. They set upon their victims mercilessly, giving them up only after they sated their instincts. The other frightened passengers had stopped their ears and closed their eyes. Santos, his eyes glinting, planted himself before them and forced them to listen to him.

"That one has paid his passage. As you can tell, I'm easy to please I accept gold as well as any other precious possessions. Must I prove it to you once again?"

Then they feverishly pooled whatever little they had left and gave it to have their lives spared. It must have been enough, because Santos asked for nothing else and brought them to Morocco. Similar scenes took place on other ships. One captain, blaming weak winds, slowed the voyage until the exiled used up their provisions. He then sold them food at exorbitant prices. Often, as ships were nearing Moorish territory, the exiled penned up in the hold of ships were sold as slaves to rich Arabs or left behind on some deserted coastal area of Africa. Thievery or rape or murder, all was fair to take advantage of their extreme helplessness.

And if ship captains happened to be honest men, nature took a hand in turning some crossings into nightmares. Rabbi Juda ben Hayyat embarked in Lisbon with his wife and more than two hundred and fifty people. Health conditions were such that plague broke out on board. By the grace of God there were only four dead, and the outbreak was quickly checked, although no harbor wanted to accept the ship, which roamed the seas for four months. Pirates from Biscay seized it without meeting any resistance and beached it in the nearest harbor once they realized there was little to steal.

They had landed back in Spain, in Málaga. They counted their dead and tended to the sick, but when the Jews readied to disembark the authorities turned them down. "You shall set foot on this land only if you convert."

The rabbi tried to reason with them. "Let us buy food! We have been eating mildewed cereals for the past two weeks, some of our children died of hunger, pirates locked us up in the hold of the ship for three days. Let us have food and we'll leave!" But he remained unable to move the priests, who stood their ground, happy at the opportunity to make so many new Christians.

After a few days, exhausted, half the survivors, a hundred of them agreed to be baptized. The others held fast. As days went by, more Spaniards came to swell the crowd of spectators, sometimes from far away, to see a handful of mad men in the throes of death. Wagers were taken on how many would perish. "Those Jews are so stupid, they'd rather die than become Christians!" "Wait a few more days and they'll give in."

First there were ten dead, then twenty, then the rabbi's wife died. The Hebrews, however, didn't give in; the weakest among them had already left the ship. Spaniards began to tire of the macabre spectacle; their frenzy subsided, and a few voices began to be heard in favor of helping the wretched souls. After a hellish two months they were brought bread and water, and the emaciatedd survivors were allowed to set sail for Africa again. Their ordeal, however, was not yet over; a few cases of dysentery broke out on board. Believing it was cholera, harbors refused to let the ship come ashore. Finally they disembarked on a deserted Moroccan beach where a nomadic tribe led them away before enslaving them.

Rabbi Hayyat was thrown into a cell teeming with rats and salamanders. After so many trials he had decided to let himself die rather than renounce his faith. Was God with him? He survived his persecutions and was later set free.

There was such a famine then that to earn his daily meal the rabbi had to do back-breaking work turning a grindstone. A rumor reached Fez that Rabbi Hayyat, a martyr in Spain, was still alive. The community collected monies to buy his freedom. Blessed be the Eternal, Who allowed this miraculous rescue.

In Portugal, those who had waited for the eight months to elapse before leaving the country learned of the horrendous events. They became scared about leaving. Rabbis pleaded with the king to allow them to stay, but the king refused.

When the deadline passed there were still tens of thousands of Jews in Portugal. True to his word, Joao II sold them as slaves to members of his aristocracy. Some horrific scenes erupted. Children aged three to ten were torn away from their parents before being converted and sent to people in faraway lands. They even shipped a boatload of children to the island of Saint Thomas, where venomous snakes abounded. Most of the children perished. Mothers threw themselves in the waters with their children. Others killed their offspring before ripping open their own bowels. Yet others hid in the mountains while some went back to Spain.

Abraham and Myriam heard only a few of these stories. Once in a while they heard that some families had reached Egypt, Crete or Albania. They waited a long time for news from Simon, but they never received any. Myriam no longer asked the Eternal to return her brother to her; she only beseeched Him to keep him alive.

Chapter 54

By the time Myriam's second message had reached him, Simon had already learned of the atrocities committed on the roads to exile. It was now pointless to think about going to Portugal. But how would he go about looking for his sister? Africa was so vast! She had wanted to embark for the Atlantic coast of Morocco, but had she reached her destination safe and sound?

During the month of January, 1493, he informed the authorities of the results of his mission: "I have met with families that have willingly accepted their new faith. Sometimes they wax nostalgic about the past, as could be expected. Some are saddened, others resigned to the change, but none will betray it, for all are most desirous to enter into the service of the New Spain."

"I, for one, will admit to being tired and weary of traveling the roads of Spain. I have a need to settle down. I would like to devote myself entirely to my new life by ridding myself of everything I have ever known before. Toledo has been the scene of past personal misfortunes, and thus I would gladly move to another city. I once liked Valencia, and settling there would suit me perfectly."

Since he had fought in Granada, had saved men's lives on the front and now reported on the new converts, Simon was in a position to barter for a few months of respite. In fact, it was high time for him to think about his escape. He needed to be close to a harbor. His request was met favorably. Six months had passed since July ended, and the exile of the Jews was hot news only along the borders. To show his appreciation, the king even offered him the beautiful Valencia residence of the Darmons, who had left for Italy. By uncanny happenstance, the crown was now helping him realize his plans.

The Benavista family was glad to leave Toledo one February morning of 1493. Judith took leave of her suitors; David sought strength in his father's embrace; Rachel threw the key to the house she had grown to dislike since her conversion as far as she could, and Simon carefully wrapped his grandfather's parchments and bow. He sighed with relief. "Had we stayed, we would never have left," he said. "By pretending to be good converts we would have naturally turned into true Christians."

"Never!" Judith let out. "I would never have let it happen! I am a Jew!" That affirmation straight from the heart dissipated in the surrounding thickets. A happy Simon kissed his daughter.

"What about you, David?"

"I read the Bible during the day, but each evening I forget everything they taught me during catechism."

Simon and Rachel embraced him. They felt joy and fear all at once with, at the end of the road, hope.

They went through Aranjuez one last time to meditate over Yasmina's and Abraham's graves, then they went across La Mancha. It was dry and cold, but on the second day the atmosphere changed. The sky took on a blue hue, the winds died down, and the rivers rolled their silvery ribbons. The adolescents marveled at the new landscapes. At night, in Tarancon, they found a comfortable inn. Simon had entreated them to "play the Christian well."

Their third night, in Motilla del Palancar, they dealt with a convert, and all went smoothly until Simon and the innkeeper, without revealing the tiniest bit of their inner thoughts, exchanged a conspiratorial smile. After the suffering and the anxiety they had endured the first two months the populace was trying to get used to its new status. Those who didn't want to give up, however, communicated among themselves via signs so discreet they would go undetected by Christian-born. That smile of complicity gladdened Simon, who was so disconsolate when visiting new Christians for the crown. A trace of the Jewish spirit still hovered over the country, even if driven underground.

They took it easy on the fourth day. Far away, at the end of their journey, was the sea the children had never seen. The air was noticeably warmer. All of a sudden a delightful clearing came into view, an idyllic tableau of greenery, shadows and water reflections. Judith asked to stop. Simon stopped the horses, and they all ran and sang in the spot blessed by God.

The whiled the afternoon away. They were less than four hours from Valencia, but they agreed to spend one last night at the inn. They knew they should not be wasting their money, but this had been their first truly blissful day, and no one knew what tomorrow would bring. While David and Judith went to look at the water of a small stream Simon lay next to Rachel.

A little later David came to get him to show him, in the south, an immense plain surrounded by snow-topped mountains. Judith lay down next to her mother to rest. "Father," she whispered, it's so beautiful here. And to think we shall never come back to this place!"

Simon nodded. He left the two women to stroll the grounds with David.

"We will see Myriam again, won't we, Father?"

"We'll do all we can."

"Perhaps one day we can come back here."

"Hmm! I doubt it. A chapter is closing. Yet if you only knew how much I love this land …"

"And elsewhere? It is as beautiful?"

"I only know Portugal. I studied there. Life was peaceful then, although everything seems to have changed in a short time. The news that we received is frightening. They say Italy is wonderful."

"Then, that's where we shall go."

"Yes, Valencia is the perfect harbor at which to embark when the time is right."

"Will we be able to live as Jews?"

"We shall live there as Jews. In Italy the pope will protect us. We will be free, and we will be able to give thanks to God for giving us days like today."

They reached Valencia the following morning. The magnificent Darmons' residence was waiting for them, with its walls full of the history of another family. Aware she was "stealing" some of the intimacy of the previous owners, Rachel looked with much emotion at the used books, the carefully stored dishes, the clothes left behind in a rush. The house, bought by the crown, had escaped looting. Only isolated homes that hadn't found a buyer were ransacked. Darmon had renounced every worldly possession to keep his faith whole.

The next day Simon was paid a visit by the king's representatives; they wanted to make sure he was comfortably settled in. He was soon called to the bedside of rich Valencians who had learned of his presence among them. He earned gold that would be most useful to him later. He planned on leaving in June, in the renascent spring, to avoid the cold currents of winter and the dog days of summer. Once there he would look for his sister, and the year 1492 would become a bad memory.

Sometimes, during the afternoon, he would take David along on a walk down to the harbor, where they'd overhear terrifying testimonies. There the news was more current than in Toledo: in taverns crews recounted the deadly expeditions. Simon often balled his fists before the loud laughter of sailors mocking the exiles. Plague, pirates, diseases, unwelcoming harbors, cruelty from Moorish authorities. He could well imagine the hellish journeys of many of his brethren. It was all over now; another diaspora was born. The summer of 1492 would be a topic of conversation for a long time around rounds of wine until the adventures in the New World pushed into oblivion the expulsion of the Jews.

Simon carefully noted what might be useful in their escape: the names of captains, the safest merchant ships, the best time of the year. He learned that sailors always sailed close to the coastline when going east, guiding themselves by the distant fogs and the cries of birds. At night they followed the fixed star, the one Arabs called Alrouk-Kabah, the guide. Older ones knew the shark-infested areas, the years of the medusas, the treacherous currents. People in this part of the world lived from the sea, according to her cycles and her laws.

It was on one of those afternoons, as he returned from the harbor with David, that he found his house ransacked, the door open and, in the garden, the bodies of Judith and Rachel. One had her neck broken; the other had been stabbed in the back. Simon screamed. With tears rolling down his face he ran to David, who stood paralyzed at the entrance to the garden, his eyes, and the two of them stood motionless, frozen in their affliction.

Judith, crowned by her long black hair, showed surprise in death. Rachel had tried to protect her before being slain. After a quick investigation the militia found out that the murderers had benefited from the complicity of the day guard whose duty it was to keep an eye on the crown's residences. The murderers were found and hanged then and there. They were small-time hoodlums who targeted converts as easy prey.

Fervid and despondent, Simon made sure that the money hidden in the garden was still there. He would leave as soon as possible, as soon as he found a boat, right after the burial. He addressed Lazarus, who, he thought, must be watching them in the heavens:

"How did you go on living, Grandfather, after seeing Yael die? How did you survive fifteen years of jail, your brother's betrayal, your daughter's death? Where did you find the strength to see Myriam go forever, what was your secret?... Give me hope, tell me that I have to live for the quiet child I raised as my own, give me a sign so that I can continue on this difficult path."

He felt a glow in his heart in the darkness of the room to which he had retreated. He tightened his fists and closed his eyes. Lazarus was there; he had been heard.

Judith and Rachel were buried according to strict Christian rites, thus exacerbating Simon's suffering. He could still hear his daughter affirm, "I am a Jew!" The cross of Jesus cast its shadow on her grave. David, still quiet, followed the entire ceremony with unflinching eyes. That afternoon they went back to the cemetery. Simon could not have left without saying one last prayer in Hebrew. He placed his hand on David's shoulder, and together they tearfully recited the prayer for the dead. They remained standing a long time.

Suddenly a man came out of the chapel nearby, smiling devilishly. "Ah! I was right to follow you and to hide here. I haven't wasted my time! I often wondered if the good doctor Benavista had truly become a good Christian, and now I have the proof I needed! The authorities will be pleased to be rid of a renegade like you. You're as good as dead!"

Simon recognized the alchemist Pedro Delvallo, whom he had alienated when he settled in the house the other had his eye on.

"I have just buried my wife and my daughter! Can't you show any mercy? If it is the house you want, you can have it, but leave me alone!"

"The house, what house? Do you think I have another motivation than my duty? Don't you remember Isabella's edict? Every Jew must vanish from Spain. You're a Jew, therefore you must disappear. Farewell."

David belted out a terrifying scream. Jolted back to reality, Simon rushed the man. They scuffled, but Simon's survival instinct was stronger. He knocked out Delvallo, who fell heavily to the ground. Then, picking up a rock, he crashed it on the man's face.

He got up to his feet, shaking. "We have to leave," he said to his son. "Someone might come. We can't hide the body far enough away from their graves, and we can't run the risk of being suspected of this murder. I didn't want to give in to violence, but I had no choice; it was either him or us. It must have been people of the same ilk who attacked your mother and sister. But time is of the essence. We can't take any more time praying for them. Let's carry the body to a thicket and run out of here. With a bit of luck his body won't be discovered for a few hours. If we want to stay alive, we'll have to make the best of whatever time we have left. Let's go back home and grab a few of our belongings. We'll escape as soon as we can. We'll find a boat along the coast. Once the authorities figure out what went on we'll already be far away, and then we'll be able to think and cry."

They gathered money, food, warm clothing and Lazarus's treasures. Then they climbed into their cart and headed south at a good pace.

With nightfall they arrived close to a small bay Simon had spotted some time before. There were a few houses and four or five boats. A man, obviously a fisherman, came toward them.

"What do you want here?" he asked distrustfully.

"Could you sell us a small craft?"

"I only own two fishing boats, and it's hardly enough. I can't sell you anything! Come back tomorrow."

"Tomorrow will be too late. My father is in very poor health over there in the Balearic Isles. I must see him before our Lord Jesus Christ calls him to Him. I leave you the horse, the cart and these gold coins. That should be enough!

"You want to leave now? It's too dangerous!"

"Yes, but the night is clear, and my son and I are good sailors."

"This is a strange story."

The man with the furrowed face was frowning. David, seeing his father flushing with trepidation, began to cry. Simon begged, "Name your price! I can't bear my son's sorrow. You must take pity!" Whereupon he proffered four gold coins, a small fortune.

At first the man frowned, but then he pocketed the money without pausing to think. Simon was pulling the boat into the water when he let out a piercing scream; in a bad move he had just fractured two ribs.

That was how, in the moonlit night of May fifth, 1493, he and his adopted son left Spain forever.

And so, little David, all alone on your boat, you wait for a sign from fate. The sky, the sea, the earth and fire all blend together. A century of history has unfurled before you, yet you are but a speck on the vast sea, although you have been entrusted with so many lives. Everyone around you has died, and that is why you must live. God will not forsake you. If He lets you live long enough, you might find sweet Myriam somewhere in the world.

Chapter 55

Days went by. Inclement weather blew in over the calm seas. The strong wind tore apart the pages of the book one by one as David stood by powerless. The boat pitched and almost capsized many times. Holding onto ropes, David awaited his death. Lying down on the bridge, he saw the houses ablaze and the murderers' lances again. He groped for his mother's arm, his sister's smile, the powerful hand of his father but could not find anything. He cried and reflected a long, long time. The setting sun over the grapevines, the pride of generations of Benavistas. Lazarus's winning arrow! It broke the silence with its sharp hissing sound, mindless of the spectators' cries. He thought he heard not the clicking of waves but rather the sound of trumpets heralding Lazarus's victory.

The roll made him fall. He caught himself on the ropes again. The sea carried him farther away steadily. He touched Lazarus's trophy, the last testimonial to that tragic period. Nothing was left of the book except for some disheveled pages. Yet, in his memory, it remained complete and untouched.

New images flashed in quick succession in his feverish mind: the burning fortress, the forbidding Alcazar, the beautiful property on the banks of the Tagus, the horror-filled Inquisition, and Manuel, his father, of whom he had but a few vague childhood memories.

Though he wasn't hungry, he nibbled on the few provisions he had left. He was neither hot nor cold, but he was slowly becoming lethargic.

Night came and then morning. Little David was asleep. The sea was calm. Strange, pleasant noises awoke him. He thought he heard someone's laugh. A ghostlike shadow hovered above the boat, and he raised his eyes: seagulls! He followed their strange and harmonious ballet. These images brought him some comfort. All at once he stood up. "Birds! There are birds! Land, then, cannot be far away!" He peered at the horizon, made a million careless moves and almost went overboard a few times before he finally caught sight of it… land, Italy.

He screamed, he sang, he called Simon's, Rachel's, Judith's and Manuel's names. He cried. The boat was imperceptibly drawing closer to the coast. Slowly, very slowly it came closer, sailed over sand and finally beached itself.

David grabbed the trophy as well as the pages of the book the tempest had not blown away and let himself fall on the warm sand. But he got back on his feet quickly. "Dear God! What if the boat went in circles and I'm back in Spain?" He became very frightened. He thought of the Inquisition. He was certain he'd be tortured. Maybe not, because of his age, but they'd force him to convert. He decided to trust his fate to God.

He gathered whatever strength he had left and walked away from the beach in quest of his future. It was a beautiful day, and it was already getting hot. The landscape was different from the landscape he had always known—few trees, little vegetation, and the earth was hard and cracked.

He had walked a very long time when, from the top of a hill, he spotted what looked like a hamlet. He had never seen such a thing in Spain. The place was small, with no streets and a few white houses that looked more like huts of mortar and straw. There were a few goats bleating meekly, pungent odors, men dressed strangely, their heads covered with amazing hats; women covered in veils. What to do? He never had the opportunity to answer his own question. Someone tapped him on the shoulder. Frightened, he turned around.

A young man more or less his age was smiling at him. He had a dark complexion and black eyes and spoke a language David didn't understand. He was an Arab, an Algerian Arab. He extended an amicable hand to David.

"Salam alaikum," he said.

Realizing that he was safe, David answered, "Shalom."

-END-